DATE DUE

DESIRE
AND
TRUTH

DESIRE

AND

TRUTH

FUNCTIONS OF PLOT IN
EIGHTEENTH-CENTURY
ENGLISH NOVELS

PATRICIA MEYER SPACKS

THE UNIVERSITY OF CHICAGO PRESS
CHICAGO AND LONDON

Patricia Meyer Spacks is the Edgar F. Shannon Professor of
English at the University of Virginia.

The University of Chicago Press, Chicago 60637
The University of Chicago Press, Ltd., London
© 1990 by the University of Chicago
All rights reserved. Published 1990
Printed in the United States of America
99 98 97 96 95 94 93 92 91 90   5 4 3 2 1

Library of Congress Cataloging in Publication Data

Spacks, Patricia Ann Meyer.
  Desire and truth : functions of plot in eighteenth-century English
novels / Patricia Meyer Spacks.
      p.   cm.
  Includes bibliographical references.
  1. English fiction—18th century—History and criticism.
2. English fiction—18th century—Stories, plots, etc.   3. Women and
literature—Great Britain—History—18th century.   4. Psychoanalysis
and literature.   5. Sentimentalism in literature.   6. Desire in
literature.   7. Sex in literature.   I. Title.
PR858.P53S63   1990   89-27725
823'.50924—dc20   CIP
ISBN 0-226-76845-7 (alk. paper)

FOR MARGERY SABIN

Friendship . . . redoubleth joys, and cutteth griefs in halves.
—FRANCIS BACON

CONTENTS

ACKNOWLEDGMENTS

Parts of this manuscript, usually in considerably different form, have appeared in print earlier: in *Studies in the Novel, Modern Philology, Eighteenth-Century Fiction*, and *Explorations: The Age of Enlightenment*. A different version of parts of chapters four and six was printed in *Rhetorics of Order/Ordering Rhetorics in English Neoclassical Literature* (Associated University Presses, 1989).

I am grateful to several friends and colleagues who read parts of this book in earlier versions: Alan Bewell, J. Paul Hunter, David Marshall, Margery Sabin, Gordon Turnbull, and Aubrey Williams. All provided insight, criticism, encouragement, and on occasion bibliographical suggestions that made my undertaking easier and improved the quality of the finished product. Deborah Kaplan read the entire manuscript rigorously and speedily, with acute understanding of my purposes and generous imagination of the book's potential. My readers and I owe a great deal to her. Mary Patricia Martin labored mightily as my research assistant. I am indebted to her and to the graduate students at Yale who have pondered with me the complexities of the eighteenth-century novel.

P. M. S.

PREAMBLE:
DESIRE AND TRUTH

"Desire" has become an indispensable term for late-twentieth-century critics investigating psychological intricacies of narrative. The word suggests the emotional force implicit in the acts of reading and writing fiction; it provides a means of linking the energies of characters within a text to those involved in creating and in responding to that text; it calls attention to latent as well as overt erotic elements in fiction. Such critics as Nancy Armstrong, Peter Brooks, Ross Chambers, and René Girard have refined "desire" as a tool of exegesis. The explicit association of desire with fiction, however, long antedates the twentieth century, and the terms of the early discussion illuminate issues involved in reading and in writing eighteenth-century novels.

Samuel Johnson, for instance, appears to consider desire and fiction inextricably linked; he constructs a fable to illustrate the point. *Rambler* no. 96 (16 Feb. 1751) opens with a discussion of truth: "Truth is . . . not often welcome for its own sake; it is generally unpleasing because contrary to our wishes and opposite to our practice" (Johnson, *Rambler* 4: 148[1]). In the story that follows, the personified figure of Falsehood gains popular approval "because she took the shape that was most engaging, and always suffered herself to be dressed and painted by Desire." Trying to win the hearts of the people, Truth arrays herself the same way.

The Muses wove in the loom of Pallas, a loose and changeable robe, like that in which Falsehood captivated her admirers; with this they invested Truth, and named her Fiction. She now went out again to conquer with more success; for when she demanded entrance of the Passions, they often mistook her for Falsehood, and delivered up their charge; but when she had once taken possession, she was soon disrobed by Reason, and shone out, in her original form, with native effulgence and resistless dignity. (4: 152).

Truth, dressed—like Falsehood—by Desire, becomes Fiction. The fable encapsulates Johnson's ambivalent attitudes toward desire and fiction alike. It also calls attention to the importance of

1

truth—not realism: *truth*—as an issue in fiction. From the point of
view of Johnson and many of his contemporaries, fiction justifies
itself by the truth it tells. Johnson's distaste for realism is notorious:
"If the world be promiscuously described, I cannot see of what use
it can be to read the account; or why it may not be as safe to turn
the eye immediately upon mankind, as upon a mirror which shows
all that presents itself without discrimination" (*Rambler* no. 4, 31
March 1750; 3: 22). He considers it neither useful nor appropriate
for the novelist merely to imitate actuality. On the other hand, fiction can make "truth"—by which Johnson obviously means moral
or ethical truth ("contrary to our wishes and opposite to our practice")—palatable: partly, the fable suggests, by addressing our passions. The need for fiction's disguises, as James Beattie points out,
reflects the moral insufficiency of human beings: "It is owing, no
doubt, to the weakness of human nature, that fable should ever
have been found a necessary, or a convenient, vehicle for truth"
(505). Neither Beattie nor other critics of the late eighteenth century, however, ever seems to doubt that fiction *can* convey truth.

The distinction between truth and verisimilitude, obvious to
Johnson, appears less manifest to others. Clara Reeve, for instance,
comments on the parental obligation to give children "a just and
true representation of human nature, and of the duties and practice of common life." In order to fulfill that obligation, parents
should control their children's reading, watching out in particular
for "Eastern tales," "certainly dangerous books for youth" because
of their lack of verisimilitude (2:59). Truth of representation, to
Reeve and others, appears essential for truth of doctrine. Paul Ricoeur speaks of the "concern for being true—in the sense of being
faithful to reality, or for equating art and life" as a central doctrine
of early novel critics (11).

The story of eighteenth-century fiction that I hope to tell will
investigate the kinds of truth it conveys and how it conveys them,
concentrating less on truths of verisimilitude than on those of
desire. I begin with a working hypothesis: fiction creates and
conveys its truths through plot. The dynamic narrative organization of events we call plot engages our desire (as Peter Brooks has
most fully demonstrated) and controls our comprehension. Modern theorists have explained in various ways the nature of plot.
They have paid less attention to its functions—not only its meanings as a component of "art," but its ways of reflecting "life."

In particular, critics have largely neglected the uses of plot in
eighteenth-century fiction. The plots of eighteenth-century novels,
we may be accustomed to think, are largely "conventional," heavily

dependent on romance tradition. Neither "realistic" in any readily recognizable sense nor, to most twentieth-century eyes, daringly experimental, these plots belong to the novel in its early adolescence. Critics have on the whole interested themselves more intensely in the form's putative maturity or yet more putative decline.

To think about the old-fashioned question of truth and the more modish notion of desire in relation to eighteenth-century plots helps one to see how plot both shapes and conveys meaning. I shall argue that eighteenth-century fiction is both profoundly realistic—that is, its plots speak the realities of the culture from which they emerge—and consistently daring in its exploration of formal, psychological, and social possibility. The patterns that emerge through examining numerous examples of the period's fictional narratives convey complicated attitudes toward such matters as the relations of parents and children and the viability of power as a principle of social organization.

If truth, like desire, can assume multiple forms, perhaps male and female versions are different. The story this book tells delineates struggles between "masculine" and "feminine" values. Gender terms loom large in eighteenth-century discourse, and they underlie the action of many novels. The tension between meanings perceived by men and by women, between assumptions associated with one sex and the other, informs and invigorates the century's fiction. Such familiar eighteenth-century problems as the relative value of reason and feeling turn out, when given fictional embodiment, to bear on complexities of gender, which assume central importance in my reading of early fiction. Awareness of such complexities helps to give familiar novels fresh meaning and to reveal the power of unfamiliar texts.

Robert Caserio, one of the few critics to take plot seriously as a reflection of experience, has made an eloquent case for plot as bearer of meaning in the Victorian and modern novel. Insisting that plot "makes sense emotionally or morally as well as intellectually," he goes on to observe that story and plot "dissolve the differences whereby we usually discriminate thought from feeling, theme from treatment, cognition from evaluation" (7). Caserio concerns himself with the effects of plot on readers. Ways of interpreting experience, our own and other people's, derive partly from the reading of fictions: "we *think through* them" (8). Although Caserio asserts no equation between art and life, he argues forcefully that art makes things happen in life, partly by altering perceptions. "By positing a directness of relation between narrative motions of consciousness in the novel and in ordinary living we are able to see

that changes in the sense of plot, over any stretch of time, make up
a continuing argument about the problems and possibilities of human purpose and activity" (8).

To make a case for this controversial position seems easiest with
relatively recent fiction. Works such as *Tom Jones, The Man of Feeling, Evelina* (which share little more than a common century) speak
of a past so remote in its assumptions about fiction and about human experience that we may not readily see how its arguments
"about the problems and possibilities of human purpose and activity" bear on our own purposes and acts. I do not propose to
demonstrate how Evelina's social mistakes in London might help
an aspiring young actress in late-twentieth-century New York City.
Dr. Johnson's notion of Truth dressed by Desire helps to define a
more fruitful problem. To inquire of eighteenth-century novels,
What truth? *What* desire? may enable us to locate ways in which
these works continue to speak to us.

These questions derive from an eighteenth-century source:
their terms are Johnson's. My procedures in this study will often
draw on hints by critics writing at the same historical moment as
the novelists who interest me. Although the eighteenth century in
England produced no systematic body of theory or criticism on the
novel, several writers (including novelists) touched on problems
they found inherent in the developing genre. I summarize some of
their contributions in Chapter Two, but they have influenced me
throughout the book. This is not to say that I attempt to recapture
eighteenth-century readings of eighteenth-century texts. On the
contrary, I hope specifically to indicate ways of reading eighteenth-
century works with the perspective of twentieth-century assumptions, in search of the truth they tell *us*.

The notion that "truth" depends on interpretation, a current
cliché, possesses eighteenth-century authority. "It seems that the
impression we derive from a book, depends much less upon its real
contents, than upon the temper of mind and preparation with
which we read it" (Godwin, "Of Choice" 135). William Godwin believes that books have "real contents," but that different ways of
reading in effect create different books. On the basis of this conviction, he distinguishes between "moral" and "tendency." "The moral
of any work may be defined to be, the ethical sentence to the illustration of which the work may most aptly be applied. The tendency
is the actual effect it is calculated to produce upon the reader, and
cannot be completely ascertained but by the experiment" (136).
Tendency matters far more than moral: "the moral of a work is a
point of very subordinate consideration, and . . . the only thing

worthy of much attention is the tendency" (137). Despite the ambiguity of *calculated* ("the actual effect it is calculated to produce"), Godwin's distinctions imply a split between the author's intent, perhaps embodied in a work's "moral," and readers' impressions of what they have read, dependent on "temper of mind and preparation." And they suggest a view of narrative as what Barbara Herrnstein Smith calls "a *social transaction*" (233), a situation involving, in any act of reading, two persons. It would seem to follow—although Godwin does not explicitly make this point—that the tendency of a work changes over time, as cultural presuppositions change. It follows too that moral and tendency will often be at odds.

Recent readers, especially of "minor" novels from the eighteenth century, have sometimes allowed morals to blind them to tendencies. Eighteenth-century novels may emphasize the ethical import of their fictions to a degree that makes it hard to notice anything else about them. Yet Godwin implies that morals are almost always irrelevant:

If the moral be invented first, the author did not then know where the brilliant lights of his story would fall, nor of consequence where its principal power of attraction would be found. If it be extracted afterwards, he is often taken at a disadvantage, and must extricate himself as he can. (134)

This putative irrelevance makes novelists perhaps all the more insistent about their moral impeccability. I agree with Godwin, though, that "the only thing worthy of much attention is the tendency." It is "tendencies" that I propose to examine: aspects of eighteenth-century novels apparent to a twentieth-century woman reader with a feminist "temper of mind" and highly literary "preparation."

John Bender has written that

we can see more in works of art than mere reflections. They clarify structures of feeling characteristic of a given moment and thereby predicate those available in the future. This is the specific sense in which they may serve as a medium of cultural emergence through which new images of society, new cultural systems, move into focus and become tangible. (7)

Nancy Armstrong expresses the same point even more concisely: "I regard fiction . . . both as the document and as the agency of cultural history" (23). Recent critics have called attention to a special kind of "tendency" in fiction: the degree to which narrative both delineates and helps to shape cultural reality. I propose that plots of eighteenth-century novels illuminate the history, politics, and manners of their age not only by embodying prevailing ideology but, often, by reshaping ideology closer to the heart's desire. I differ thus from such critics as Armstrong and Terry Eagleton, who see in fiction only the expression of power relations prevalent in society. "Fictions are for finding things out," Frank Kermode has written, "and they change as the needs of sense-making change. Myths are the agents of stability, fictions the agents of change" (39). Eighteenth-century novels contain their society's myths: the virgin and the whore, the wise father, the fortunate orphan. But by the patterns of action they represent, they also modify the meanings of those myths. They "find things out" by expressing authors' desires and satisfying readers'. Desire and truth, as far as plot is concerned, thus coincide.

I shall try to sketch a history of the eighteenth-century English novel and its transformation into the nineteenth-century novel by concentrating especially on the working out of sexual assumptions in novelistic plots. To adumbrate the argument in schematic fashion: I will argue that preoccupation with the vicissitudes of phallic power shapes major fictions of the 1740s and 1750s. For these decades, the distinction between "male" and "female" plots (see N. Miller, *The Heroine's Text*) has little relevance. *Tom Jones* and *Clarissa* exemplify comic and pathetic versions of a single structure; they resemble one another more importantly than they differ. By the late 1760s, however, the concentration on power begins to weaken; new ideological possibilities emerge, as plot structure also weakens. In important novels of the 1760s and the early 1770s, plot breaks down, its breakdown often providing the implicit or explicit subject of the fictional work. I am thinking of such books as *Tristram Shandy* and *A Sentimental Journey*, where the impossibility of telling a coherent story preoccupies the narrator; *Humphry Clinker*, in which the title character appears late and plays a peripheral role in the action, and in which the epistolary mode produces an obliquely related series of disparate texts; Henry Mackenzie's *The Man of Feeling*, rarely read though frequently cited in literary histories, a work that flaunts its own incoherence; Henry Brooke's *The Fool of Quality*, which attempts to deny the claims of "self" and provides only repetition as a principle of organization. These works show themes of sexuality and of power assuming radically new forms; their near rejection of plot implies an ideological challenge.

In the late 1770s, and more insistently as the century nears its end, novelists (Burney, Holcroft, Bage, Radcliffe, Wollstonecraft) begin to experiment with an ideology of relationship. Sexual relations are presented as a form of connection, not of power; familial relationships sometimes assume new importance. On the basis of eighteenth-century views of the "feminine," which stress women's alleged interest in human relations, one might call this pattern a "feminizing" of plot. At any rate, it soon yields to more ambitious ideological attempts. The narrative problem toward the end of the century is to incorporate the discourse of power—a discourse involving both men and women, despite stereotypical notions that women do not concern themselves with power—into a harmony that will not allow this discourse automatic hegemony. The nineteenth-century novel, I believe, grows out of this attempt.

Of course, novels do not follow such a neat chronological sequence; some novels of the 1780s demonstrate the same structure as those of the 1740s. The interplay between a discourse of relationship and one of power cannot be easily defined. For one thing, it may be argued—although I would on the whole argue otherwise—that the first discourse only mystifies the second. And certain novels do not lend themselves readily to description in these terms. Nonetheless, such a developmental scheme at least provides a sketch of my path.

Words like *ideology* suggest that the "truth" of novels belongs to the public realm. Looking at works of the past, we may see cultural import more readily than we discern idiosyncratic, subjective meanings. Similarly, the forms of desire duplicated in one text after another, the forms that speak of a shared sense of possibility and of limitation, present themselves to us more vividly than do more personal yearnings. Yet my key terms in fact designate both public and personal vision. Barbara Herrnstein Smith reminds us that "a recognition of the variety of possible narrative transactions and the range of interests that they may thereby serve should encourage us to acknowledge and explore the *multiplicity* of functions that may be performed by narratives generally and by any narrative in particular" (235). The notions of *desire* and *truth* in their full ambiguity help direct attention toward multiplicity.

Dr. Johnson, suspicious of desire (I shall examine his attitudes more extensively in Chapter One), insists on its universality. In his view, one must struggle to resist desire, whatever its object. As "imagination" and "reason" battle in Johnson's psychomachy, so too do "desire" and "virtue." Consider three typical Johnsonian formulations of the antithesis: "Nature will indeed always operate, human desires will be always ranging; but these motions, though very powerful, are not resistless; nature may be regulated, and desires governed" (*Rambler* no. 151, 27 August 1751; 5: 42). Again: "The greater part of mankind are corrupt in every condition, and differ

in high and in low stations, only as they have more or fewer opportunities of gratifying their desires, or as they are more or less restrained by human censures" (no. 172, 9 Nov. 1751; 5: 146). And
finally: "To enumerate the various motives to deceit and injury,
would be to count all the desires that prevail among the sons of
men; since there is no ambition however petty, no wish however
absurd, that by indulgence will not be enabled to overpower the
influence of virtue" (no. 175, 19 Nov. 1751; 5: 162). These sentences suggest varying degrees of pessimism about the possibility
of withstanding desire, but all imply the necessity of restraint,
regulation, government. And all assign desire to the realm of nature ("Nature will indeed always operate, human desires will be
always ranging . . ."), its government to that of culture—although
Johnson in fact demonstrates his awareness that the actualities
rather than the theoretical possibilities of social existence create the
objects of desire and encourage desire's development.

Although modern readers are unlikely to share Johnson's sense
of the great danger of desire, we may concur in finding desire universal in presence while infinitely diverse in manifestation—like
truth. (Johnson himself, of course, believing truth in all times and
places the same, would not accept the analogy.) Both are subject to
social definition and manipulation. The recognizable forms of desire depend, as Johnson suggests, on cultural pressure. The recognizable shapes of truth likewise diverge from one culture to
another. Like novels, ideas of truth and desire draw their energy
from the mutual intensification and the unpredictable tension of
the social and the personal. In novels, desire impels characters
whose struggles uncover what readers accept as truths of feeling
and of intellection. Johnson feels far more comfortable with por-
tentous words like *truth* than most twentieth-century readers do,
but we too (most of us) accept fiction as knowledge and learn the
dimensions of the human partly by reading novels.

Thinking about the place of plot in our learning, I propose not
to offer detailed exegeses, but to suggest ways that plot generates
meaning. Small happenings and large patterns alike reveal dynamics of desire. They create our sense of character, they limit textual
possibility. Plot arrangements locate a novel's thematic concerns
and chart the intellectual and ideological issues implicit in action.
Diagramming the movements of power, plot defines the politics of
fiction. Moreover, to plot—in the literary as well as the "real-world"
sense—is itself a political act. It establishes the narrator's power
and indicates his or her relation to power. Eighteenth-century novelists, using different terminology, show themselves conscious of

these issues and adept at dramatizing them. To examine their plots helps to reveal the power and the intricacy of the novelistic enterprise in eighteenth-century England.

A common way of understanding the shift from the eighteenth-century to the nineteenth-century novel has been to speak of a movement from emphasis on "plot" to stress on "character." Subterranean value judgments often lurk in such a description. Given our belief in the importance of "personality," we may feel that who a person is matters more essentially than what he or she does. Moreover, eighteenth-century plots, as they generalize themselves in the mind, displaying often a providential structure and specializing in the neat working out of all problems, seem false to experience. Nineteenth-century novels have plots too, of course, and Dickens's structures prove no more "realistic" than Fielding's. But Dickensian theatricality calls attention to kinds of doubt one fails to find in Fielding, and novelists like Eliot and Gaskell and even Hardy use their plots to demonstrate how character and society create fate—a view more congruent with modern assumptions than Fielding's or Richardson's.

I shall argue for a less obviously value-laden way of comprehending how the eighteenth-century novel turned into its nineteenth-century successor. If character makes plot, plot also makes character. That is, our sense of persons created in and by a fiction depends largely on the invented actions that reveal their natures. Instead of positing a shift in the kind of novel written in the nineteenth century, I would claim the primary importance of a shift in the intellectual and ideological freight borne by plot in the nineteenth-century novel. My argument is thus loosely historical. Although no neat demarcation points present themselves, large movements of thought become manifest as one examines plot's shifting functions. Because those movements interest me, I have found it necessary to touch on many novels—not only the ones that define for us the central novelistic tradition of the eighteenth century.

Canonical and noncanonical texts mingle in this study. Both participate in the same literary history. *Clarissa* and *Tom Jones* are endlessly fruitful and delightful objects of study, but for my purposes, relatively unfamiliar novels often prove more revealing than their better-known counterparts, more transparent in their ideological commitments, and almost equally delightful. I have sometimes treated these lesser-known novels at considerable length precisely because of their unfamiliarity. *Memoirs of Miss Sidney Bidulph*, for instance, treated dismissively in orthodox accounts of the eighteenth-century novel—as though to proclaim its sentimentality exhausted its meaning—demonstrates with particular clarity the subversive possibilities of female plotting. *The Female Quixote* (rapidly becoming "canonical") exemplifies virtually the entire range of issues implicit in the matter of plot. *The Fool of Quality* turns out to hold more thematic interest than one would dream from reading about it in conventional literary history. Such works call attention with particular clarity to what Genette calls "the singular, artificial, and problematic aspect of the narrative act" (127). Often self-conscious about their own rhetorical operations, these unfamiliar works can vividly reveal the weight of meaning plot carries. Part of my purpose here is to demonstrate what others are currently showing in other contexts: the arbitrariness of certain literary exclusions.

But of course I have my own exclusions. Defoe, Smollett, Goldsmith figure hardly at all in this study. I have neglected a number of woman writers at the century's end, although they interest me a great deal, and I have not done justice to Robert Bage, a favorite of mine. I have ignored Continental influences, even Rousseau. These exclusions, too, are arbitrary, dictated almost entirely by considerations of length. For similar reasons, I have in most instances not attempted anything resembling a "full reading" of my texts: only indications, more or less fully extended, of how my approach can illuminate both familiar and unfamiliar works and suggest ways in which familiar and unfamiliar participate in a single conversation, both social and personal.

I have tried to avoid another form of arbitrariness: that of subgeneric categories. The history of the eighteenth-century English novel has most often been written on the basis of division and subdivision. We learn of the episodic novel, the sentimental novel, the epistolary novel, the novel of manners. Novels by women become a special subgenre. There is Gothic, Jacobin, anti-Jacobin. Each of these sets and subsets indeed designates a literary type, but the effect of emphasizing them has been to suggest more fragmentation than I perceive in the novelistic enterprise. I have on the whole ignored subgeneric distinctions in this book, trying to indicate larger ways of understanding the nature of novelistic development.

That complicated conversation, The Novel, extends into our own time, with ever-changing substance. Despite dramatic transformations in the shape of what we are willing to call novels, critics have typically perceived a continuity between the nineteenth- and twentieth-century novel that constitutes the necessary ground for transformation. I am arguing for the same kind of continuity between eighteenth- and nineteenth-century modes of fiction. The nineteenth-century novel does not come out of nowhere, but neither do its eighteenth-century predecessors constitute a series of gropings toward the grand fulfillment of George Eliot. The false teleology of the novel implicit in traditional literary history corresponds to the false teleology by which we term Collins and Gray "preromantic." I hope to demonstrate the scope and range and intensity of the eighteenth-century novel as artistic and ideological form in itself and to sketch a new history of the novel that will demonstrate the essential role of Fielding, Richardson, Lennox, Burney, and the rest—not simply as precursors, but also as exemplars. And I hope to demonstrate the essential place of plot in thinking about the novel as a literary form.

Frederick Karl has argued for the essential subversiveness of the eighteenth-century novel.

From its start, the English novel has represented an adversary culture. Although it seemed to bow to the tastes and needs of the new bourgeoisie, it also stood for new and often dangerous ideas, criticized the predominant culture, and displayed what were often subversive forms of behavior. It upset familiar assumptions, questioned realistic presuppositions, and tested out, however sparingly at times, new ideas, forbidden desires, secret wishes. (5)

This comment returns us to the question of what truth fiction tells. Because novels speak of desire, always experienced as individual, and because desire (as both Johnson and Karl remind us) frequently takes forbidden forms, fiction necessarily has subversive as well as conventional aspects. Its moral may support the proclaimed standards of society while its "tendency," to return to Godwin's term, encourages questioning and challenge. Even when a novel tells a story of efforts toward conformity, as almost all eighteenth-century novels except *Tristram Shandy* do, its revelation of the efforts' costs may indicate a counter-message. In the chapters that follow, I investigate—varying my method from summary to detailed analysis, referring to some texts in more than a single context—how messages and counter-messages emerge through plot. I hope to locate a series of moments in the "continuing argument" Robert Caserio describes—the novel's endless argument about "truth," about "the problems and possibilities of human purpose and activity."

1

SUBTLE SOPHISTRIES OF DESIRE:
THE FEMALE QUIXOTE

In 1752 (when all of Fielding's novels had already appeared, and all but one of Richardson's, but before Sterne and most of Smollett) Charlotte Lennox published *The Female Quixote*. A fiction about the reading and making of fictions, the novel establishes, by its practice and by its discussions of fiction and fiction's effects, a complex thematic of plot. Indeed, it embodies, explores, or at least touches upon precisely the aspects of plot that will concern me in this book: plot as convention, as power, as prophecy, as interpretation; plot as ideology; plot as a dynamic of desire.

"It is the function of a plot," Paul Ricoeur writes, "to bend the logic of *possible* acts toward a logic of *probable* narratives" (43; Ricoeur's italics). The formulation's clarity may obscure the difficulty of demarcating the reference of the italicized adjectives. Both the possible and the probable define themselves always in specific social contexts; individual desire may deform both concepts; both maintain conceptual existence only within the limits of convention. The study of plot, accordingly, implies more than formal considerations. If plot serves as a principle of arrangement and as a generator of narrative interest, it also describes—and, I shall argue, on occasion enlarges—a society's sense of the bounds of possibility.

The Female Quixote will provide a preliminary case history of plot's workings, its power, and its potential. Because it makes fiction its subject as well as its method, and because it demonstrates with particular clarity the possible opposition between "moral" and "tendency," Lennox's novel exemplifies the subtlety with which fiction can embody meaning. Ronald Paulson considers a sense of division characteristic of the eighteenth-century novel. "There is very often a lack of congruence between stated intention and the total book, between logical and psychological progressions, between plot and symbolism, and between differing conventions" (*Satire* 49). The gap opened up by various "lacks of congruence" provides a space for meaning especially useful in a work concerned with the situation of women—and simultaneously concerned to insist on its own respectability.

Lennox's novel turns on meanings of narrative plot. Its protagonist, Arabella, reared in isolation by her disaffected father, conceives possible plots for her own experience on the basis of her reading, exclusively in romance. Because she naively assumes that literary and social conventions duplicate one another, she repeatedly violates other people's sense of probability and even possibility. Her plotting falls often into a prophetic mode: enlightened by her reading, she believes herself capable of predicting her own and others' futures, because she understands life's necessary patterns as those of literary romance. She can also readily interpret happenings in the present, knowing, as she thinks, the possible meaningful plots of female lives. Her remarkable self-confidence, a product of her reading, betrays her lack of knowledge about women's actual situation in the world.

All her prophecies, all her interpretations, declare her desire. As overtly as the romances it nominally mocks, *The Female Quixote* dwells on desire as its theme. Arabella, deprived of all contact with society, gets her ideas about reality and her formulations of acceptable desire from fiction. When a suitor approved by her father presents himself, she cannot accept him because he does not match the pattern of romance heroes. Predictable mishaps ensue as Arabella interprets experience and judges people by perverse literary standards. After she suffers a severe illness caused by her leap into a river to escape imaginary ravishers, however, an authoritative clergyman compels her to understand that romances provide inadequate guides to life. She thereupon marries her original suitor, who has remained faithful despite bouts of irritation over Arabella's absurdities; interspersed hints have announced to the reader that she really wanted him all along.

The point seems clear: foolish girls suffer from unwise reading, but they, like Jane Austen's Catherine Morland, must learn that "human nature, at least in the midland counties of England," hardly resembles character as described in romantic fiction (Austen, *Northanger* 200), and learn to acknowledge only desires that society condones. The plot's construction chastens Arabella's foolish desire.

Not only does desire control Arabella, but she values its control. Like Don Quixote's yearning for a different world, Arabella's wish to live by the rules of romance criticizes the standards of her society especially as they restrict female possibility.[1] "There is nothing at so great a Distance from true and heroick Virtue," the young woman observes, "as that Indifference which obliges some People to be pleas'd with all Things or nothing" (310). Such indifference, she elaborates, "is generally the inseparable Companion of a weak and imperfect Judgment" (311). Strength of desire, in other words, testifies to strength of intellect. Arabella herself, who deplores the "luke-warmness of Soul, which sends forth but feeble Desires" (311) and believes love "the ruling Principle of the World" (7), feels intensely about everything. Her feelings precede any specific object for them. They declare the warmth of her soul and the psychic impoverishment of her circumstances.

Obviously, this novel criticizes the absurdity of romances. Its moral is perfectly clear. Its "tendency," on the other hand, demands investigation. If the text mocks far-fetched fictions it also emphasizes their profound appeal to women, not because of female gullibility, but because women need alternatives to their socially-defined state of meaningless and powerless activity. Romances tell the truth of female desire. As Arabella puts it,

What room, I pray you, does a Lady give for high and noble Adventures, who consumes her Days in Dressing, Dancing, listening to Songs, and ranging the Walks with People as thoughtless as herself? How mean and contemptible a Figure must a Life spent in such idle Amusements make in History? Or rather, Are not such Persons always buried in Oblivion, and can any Pen be found who would condescend to record such inconsiderable Actions? (279)

Ordinary women have no place in history; ordinary life leaves no space for "high and noble Adventures." Arabella's yearning for such adventures, however ludicrous its manifestations, declares her determination to create significance. That subversive desire, a threat to the status quo, defines her as more dangerous than a woman driven by obviously erotic yearnings and raises the possibility that this novel embodies a revolutionary "tendency."

Yet this would-be heroine must learn to accept the ordinary, to welcome the fate of domesticity: with the ambiguous help of Dr. Johnson.

Johnson had a complicated relation to *The Female Quixote*, which he reviewed favorably in *The Gentleman's Magazine*. (He also thought well of its author: in the last year of his life, having dined with Elizabeth Carter, Hannah More, and Frances Burney, he exults, "Three such women are not to be found: I know not where I could find a fourth, except Mrs. Lennox, who is superiour to them all" [Boswell 4: 275]. He had known her for thirty-five years; in 1750 he organized an all-night celebration honoring the publication of her first novel.) It is possible—a long tradition says so—that Johnson wrote chapter 11 of book 9, the chapter entitled "Being, in the Author's Opinion, the best Chapter in this History." It contains the words of the wise clergyman who converts Arabella to normality. John Mitford, in 1843, first made the claim for Johnson's authorship, basing it largely on internal evidence. Miriam Small, Lennox's most authoritative modern biographer, accepts the argument (79), as does W. J. Bate (270); Carey McIntosh concurs (14). On the other hand, Duncan Isles, after considering all the evidence, concludes, "On the whole, it would seem best to regard the chapter, with all its faults, as wholly Mrs. Lennox's until definite evidence to the contrary is found" (Lennox 421).

But it hardly matters whether Johnson actually wrote the crucial chapter. As Isles puts it, "we can assume that Mrs. Lennox had discussed at least the conclusion with [Johnson]. She obviously had him in mind when she created Arabella's eventual saviour, 'the pious and learned Doctor ———', and was heavily influenced by his ideas and phraseology in the penultimate chapter" (Lennox 421). If not literally, at least metaphorically, Dr. Johnson articulates the view of the world that persuades Arabella to abandon her dream of creating meaning and interest beyond the domestic sphere.

The pious and learned doctor, however, is not the only figure available to offer sage advice. In the preceding book of *The Female Quixote*, Arabella meets a wise countess, herself a reformed reader of romances, who wishes to cure the girl of her delusions. Arabella asks the older woman to narrate her adventures; the countess explains that good women don't *have* adventures. "The Word Adventures carries in it so free and licentious a Sound in the Apprehensions of People at this Period of Time, that it can hardly with Propriety be apply'd to those few and natural Incidents which compose the History of a Woman of Honour" (327). She goes on to insist that, by Christian standards, the heroes of romance prove "impious and base." Arabella feels shaken but unconvinced. "Heroism, romantick Heroism, was deeply rooted in her Heart; it was her Habit of thinking, a Principle imbib'd from Education" (329).

The notion of "heroism" epitomizes one danger of romance reading for young women. Jane Austen joked about it: *Northanger Abbey* begins, "No one who had ever seen Catherine Morland in her infancy, would have supposed her born to be an heroine." Others treated it seriously, warning parents that a young woman who read about heroines might acquire too exalted an idea of her own potential importance. And eighteenth-century young women were *not* important, except as potential wives and mothers. Their fantasies of heroism, material for mockery, accurately register the boredom of a well-reared female's life. Conduct books of the late eighteenth and early nineteenth centuries confirm the suspicion that young ladies, females of the upper classes, had virtually nothing to do. Needlework, for instance, possessed value not for its product but for its illusory provision of meaningful occupation. Arabella's resistance to the countess's arguments suggests the urgency of her belief in heroism, rooted in her heart and in her mind, which allows her to imagine that men and women alike can act nobly. She cannot afford to relinquish such imagining. Nor, since her absolutism gives her strength, can she succumb to a woman who argues for cultural relativism, insisting that customs change over time and that Arabella is therefore guilty of moral anachronism. The Countess brings no authority to bear on the misguided girl; she operates by means of "charm," thus exemplifying a woman's limited resources. And she leaves, her work of persuasion radically incomplete, to take care of an ill mother, thus emphasizing her own conformity to "feminine" norms. Arabella will not yield to the feminine. She must be dominated by the masculine.

Enter, literally or metaphorically, Dr. Johnson.

Weakened by illness, Arabella wishes more than ever to be good. She begs the clergyman to assist her in self-knowledge, mentioning specifically the problem of desire: "If . . . you have observ'd in me any dangerous Tenets, corrupt Passions, or criminal Desires, I conjure you discover me to myself" (370). Her interlocutor thereupon offers two powerful arguments that achieve what the countess could not. He demonstrates the fictionality of the books Arabella has accepted as guides to life, and he argues that they "give new Fire to the Passions of Revenge and Love" (380). Elaborating his Johnsonian case against the dominance of love in romance, he reduces Arabella to blushes. She declares, "my Heart yields to the Force of Truth" (381) and marries, having given up, for the sake of "Truth," her tenets, passions, and desires. Her instructor has discovered her to herself as a false construction. The claims of fiction and of passion yield to those of truth and rationality: Arabella's marriage unites not only "Fortunes, Equipages, Titles, and Expence," but also "every Virtue and laudable Affection of the Mind" (383). Affection of mind rather than body: the phrase calls attention to the girl's final repression of desire.

The conflict played out by Arabella and the clergyman, between "feminine" emotionalism, fancifulness, and *desire*, and "masculine"

rationality and piety, would recur, with the same gender assignments, most explicitly in the Gothic novel. Indeed, these gender
assignments constitute eighteenth-century commonplaces. With increasing specificity and insistence, the contemporary discourse on
male and female characteristics delineates a socially constructed
opposition of qualities. (For especially lucid examples of such discourse, see Chapter Five.) The stereotypes still sound familiar:
gentleness versus boldness, passivity opposed to activity, feeling
versus thought, service versus ambition. When I use the terms *masculine* and *feminine* in this book, I allude to dichotomies of these
sorts. But dichotomizing need not depend on alleged sexual differences. Virtually all eighteenth-century plots acquire energy from
some version of the reason-feeling clash, regardless of gender distinctions. Lennox's formulation, which associates feeling with fiction and reason with truth, dramatizes the paradox at the heart of
all novelistic treatments of this subject. Fictions operate on their
readers by means of feeling, yet assign the highest value to truths
of reason that they rarely embody—although they may explicitly
support them. Eighteenth-century fiction by women often depre-
cates fiction. Fiction writers, like young ladies, must avoid self-
importance.

The scene between Arabella and the clergyman demonstrates
the power struggle implicit in their opposition as well as the degree
to which definitions of "truth" and "fiction" derive from social consent. The doctor can impose his "truth" on Arabella partly because
of the social authority he, a man and a clergyman, possesses. Her
"truth" vanishes—yet Lennox's fiction covertly preserves it.

The title of the present chapter derives from a phrase in the
dedication of *The Female Quixote* to the Earl of Middlesex. The dedication's opening sentences read,

Such is the Power of Interest over almost every Mind, that no one is long
without Arguments to prove any Position which is ardently wished to be
true, or to justify any Measures which are dictated by Inclination. By this
subtil Sophistry of Desire, I have been persuaded to hope, that this Book
may, without Impropriety, be inscribed to Your Lordship. ([3])

Although "The Author" signs the dedication, Dr. Johnson (according to Boswell) wrote it. In the dedication's opening sentences,
he aligns the fiction maker with her central character on the basis
of their self-deluding desire, but he also suggests that "almost
every Mind" will demonstrate comparable weakness. The desire
attributed to "The Author" is for "Support and Protection" to compensate for possible "public Censure" or "Neglect." The woman

Johnson here impersonates and the woman Lennox imagines share the same problem: the impropriety for a female of assuming or even fantasizing a place in the public eye. *Sophistry*, as Johnson would define it in his *Dictionary*, means "Fallacious ratiocination." Desire's false reasoning, Johnson suggests, makes Lennox ask a man to support and protect her despite her presumptuous act of publishing; she imagines comparable sophistry luring Arabella to demand that men accord her dominion and enable her life of "adventures."

In the weekly papers of *The Rambler* published during the three years preceding the appearance of *The Female Quixote*, Johnson frequently reflects about desire. Here, as so often, he articulates the dominant view of his period. (To desire, the *Dictionary* would explain, means simply "To wish; to long for.") *The Rambler*'s first issue specified "the desire of good" as one of "the two great movers of the human mind" (the other being "the fear of evil") (3 March 1750; 3: 6). Like Pope's account of passion in the *Essay on Man*, Johnson's presentation of desire stresses its function as a primary source of human energy, but also (in subsequent meditations) as a locus of danger because of the power it implies. Phrases like "the vehemence of desire" recur (no. 6, 7 Apr. 1750; 3: 34; no. 185, 24 Dec. 1751; 5: 207). We find also "the violence of desire" (no. 31, 3 July 1750; 3: 171), "the exuberance of desire" (which the "instructors of mankind" try to lop (no. 66, 3 Nov. 1750; 3: 349), "the tyranny of . . . desire" (no. 73, 27 Nov. 1750; 4: 22), and "the instantaneous violence of desire" (no. 77, 11 Dec. 1750; 4: 43). To moderate desire becomes the moralist's central endeavor, the good man's primary effort.

The trouble with desire, from Johnson's point of view, is that we want the wrong things and want them too much. The phrase "desire of the good" condenses multiple possibilities. Almost everyone considers money, for instance, a great good; the wish for it "may be considered as universal and transcendental" (no. 131, 18 June 1751; 4: 331). Equally universal, in Johnson's view, is "the desire which every man feels of importance and esteem" (no. 101, 5 Mar. 1751; 4: 175). But one need not specify particular objects of desire to emphasize how frequently people want the wrong things. "It is very common," Johnson observes, "for us to desire most what we are least qualified to obtain" (no. 61, 16 Oct. 1750; 3: 324). The richer a man gets, the more he wants: "a thousand wishes croud in upon him importunate to be satisfied, and vanity and ambition open prospects to desire, which still grow wider, as they are more contemplated" (no. 38, 28 July 1750; 3: 208). Human conflict stems from desire's importunities: "The hostility perpetually exercised between one man and another, is caused by the desire of many for that which only few can possess" (no. 183, 17 Dec. 1751; 5: 196).

The propensity to choose arbitrary or meretricious objects of desire implies less danger than does desire's tendency to become ever more violent, vehement, exuberant. One must resist indulgence. Hard enough, we know, for Johnson to forego excesses of food and drink—how much harder to withstand the temptation of psychic extravagance. "The desires of mankind are much more numerous than their attainments, and the capacity of imagination much larger than actual enjoyment" (no. 104, 16 Mar. 1751; 4: 191). That crucial association of desire with imagination elucidates Johnson's anxiety. Desire's power, derived from the dangerous prevalence of imagination, depends on the human tendency to project into the future. To resist the power of the imagined future almost exceeds human capacity.

Yet the effort to resist must be made. Arabella must relinquish her desire, which provided her power. Had Lennox not made her do so, Johnson would hardly have written his dedication.

The quotations and summaries of Johnson offered thus far fail to acknowledge *sexual* desire, which thinkers since Freud have generally assumed as fundamental, and Johnson's consistent use of the masculine pronoun and of "man" as generic noun excludes the female. From time to time *The Rambler* hints that men may desire women; the frequent association of desire with "appetite" or "passion" of course has sexual overtones. But in only two instances that I have noted do women—very young women—figure as potential agents of desire.

In a paper entitled "The mischiefs of total idleness," The Rambler observes,

For my part, whenever chance brings within my observation a knot of misses busy at their needles, I consider myself as in the school of virtue; and . . . look upon their operations with as much satisfaction as their governess, because I regard them as providing a security against the most dangerous ensnarers of the soul, by enabling themselves to exclude idleness from their solitary moments, and with idleness her attendant train of passions, fancies, and chimeras, fears, sorrows and desires. Ovid and Cervantes will inform them that love has no power but over those whom he catches unemployed. (No. 85, 8 Jan. 1751; 4: 86)

Men resist the "ensnarers of the soul" by efforts at self-regulation and self-government; women—or at least girls—must be assigned tasks to keep their imaginations under control lest they succumb to "love": not the ground but the danger of desire. Moreover, men, as the series of Johnsonian quotations makes apparent, engage in heroic struggle against their desires; women, trivial in their very natures, need only trivial occupations to distract them.

The character in *The Rambler* who most forcefully resists the injunction to moderate desire is an imagined fifteen-year-old girl. "My aunt . . . says, you are a philosopher," she writes, "and will teach me to moderate my desires, and look upon the world with indifference. But, dear sir, I do not wish, nor intend to moderate my desires, nor can I think it proper to look upon the world with indifference, till the world looks with indifference on me" (no. 191, 14 Jan. 1752; 5: 234). The narcissism of this response belongs typically to desire, in Johnson's view: desire, selfish want, assigns excessive value to the self. The girl's association of desire with the world's admiration marks her as female, one who uses her beauty—her *desirability*—as means to success. She refuses to moderate her desires because at her time of life she has the best opportunity to gratify them. A sexual transaction appears imminent.

Every woman is at heart a rake: Pope was not the only eighteenth-century writer who believed so. When he thinks of male desire, Johnson thinks of socially encouraged yearnings for wealth and power; the idea of female desire allows him to admit the presence of sexuality, from his point of view the most obvious form of female vulnerability. When the clergyman in *The Female Quixote* alludes to "love," Arabella, blushing, relinquishes her faith in her own significance; Johnson's treatment of female desire in *The Rambler* corresponds to the doctor's moralism in Lennox's novel.

The terms of Johnson's double view of desire by now have emerged: he values desire as a principle of energy, fears it as a form of misdirected imagination, of disorder. (Imagination seems for Johnson to function as source rather than agent of desire.) As for fiction: he values it inasmuch as it conveys truth, fears its potential for inculcating falsehood, another form of disorder. The association with falsehood, of course, dominates the clergyman's references to fictionality in *The Female Quixote*, although he acknowledges in passing the opposed possibility. "Truth is not always injured by Fiction," he observes (377). Arabella herself, on the other hand, declares her unmixed contempt for fiction. "He that writes without Intention to be credited," she believes,

must write to little Purpose. . . . The great End of History, is to shew how much human Nature can endure or perform. When we hear a Story in common Life that raises our Wonder or Compassion, the first Confutation stills our Emotions, and however we were touched before, we then chase it from the Memory with Contempt as a Trifle, or with Indignation as an Imposture. (376–7)

If romances are fiction—in other words, *false*—they *cannot* guide her life; if they encourage love, they *should* not guide her.

The moral responsibility of professional writers, in Johnson's view, is to combat desire. As he put it in the *Rambler* that considers the relation between authors' writings and their lives, "He, by whose writings the heart is rectified, the appetites counter-acted, and the passions repressed, may be considered as not unprofitable to the great republick of humanity" (no. 77, 11 Dec. 1750; 4: 41). This account of didactic possibilities hints literature's enmity to desire, since the essay praises writing that disciplines desire's close relations, the heart, the appetites, and the passions. As for romance, Johnson leaves little doubt about his disapproval or the grounds for it.

While the judgment is yet uninformed and unable to compare the draughts of fiction with their originals, we are delighted with improbable adventures, impracticable virtues, and inimitable characters: But, in proportion as we have more opportunities of acquainting ourselves with living nature, we are sooner disgusted with copies in which there appears no resemblance. We first discard absurdity and impossibility, then exact greater and greater degrees of probability, but at last become cold and insensible to the charms of falshood, however specious, and from the imitations of truth, which are never perfect, transfer our affection to truth itself. (No. 151, 27 Aug. 1751; 5: 39–40)

This account of literary responses occurs in a larger narrative about the inevitable stages of mental and psychological development. It glosses Arabella's career and justifies her "conversion." The first-person-plural pronoun and the declarative statements help to establish Johnson's most positive mode, in which he asserts the inevitability of moral progress. A reformed romance reader who has lost his taste for fiction, he generalizes his shifting enthusiasms into a universal. "We" move from romance to realistic fiction to history, from falsehood to truth: moral imperative disguises itself as statement of fact.

Johnson couches this moral narrative in faintly erotic terms. We "become cold and insensible to the charms of falshoood," we "transfer our affection to truth": desire remains at issue, as in the allegorical fable about Falsehood and Truth. But the allegory narrates an earlier stage of human progress when Fiction appeals by resembling Falsehood; in his later account Johnson considers fiction as more powerful through its imitation of truth.

Neither of these essays fully defines Johnson's attitudes toward fiction; the two together suggest a continuing conflict about the moral value of a literary mode ambiguously poised between truth and falsehood. The conflict centers on desire, the reader's multiform unfocused desire, which can be unpredictably activated by reading. Fiction can *take possession* of its readers, as a seducer might.

But if the power of example is so great, as to take possession of the memory by a kind of violence, and produce effects almost without the intervention of the will, care ought to be taken that, when the choice is unrestrained, the best examples only should be exhibited; and that which is likely to operate so strongly, should not be mischievous or uncertain in its effects. (*Rambler* no. 4, 31 Mar. 1750; 3: 22)

Johnson's sentence rings with anxiety about the ways that forces other than the will may dominate the mind and the imagination. The violence with which fictional examples operate on the memory corresponds to desire's violence. And desire's sophistry, which can delude us because we so ardently wish to believe, finds gratification in fiction, which also endangers the gullible through their propensity for belief.

Johnson's anxiety about the dangers of desire corresponds to his sense of the "dangerous prevalence of imagination" and to his concern about "the vanity of human wishes." He makes a powerful case. In the context of his argument about desire and his reminders that intense struggles rage in every psyche, the eighteenth-century concern over the menace of "romance," as opposed to "history," becomes more comprehensible.[2] Lennox's contribution to the attack on romance, however, calls attention to what Johnson left out. Through the character of Arabella, the novelist demonstrates the truth of fiction, although the resolution of her plot backs off from that truth. Johnson assumes that truth naturally opposes desire: "it is generally unpleasing because contrary to our wishes." Lennox raises the unsettling possibility that desire itself constitutes truth. Johnson's awareness of psychic conflict controls the "official" plot of *The Female Quixote*, but the latent possibility of quite another plot outcome reminds the reader of the suppressed authority of female needs.

Both desire and fiction, in Johnson's implicit view, threaten women more severely than they do men, because women—especially unmarried women—have fewer resources for resistance and fewer engrossing alternatives to frivolity.[3] The protagonist of *The Female Quixote*, victim alike of desire and of fiction, appears to exemplify the dangers Johnson feared for women. Particularly threatening is the fact that she challenges accepted terminology. Her identification of "history" with the extravagances of romance questions orthodox conceptions of the relationship between the two literary modes. Insistent on hearing the "history" of everyone she meets, Arabella means by the term a narrated sequence of events conforming to the plots of romance. History always has a plot, she knows—and she knows what kinds of plot are permissible. As her reaction to the wise doctor emphasizes, "history" to Arabella implies "truth." But her belief that plot provides a hallmark of authenticity calls attention to the relation between "truth" and social convention. Arabella's conventions—her assumptions about the signs of truth—differ from Dr. Johnson's, and Lennox's plot finally discredits them. But simply by daring to imagine radical disagreement over indices of truth, the novelist has announced revolutionary possibilities for fiction.

Arabella's interpretation of "history" in the large sense—the record of the affairs of nations—as well as her readings of individual lives, places women in a new position. This relocating of her sex organizes her "truth." She proclaims the agency of women and of love in national and international events, thereby confusing a foolish fop, Mr. Selvin, self-constituted authority on history who must confess his previous ignorance "that *Pisistratus* was violently in Love, and that it was not Ambition, which made him aspire to Sovereignty" (266). Arabella has replaced the stereotypically male value of ambition with a female valuation of love. One may remember Catherine Morland's complaints about history in *Northanger Abbey*: good-for-nothing men and no women at all. Arabella defies such versions of history by rewriting them, but she never *claims* to rewrite: only to read.

The heroine's role as reader merits fuller attention. First, though, it is worth emphasizing the importance of her muddling of the distinction between "romance" and "history." She values romances because she believes them to tell the truth. On one level, this aspect of her character provides grounds for ridicule: she cannot tell a petty thief from a nobleman. In another sense, Arabella's confusion provides satiric perspective on a society that deprives women of significant action. Arabella's views have powerful ideological implications. A fable of the world turned upside down, *The Female Quixote* embodies the kind of threat to order and subordination that Johnson vividly feared. After one of Arabella's passionate speeches, her lover's father expresses "much Admiration of her Wit, telling her, if she had been a Man, she would have made a great Figure in Parliament, and that her Speeches might have come perhaps to be printed in time" (311). This possibility, even couched in the subjunctive, epitomizes the dangerous potential of Arabella's fantasies. And the social implications of the character's views begin to hint how fictional plots possess ideological power. Potentially threatening by virtue of her interpretive insistence, Arabella embodies the ambiguous creative force implicit in the role of reader. The *female* reader uses that force in special ways.

Johnson's voice within the text, literal or ventriloquized, refutes Arabella's ideological threat and puts an end to her interpretations. That male voice—the utterance of the wise doctor—articulates one side of the intersecting sophistries of desire that create this novel's plot. *Male* desire defines the ideal woman in terms first hinted by the dedication: dependent, self-effacing, needy, grateful. The blushing young woman bowled over by the force of male logic belongs to the same dream. Arabella has always been beautiful; once she succumbs to the doctor's verbal power, she proves satisfactory in every other respect. Her acceptance of male wisdom, her relinquishment of her own imagined selfhood, and her willingness to dwindle into a wife all mark her as a woman able to fulfill male desire in the terms the novel has outlined.

The woman who can fill such a role, the plot suggests, must herself have no active desire. Yet that plot, in its development if not in its resolution, iterates the force and the complexity of *female* desire. Challenging the view of sexuality as sole determinant of desire, Arabella suggests desire's power to shape interpretation and questions the necessary force of gender—that force Johnson utterly assumes—in defining desire's forms. Both the plot Arabella inhabits and the plots she insistently constructs interrogate established views of womanhood.

Arabella does not lack sexuality. As Deborah Ross puts it, "post-Freudian readers will see a sexuality in Arabella beyond what Lennox openly acknowledges, expressed in symbols of considerable subliminal power" (462). Moreover, the heroine's obsession with rape, her capacity to see even her uncle as a potential ravisher, to continue seeing him thus in the face of all counter evidence—such manifestations reveal sexual preoccupation; or, possibly, exquisite sensitivity to latent eroticism.

If such sensitivity exists in Arabella's relations to men, it often deserts her in her dealings with other women. The relation of desire to interpretation emerges most vividly in two narratives of female sexuality. Both Miss Groves, whom Arabella meets accidentally, and Miss Glanville, her lover's sister, allow themselves greater sexual freedom than Arabella could condone. Arabella, however, finds her own plots in the stories they tell, in a fashion that shows how richly desire informs plot. And "desire," in this instance, proves anti-sexual, because Arabella dreams of importance for women, not of sexual fulfillment or titillation. Accordingly, she understands Miss Groves's career of illicit attachment and illegitimate children as one of female nobility and male betrayal. She attributes to self-indulgent Miss Glanville—to that young woman's dismay—excessively rigid virtue; then she reacts with horror to Miss Glanville's inadvertent revelation that she has allowed men to kiss her. Her fantasies, in both instances, assign potential sexual brutality to men and disguise female sexual feeling by elaborately codified behavior.

Arabella, the text explains at the outset, "had a most happy Facility in accommodating every Incident to her own Wishes and Conceptions" (25). (In this respect too she resembles the figure evoked by the dedication, never "long without Arguments to prove any Position which is ardently wished to be true.") Her happy facility, as demonstrated by her reinterpretations of her own and other women's histories, leads her to see men as dangerous when not dramatically subordinated to women, and ladies (not women of lower social status) as unfailingly, necessarily, noble in action. For her, "lady" equals "heroine." ("Woman" means "heroine's helper.") She desires, most of all, significance for herself and for her sex. This desire shapes the plots she imposes on "histories" she hears and creates. Claiming a kind of importance that neither she nor her sex possesses in actual social existence, she in effect temporarily alters a world that deprives women of dignity. When Miss Glanville tells her she knows nothing of "the world" (meaning, of course, the world of social convention and exchange), she responds that if Miss Glanville's "world" differs from hers, it differs for the worse. To some extent the novel supports this point. Not only does it criticize trivialities of contemporary society, it also calls attention to the trivialization of women by eighteenth-century English mores.

So Arabella's interpretations in their consistent purpose reveal the tendentiousness of all interpretive acts. Arabella embodies a powerful image of the reader. Laurie Langbauer sees her as "the ideal reader, completely given over to the sway of the text, attesting to the power of romance, a power the novelist desires for her form too" (30). This description applies to the girl as a reader of literal texts, but Arabella fills a more active role as interpreter of "histories." Indeed, the action of interpretation is her principal, in some sense her only, form of heroism; the leap into the river, which in her mind establishes her claim to importance, results directly from one of her frequent misinterpretations of appearances. Arabella demonstrates the degree to which every piece of interpretation depends on adaptation to one's own wishes and conceptions. She fails to differentiate between history and romance because her principles of interpretation obviate the difference. Desire defines meaning. Without it, this novel suggests, meaning hardly exists.

This idea seems less startling now than it may have appeared in the mid-eighteenth century. Peter Brooks has recently restated the essential connection between fiction and desire. In a chapter called "Narrative Desire," he argues that plot is

perhaps best conceived as an activity, a structuring operation elicited in the reader trying to make sense of those meanings that develop only through textual and temporal succession. . . . We can, then, conceive of the reading of plots as a form of desire that carries us forward, onward, through the text. (37)

The formulation calls attention to the double aspect of Arabella's reading, both her literal reading of romances and her ongoing interpretations of her own and others' lives. Desire shapes her reading and is shaped by it. She finds in books what she wants, she learns what she wants by reading them. One text influences her understanding of the next, literal or metaphoric. She plots the "histories" of those she meets as functions of her mediated desire.

Arabella cannot distinguish romance from history, in people or in books, precisely because of the emotional intensity of her reading. In Clara Reeve's *The Progress of Romance* (1785), Euphrasia, the author's surrogate, observes, "The effects of Romance, and true History are not very different." Elaborating her point, she continues,

When the imagination is raised, men do not stand to enquire whether the motive be true or false.—The love of glory has always a certain enthusiasm in it, which excites men to great and generous actions, and whatever stimulates this passion, must have the credit of the actions it performs. (1: 102)

If the reader (in this case the male reader) allows himself to be moved, in other words, his imaginative incorporation of literary experience obviates generic distinctions. Arabella, as reader, resembles the men Euphrasia imagines. She too uses romance to inspire "great and generous actions."

It is by no means arbitrary that Reeve's Euphrasia writes of *men* as those potentially motivated by "love of glory." Arabella's fantasies, although they center on the special role of women, in effect

preempt a masculine mode. As Leland Warren puts it, "Perhaps
the most quixotic thing our Female Quixote does is to refuse the
role allotted to women and to insist on becoming an active partici-
pant in the discourse of truth usually reserved for men" (377). And
not only discourse. Those fantasies of Arabella's, as I have already
suggested, insist upon direct female force: either that of heroic action or that of determinant influence over men. In Arabella's mythology, women absolutely control male destinies. The man who
presumes to love becomes totally vulnerable to the will of the beloved. At her order or at the sight of her displeasure he must gladly
die; if she commands him to live he will overcome any disease to
do so. Arabella sees herself as the cause of every apparent expression or action in every man around her—gardeners, fops, high-
waymen—and as the possessor of life-and-death power over men.
She reverses the social convention that makes women compliant
and dependent.

But she goes further. The text is at pains to point out Arabella's
"feminine" characteristics. She blushes and weeps, she looks unfailingly beautiful, she is "sweet" as well as witty. Nonetheless, the
subversive power of *The Female Quixote* derives from the fact that
its heroine has appropriated "masculine" values; her desire strikingly resembles forms of male desire chronicled in *The Rambler*,
and no trivial avocation will distract her from it. Arabella concerns
herself obsessively with honor and fame. Early in *The Female Quixote*, she describes the romances she loves as books

which give us the most shining Examples of Generosity, Courage, Virtue,
and Love; which regulate our Actions, form our Manners, and inspire us
with a noble Desire of emulating those great, heroic, and virtuous Actions,
which made those Persons so glorious in their Age, and so worthy Imitation in ours. (48)

The "noble Desire" to which she alludes dictates her subsequent
actions. Just before she leaps into the river to escape anticipated
assault, she urges her female companions to join her.

'Tis now, my fair Companions, said she, with a solemn Accent, that the
Destinies have furnish'd you with an Opportunity of displaying in a Man-
ner truly Heroick, the Sublimity of your Virtue, and the Grandeur of your
Courage to the World.

   The Action we have it in our Power to perform will immortalize our
Fame, and raise us to a Pitch of Glory equal to that of the renown'd *Clelia*
herself.

   Like her, we may expect Statues erected to our Honour: Like her, be
propos'd as Patterns to Heroines in ensuing Ages: . . . And the Admiration

and Esteem of all Ages to come, will be the Recompence of our noble
Daring. (362–3)

This fuller delineation of her "noble Desire" emphasizes her
need for a response from "the World" for her heroism, virtue,
and courage. She wishes, without relinquishing her femininity—
indeed, by virtue of her redefined femininity—to inhabit the public sphere.

Her yearning constitutes principled desire of a traditionally
masculine sort. Arabella's appeal to her friends recalls Sarpedon's
injunctions in *The Iliad* (here quoted in Pope's version):

> Why on those Shores are we with Joy survey'd,
> Admir'd as Heroes, and as Gods obey'd?
> Unless great Acts superior Merit prove,
> And vindicate the bounteous Pow'rs above.
> 'Tis ours, the Dignity They give, to grace;
> The first in Valour, as the first in Place.
>
> (12: 377–382)

Pope himself transformed these words, in Clarissa's speech in *The
Rape of the Lock*, into a conventionally feminine mode, with "good
Sense" and "good Humour" as operative terms. But Arabella has
no interest in the conventionally feminine, desiring as she does heroic rather than social virtue; the Countess's appeal to social convention unsettles but does not dissuade her. And this "female
Quixote" is not merely narcissistic, or merely silly; indeed, her rigorous principles enable her to offer penetrating criticism of social
follies. She yields to the clergyman's arguments only because he
persuades her that his principles of Truth and Chastity are more
uncompromising than her own.

Arabella's consistent commitment to principle and her contempt
for meretricious social enticements make her potentially more
threatening to a male-dominated order of things than seventeen-
year-old fictional heroines customarily appear. She claims male
prerogatives, welcomes male responsibility—and declares both "female." But jumping into the river, her final attempt at heroism,
proves self-defeating: it causes the illness that makes Arabella vulnerable to the clergyman's persuasion. As a moment in Lennox's
plot, it marks the novelist's withdrawal from the full implications of
her fable. Until that moment, Arabella, though intermittently ridiculous and occasionally even destructive (as when she encourages
her lover to fight duels; see Paulson, *Satire* 275), has exercised a
great deal of force.

Recent commentators on *The Female Quixote* have noted that

Lennox's novel both celebrates and ridicules romance. The river episode exemplifies how the plot, until this point partaking consistently of ideological ambivalence, must finally resolve itself. Episodically structured, the novel has proceeded by a series of inconclusive encounters between Arabella and others, none of whom share her guiding assumptions. Although almost everyone thinks the girl misguided and wrong, she often influences other people's conduct. Her servant follows her lead as well as she can; her lover, although he does not accept her decree of total banishment, rescues her beloved books from the flames in order to restore himself to favor. The dramas she manufactures tend to trail away: the gardener whom she imaginatively elevates to the nobility simply disappears in bewilderment, mumbling about how he thought she thought better of him; the attendant males at Bath drift off after Arabella has invented for them stories of unrequited love. But the leap into the river demands resolution. It is Arabella's most important willed nonverbal action, her most conscious attempt to achieve the fame for which she yearns. Either she must win recognition for her courage and ardor, or she must come to know her folly.

The courage and ardor are real enough, within the fictive context. Arabella's appeal as a character comes not only from the poignance of her desire but from her determination to fulfill it: to remake her world with room for genuine female achievement. But Lennox's plot cannot finally allow such achievement. Arabella must come to her senses and accept her overdetermined destiny. The gesture she imagined as heroic defiance turns into self-destruction: spiritual if not literal drowning. The plot, in the few pages remaining after Arabella's immersion, loses its double valence.

Arabella's plots, like Lennox's, challenge the status quo yet finally succumb to it. The plots shaped by her desire focus on questions of power. In the life imagined for her by Lennox, the capacity to plot provides Arabella's most effective mode of control. Reimagining other people's lives, she incorporates those lives into her own story; and that story, too, she constantly plots. The psychologist Jerome Bruner is quoted in *The New York Times* (20 October 1987, C-13) as saying that people's ways of telling their own stories "finally become recipes for structuring experience itself." Arabella illustrates the point: her experience is recognizable to her only as product of a previously imagined story, a narrative as rigidly controlled by convention as is the single story her society allows a well-reared young woman, but nonetheless freeing to the female imagination. By replotting experience she makes bold claims for herself. She exerts power over her world by the way she reads it.

Yet her imaginings come only to prearranged marriage. Her power, after all, is merely verbal—not enough to change the world, only enough to criticize it.

The real power in *The Female Quixote*, unsurprisingly, rests with men. Sir George Bellmour, a determined suitor more enamored of Arabella's money than of her person, engages the energies of plot more actively than anyone else in the novel can or will. Unlike Arabella's plotting, his is not merely verbal: he controls events as well as their interpretations, Lovelace-like (although much less diabolical) in arranging an elaborate charade to deceive Arabella. His manipulations, however, do him no good. In contrast, Glanville makes little attempt to control by his own action the course of events. Although he once asks his father to act on his behalf, and although he is finally deluded into fighting a duel, his main role is passive: frustrated waiting. Nonetheless, he wins the woman he has wanted all along, thus triumphing over his aristocratic rival. The most powerful man on the scene is, of course, the wise clergyman, who, like Arabella, possesses only verbal force. He too wins.

In other words, the plot's outcome conveys that women's language—women being excluded from Parliament and other public forums—possesses no performative power (not even the benevolent countess can effect change). Men's language, reinforced by public authority, makes things happen. Men, however, have no business entering the realm of fantasy; Bellmour makes himself as ridiculous as Arabella by doing so. Male power often depends less on action than on role. Female efforts at heroic action are doomed to frustration partly because role must reinforce action to make it meaningful. Thus Arabella's father can respond to his perception of social corruption by fleeing the world; Arabella cannot. Plot outcomes throughout the eighteenth century will tell the same story.

Lennox's plot finally succumbs to social and literary convention. As for Arabella's plots—Arabella stops plotting, acknowledging her desire's incommensurability with her social environment. In both cases, the laws of the probable—to return to Ricoeur's terminology—triumph over a woman's imagining of the possible. But a dilemma remains for the reader of Lennox's text, a dilemma that has been figured by Arabella within that text.

Possibilities for the reader's desire can best be understood in relation to the protagonist's feelings. Despite all of Arabella's follies, she represents something important, and never more so than in her fashion of taking seriously words on a page. Johnson himself had eloquently described the mental action of identification with figures evoked by a text.

All joy or sorrow for the happiness or calamities of others is produced by
an act of the imagination, that realises the event however fictitious, or ap-
proximates it however remote, by placing us, for a time, in the condition
of him whose fortune we contemplate; so that we feel, while the deception
lasts, whatever motions would be excited by the same good or evil happening to ourselves. (*Rambler* 60, 13 Oct. 1750; 3: 318–19)

Although they raise the possibility of the "fictitious," these words
refer specifically to biography—to what Arabella would call "History." The process of identification Johnson describes, however,
applies equally well to the experience of reading fiction.

The romances that delude Arabella provide her with enabling
fictions to express the truth of her desires, with plots through
which she can reshape her impressions of the world. Performing
the act of imagination which Johnson declared inevitable in reading about human experience, she identifies with personages whose
heroism and glory supply her with images of possibility. "Truth . . .
is generally unpleasing because contrary to our wishes." Wishes,
however, possess their own truth; *The Female Quixote* tells its story.

Neither Dr. Johnson nor the moralist who stands in for him, that
moralist horrified by Arabella's self-imagining, however, hears this
story the novel tells. Desire involves true feeling, but it implies false
reasoning: "sophistry." This conjunction lies at the heart of Johnson's anxiety about fiction, which, dressed by desire, arouses feeling
and threatens rationality. Arabella, heroine of a didactic novel, responds readily to a wise man's *naming* of her experience, which
registers his verbal force. She thinks she has read truth; the moralist names it fiction. She believes herself motivated by desire for
virtue and fame; the clergyman names her desire as directed toward love and revenge. Accepting conventional names, she accepts
her conventional fate. Control of language implies control of action: the novel demonstrates what Johnson had long asserted.

But it also embodies what he fears. Even *The Female Quixote*—for
that matter, even *Clarissa*, Johnson's type of the ethically sound
novel—exemplifies truth dressed by desire, thus unpredictable in
its effects. As Arabella's desire responds to that expressed in the
romances, creating (Johnson would say) its own sophistries, so every reader brings his or her own desire to the text, reiterating in
unexpected ways the desire of the novel. The clergyman hears a
story of a foolish girl, her noble mind o'erthrown by fiction; he
reforms her. The reader whose desires are answered by affirma-
tion of social stability may read the same story, but the text allows
confirmation also of other wishes.[4] The "tendency" of Arabella's
story reveals an amateur social critic able to demonstrate her wis-

dom even in her folly, and it shows her ultimate defeat by social fact and convention.

Clara Reeve's argument about the identical effects of "Romance" and "true History" goes on to praise the spirit aroused in readers by both genres at their best. "Whenever this spirit, and this enthusiasm, become the objects of contempt and ridicule," she maintains, "mankind will set up for themselves an idol of a very different kind.—They will then devote themselves to mean or mercenary pursuits which debase and corrupt the mind" (1:102). Reeve also points out, in relation to *The Female Quixote*, that by the time the novel appeared, "the taste for those Romances was extinct, and the books exploded" (2: 6). Perhaps, then, Lennox's satiric target was not so much romances as those "mean . . . pursuits which debase and corrupt the mind." In any case, she leaves open for the reader the possibility of understanding that the "contempt and ridicule" leveled against Arabella, like more general attacks on the enthusiastic spirit encouraged by reading romance and history, reflects the debasement of her critics more than the ridiculousness of her aims.

Nancy Armstrong suggests that twentieth-century readers are "likely to feel that the success of repeated pressures to coax and nudge sexual desire into conformity with the norms of heterosexual monogamy affords a fine way of closing a novel and provides a satisfactory goal for a text to achieve" (6). The most remarkable accomplishment of *The Female Quixote* is to raise questions about just these matters: not only about marriage as a goal for a girl to seek as rapidly as possible, but about where the richest possibilities for story lie. The novel ends as it must; but it does not leave all readers confident that this is a fine way of closing a novel.

Partly because Lennox's book raises more questions than it resolves, it provides an appropriate starting point for investigation of the eighteenth-century novel. Its central questions concern the nature of desire (including desire for fiction) and of readers' relation to it; the boundaries of responsible interpretation; the scope of fiction's appropriate emotional effect and its consequences; the relative place of rationality and passion in understanding; the interpenetration of fiction and history. As it examines desire's sophistries, it generates awareness of the social determinants of desire. As this novel examines the character of a fiction-deluded girl, it announces the possibility of new forms of female power: not merely the power of sexual desirability, but the force of self-imagining. Acknowledging desire's capacity to deceive, Lennox's work also demonstrates desire's authority and energy.

To be sure, although the novel in its meditations on plot articulates or implies these issues, its own plot does not confirm the radical implications concealed within it. Like her contemporaries, Lennox understood plot structure as based on lines of power. There is no way for Arabella to win: controlling social facts limit plot's possibilities. A young woman cannot triumph over a wise clergyman, fiction cannot overcome fact, a girl cannot sustain her dominance over a lover beyond conventional limits. Reality must subdue desire. Yet the possibilities raised before probability triumphs express themselves also in various ways in other fictions of eighteenth-century England. Johnson's understanding of fiction as the union of truth and desire implies the uncontrollability of texts: like that of desire itself, a source of danger and of appeal. The eighteenth-century novel would go on to explore both aspects.

2

INVENTING GOOD STORIES

To invent good Stories, and to tell them well, are possibly very rare Talents. (Fielding, *Tom Jones* 488; bk. 9, ch. 1)

There can be no kind of writing which relates to men and manners where it is not necessary for the author to understand poetical and moral truth, the beauty of sentiments, the sublime of characters, and carry in his eye the model or exemplar of that natural grace which gives to every action its attractive charm. If he has naturally no eye or ear for these interior numbers, 'tis not likely he should be able to judge better of that exterior proportion and symmetry of composition which constitutes a legitimate piece. (Shaftesbury 216)

The relation between the "interior numbers" that constitute moral harmony and the gift for inventing good stories remained a problem throughout the eighteenth century. Shaftesbury wrote before the novel, as we understand it, existed. Yet his desiderata for every kind of writing called attention to a problem implicit in the new form as well as in its predecessors. Given a mimetic enterprise—and the claim of realism by which novels distinguished themselves from romances of course implied mimesis—the problem of what to imitate demands attention. Shaftesbury assumes the writer's universal obligation to imitate the ideal forms of things, the Platonic pattern available for one to "carry in his eye" but not accessible in the actual world. Most eighteenth-century novelists, however, consciously rejected ideal forms in favor of models from actuality. Hence the anxiety about fiction exemplified most familiarly by Dr. Johnson. Ira Konigsberg argues that Johnson felt threatened by novels "because the reader's mind and imagination were filled with experiences and thoughts not his own, allowing memory and hence identity to be too easily exchanged for those of the fictional character" (5). Many critics contemporary with Johnson expressed comparable concerns.

Shaftesbury claims a necessary connection between moral awareness and capacity to generate "exterior proportion and symmetry of composition." In novels, elegance of plot construction declares such proportion and symmetry. What kind of relation can we per-

ceive between the desire that drives plots and the "truth" that novelists claimed to promulgate, between the invention of good stories
and the furthering of good character? Johnson's notion that desire
dresses truth to constitute fiction suggests a hopeful view of the
relationship, although his discussions of desire as a dangerous
human impulse often imply necessary divergence between desire
and ethical behavior. Other eighteenth-century commentators perceive—as Shaftesbury implicitly does—a possible conflict of desire
and truth, recapitulating the familiar, troubling clash of feeling
and thought.

Particularly emphatic in their implicit and explicit awareness of
plot, *Tom Jones* and *Tristram Shandy* provide good starting points for
trying to locate eighteenth-century understanding of plot's meaning and energy. Coleridge's claim of a "perfect plot" for Fielding's
novel, a claim earlier articulated by Fielding's contemporaries, has
been echoed by subsequent critics, most notably R. S. Crane, who
specifies just what such a characterization of the novel might mean.
But *Tom Jones* not only embodies an arguably perfect plot (some
dispute the point: see, e.g., Goldknopf), it also abounds in reflections about the form and content of adequate storytelling. *Tristram
Shandy*, on the other hand, ostentatiously flouts orthodox rules of
narration. As Gabriel Josipovici puts it, "Plot, in the sense in which
it exists in George Eliot or Dickens, does not exist in *Tristram
Shandy*. That novel's movement is all sideways, never forward towards the final revelation inherent in plot" (23). Yet the famous
assertion by the Russian formalist Victor Shklovsky, that "*Tristram
Shandy* is the most typical novel in world literature" (57), appears
to rest on Shklovsky's conviction that Sterne's violation of conventional form "forces us to attend to it" (30), the violation becoming
the very content of the novel (31). Only defiance of plot, in other
words, makes plot's meaning fully manifest.

The issue of truth concerns the narrator of *Tom Jones* most insistently. Emphatic about his difference from writers of romance, he
claims the historian's powers, recording private rather than public
history. The "truth" of his enterprise inheres in his conformity to
the laws of "nature." "As we have good Authority for all our Characters, no less indeed than the vast authentic Doomsday-Book of
Nature, . . . our Labours have sufficient Title to the Name of History" (489; bk. 9, ch. 1). Unlike other historians, he does not draw
his information from written records, he can cite no supporting
testimony, but his narrative does not therefore lack authority. The
order of historians to which he belongs must possess "Genius," con-
sisting of Invention and Judgment. Invention, however, does not

imply making things up. "By Invention is really meant no more, (and so the Word signifies) than Discovery, or finding out; or to explain it at large, a quick and sagacious Penetration into the true Essence of all the Objects of our Contemplation" (491; bk. 9, ch. 1). The novelist's ultimate claim to authority rests on his capacity to discern truth—"true Essence."

The narrator expresses his contempt for the supernatural as plot device: for the exploded fictions of the ancients, for the sacred agents of Christian belief when used as novelistic counters, even for ghosts, although authors may be permitted to make "sparing" use of them.

These are indeed like Arsenic, and other dangerous Drugs in Physic, to be used with the utmost Caution; nor would I advise the Introduction of them at all in those Works, or by those Authors to which, or to whom a Horse-Laugh in the Reader would be any great Prejudice or Mortification. (399; bk. 8, ch. 1)

Readers, however, often enjoy the supernatural. The narrator's scrupulosity about eschewing it, which reflects his primary concern with truth, on occasion implies his willingness to reject his readers' desires.

The narrator's apparent awareness of the reader's desire, at various levels, permeates the text and influences many of his comments on the making of his own fiction. He remains vividly conscious of what readers may be expected to think, to want, or to hope. His tone toward them shifts, but his awareness of those metaphoric travelers who may or may not choose to dine at his inn seldom wavers. He understands that they want a satisfying structure in the books they read; he knows that they possess universal human wishes and hopes. The shape of their desire will control the reception of his text. At the end of the chapter in which Tom has arranged the marriage of young Nightingale and his Nancy, the narrator comments,

Those Readers who are of the same Complexion with him will perhaps think this short Chapter contains abundance of Matter; while others may probably wish, short as it is, that it had been totally spared as impertinent to the main Design, which I suppose they conclude is to bring Mr. *Jones* to the Gallows, or if possible, to a more deplorable Catastrophe. (816; bk. 15, ch. 8)

Readers, in other words, shape a plot (or "Design") in their minds in accordance with their natures; they accept or resist the novelist's attempt to impose a plot insofar as they share or oppose his assumptions and wishes. Although the narrator often adopts a contemptuous or patronizing tone toward hypothetical readers whose desires lead them in different directions from his own, he recognizes their troubling power to refuse the feast he offers, to seek out a new bill of fare.

His most aggressive—and most anxious—address to the reader occurs at the beginning of Book 10, in the middle of the episodes at Upton:

> Reader, it is impossible we should know what Sort of Person thou wilt be: For, perhaps, thou may'st be as learned in Human Nature as *Shakespear* himself was, and, perhaps, thou may'st be no wiser than some of his Editors. . . .
>
> First, then, we warn thee not too hastily to condemn any of the Incidents in this our History, as impertinent and foreign to our main Design, because thou dost not immediately conceive in what Manner such Incident may conduce to that Design. This Work may, indeed, be considered as a great Creation of our own; and for a little Reptile of a Critic to presume to find Fault with any of its Parts, without knowing the Manner in which the Whole is connected, and before he comes to the final Catastrophe, is a most presumptuous Absurdity. (523–25; bk. 10, ch. 1)

The narrator goes on to justify himself for presenting similar characters in similar roles (the landlady in the seventh book and the one in the ninth) and, lengthily, to claim the value of characters who display both virtues and vices; he warns the reader "not to condemn a Character as a bad one, because it is not perfectly a good one" (526). His concern focuses not only on the danger of negative critical judgment but on the possibility that the reader will not submit to his "Design," both his plot and its purposes.

The issue, finally, simply, and almost explicitly, is power to control assignments of truth and to direct desire. The "great Creation" of the novelist must be acknowledged as great, its controlling "Design" submitted to. If the reader will admit the comparative inadequacy of his own conceptions and yield to the novelist's authority, all will be well. But the reader may have competing claims. In Godwin's terms, "tendency" need not recapitulate "moral." Sometimes the narrator jokes about this fact, sometimes he expresses anger, sometimes he argues his points. Often he taunts readers with his own superior knowledge, pointing out that he neglected to convey some vital bit of information earlier because an apparent rather than genuine cause would suffice to satisfy the reader at a given juncture, or simply emphasizing his capacity to choose either to divulge or to conceal. Always he implies the recognition exemplified in *The Female Quixote*: plot is power.

One of the novel's early digressions raises a question about the relation between character and event. "It is a more useful Capacity," the narrator asserts, "to be able to foretel the Actions of Men in any Circumstance from their Characters; than to judge of their Characters from their Actions" (117; bk. 3, ch. 1). He invites his readers to exercise the former skill, but in fact the novelistic enterprise depends on the latter. Tom's reported actions and the tone in which they are reported create the reader's impression of his character; thus plot controls fictional character, although virtually all eighteenth-century commentators assumed the converse. The narrator's apparent anxiety lest readers should continue to wish and expect Tom to be hanged—an outcome early suggested by the narrator himself—reflects concern that those readers may not submit to the authority of his design. Look how clever I am, he says over and over: I kept these two characters apart, I accounted for this event in this misleading fashion. . . . But cleverness is not enough. Only if readers accept the propriety of the happy ending, coerced by the plot into believing that Tom indeed deserves Sophia and might plausibly get her—only such acceptance, such submission, can declare the triumph of the author's "Design" and justify his enterprise.

If readers *do* accept the plot's design, they have accepted a corresponding version of truth. Fielding's announced moral purpose includes leading others to acquiesce about the mixed nature of human character. If readers acknowledge that Tom has earned his reward, they have agreed that virtue deserves recognition even when mingled with vice. Moreover, the reader has concurred in the novel's definition of acceptable and unacceptable kinds of vice. Blifil deserves punishment, Thwackum is worse than Square, fornication is a venial sin: the judgments to which we consent outline a moral universe (see Sacks on this point).

Tristram Shandy as narrator of his own career reflects on the structure of his narrative both in order to taunt and to educate the reader. Whereas Fielding's narrator claims absolute control of his "Design," Sterne's calls attention to the fact that all designs issue from fallible and wavering human minds. Given the associative structure of mental process, any fictional structure must reflect a more personal version of truth than Fielding's novel implicitly claims. Truth nonetheless: Tristram flaunts his authenticity and his narrative's consequent integrity.

Although Tristram at one point claims to be approaching a straight line in his narrative form, he suggests more often that straight lines of narrative are necessarily inauthentic.

Could a historiographer drive on his history, as a muleteer drives on his mule,—straight forward;—for instance, from *Rome* all the way to *Loretto*, without ever once turning his head aside either to the right hand or to the left,—he might venture to foretell you to an hour when he should get to his journey's end;—but the thing is, morally speaking, impossible: For, if he is a man of the least spirit, he will have fifty deviations from a straight line to make with this or that party as he goes along, which he can no ways avoid. He will have views and prospects to himself perpetually solliciting his eye, which he can no more help standing still to look at than he can fly; he will moreover have various

> Accounts to reconcile:
> Anecdotes to pick up:
> Inscriptions to make out:
> Stories to weave in:
> Traditions to sift . . . (41; bk. 1, ch. 14)

Morally speaking, impossible. Tristram finds a moral issue in the choice between straight line and squiggle. Abundant verbal possibilities (preexistent accounts, anecdotes, inscriptions, stories, traditions), like possible visual distractions ("views and prospects") and the incalculable demands of other people ("this or that party"), imply the need to incorporate. This need is not merely wish but genuine necessity; Tristram can no more help looking at what the world presents than he can fly. But there remains the implicit alternative of exclusion, which alone makes possible straight lines of narrative. And exclusion is morally unacceptable: impossible.

Josipovici calls attention to the fact that the failure of plot in *Tristram Shandy* results from the narrator's unsuccessful struggle to triumph over time.

> Plot and metaphor suggest a triumph of the artist over time. It is not surprising that aestheticians, concerned to replace religion by art, have made so much of these things. *Tristram Shandy* enacts the effort to achieve them and the failure of that effort. The book is all extension and no meaning, all analogy and metonymy and no metaphor or plot. (29)

The apparent rejection of plot in Sterne's novel, however, conveys not only failure but the narrative's central assumption, its conviction that truth can only be located in totality—or the nearest possible approach to totality, since Tristram soon admits the impossibility of keeping up with his own experience in a verbal record. Indeed, plot's impossibilities receive a good deal of textual attention. Tristram invokes the "POWERS . . . which enable mortal man to tell a story worth the hearing,—that kindly shew him, where he is to begin it,—and where he is to end it,—what he is to put into it,—and what he is to leave out,—how much of it he is to cast into shade,—and whereabouts he is to throw his light!" (244; bk. 3, ch. 23). The choices invoked—where to begin and where to end, what to include and what to omit, how to determine light and shade—specifically involve arrangements of plot. And those arrangements often seem, in *Tristram Shandy*, altogether arbitrary. When Tristram introduces into his narrative a rhapsody on the goodness of Uncle Toby, he begins, "Here,—but why here,— rather than in any other part of my story,—I am not able to tell;— but here it is" (265; bk. 3, ch. 34). "Is a man to follow rules—or rules to follow him?" he inquires later (337; bk. 4, ch. 10), sounding rather like Lewis Carroll's Humpty Dumpty. His answer to this rhetorical question is obvious. But plot is by no means only a matter of rules. Events *demand* narration. Even hypothetical events thrust themselves in, such as Uncle Toby's death at some time in the future. Tristram narrates the funeral as an imagined scene, then appeals once more to the "powers" to help him tell a story so profoundly involved with his personal feeling (545; bk. 6, ch. 25). Emotions determine significance, but even events of significance—*especially* such events—require skill in the telling in order to arouse corresponding emotions in the reader. The connections between feeling and narrative expertise remain an explicit problem throughout Sterne's novel.

For Tristram as for the narrator of *Tom Jones*, plot implies relationship with the reader. Tristram comments on his difficulty, given his peculiar way of storytelling, in conveying a unified impression: "when a man is telling a story in the strange way I do mine, he is obliged continually to be going backwards and forwards to keep all tight together in the reader's fancy" (557–8; bk. 6, ch. 33). "Much unexpected business [may] fall out betwixt the reader and myself," Tristram observes (39; bk. 1, ch. 13). Just so. The reader's fancy, here and elsewhere, collaborates with his own. At the level of wordplay, Tristram draws upon the bawdy imagination he assumes in his audience. (As Robert Alter points out, in *Tristram Shandy* sexuality is "the universal preoccupation that binds us while systems sizzle, hypotheses hatch, and ratiocination goes its merry solipsistic way" [*Partial* 39].) At the level of plot, the novel duplicates the narrator's sexual problems of impotence and failure of climax. Let us drop the story, Tristram says at one point,

for though I have all along been hastening towards this part of it, with so much earnest desire, as well knowing it to be the choicest morsel of what I had to offer to the world, yet now that I am got to it, any one is welcome to take my pen, and go on with the story for me that will. (779; bk. 9, ch. 24)

The storyteller's desire generates the plot and conceives its climax, but the reader's desire might be equally authoritative.

In *Elements of Criticism*, an important eighteenth-century theoretical work which attempts to account for literary power in psychological terms, Lord Kames observes that "It is a law of our nature, that we never act but by the impulse of desire; which in other words is saying, that passion, by the desire included in it, is what determines the will" (96). *Tristram Shandy* in effect analyzes the implications of that statement by investigating relationships of desire and will. If the stories Sterne's novel tells repeatedly dramatize tensions of desire and will, the structure that contains them, haphazard though it seems, illustrates how inevitably but how deviously desire expresses itself. Tzvetan Todorov, in "Speech According to Constant," raises the possibility that desire may "be one of those constants which permit us to define literature itself" (*Poetics* 106). Tristram seems to think so too—as does Lord Kames. In Tristram's view, the hypothetical reader's desires lend themselves to codification as little as do his own. The difficulty of achieving straight lines, or straightforward plots, directly reflects desire's incalculability. Tristram's narrative desire vacillates between eagerness to reveal and delight in concealing. To tell a story, he demonstrates, can never be easy: Corporal Trim never manages to relate his tale of the king of Bohemia, for reasons partly dependent on his listener's wishes. To hear, or read, and understand a story is not easy either. The narrator cannot assume that the reader's will and desire will correspond to his own.

So Tristram's declarations of narrative power—specifically of the power of his plots—sound less authoritative and more desperate, though also more teasing, than those of Fielding's narrator. He can control his text, he keeps telling us, no more than his own desires. But he possesses some control over his readers; specifically, the ability to play with them. He can demand that readers attend closely to tiny details of narrated happenings; he can force them to listen to his stories; he can refuse to tell them stories. The arbitrariness of structure to which he repeatedly calls attention signals his inability to dominate his text but his power to dominate his readers. The narrator of *Tom Jones* acknowledges the possibility that guests at the inn may not like his bill of fare; Tristram Shandy acknowledges nothing of the sort. Theoretically, readers can choose not to read. Tristram implies, however, that they have no choice at all, that they must submit to his narrative desire even when it produces only a cock-and-bull story.

He claims, then, both more and less authority than does the narrator of *Tom Jones*: more, in assuming that readers must read; less, in verbally abrogating control over his own text. Or perhaps he only achieves his authority in different ways. Ross Chambers, reminding us (as does Tristram, after his fashion) that "stories are not innocent" (7), differentiates devices by which storytellers declare their power.

> One is . . . the tranquil assumption of a mastery that is, literally, *taken for granted*. . . . In this connection, secrecy—the claim to be in possession of a secret, together with an implied willingness to divulge it—forms the paradigm of all such tactics of narrative authority. (214)

Such is Fielding's method, in his narrator's explicit comments on his own procedure, his hints about an outcome he knows and the reader does not—although perhaps the assumption of mastery is less "tranquil" than Chambers's paradigm suggests.

Chambers goes on to point out that "authority" necessarily depends on the existence of another. "There can be no narrative without the authority to narrate, and no authority without the authorization of another, whose desire must consequently be inscribed, however spectrally, in the narrative discourse itself" (218). It follows, therefore, that narrative—often or always—involves a process of seduction: by narrator, of reader. Chambers focuses his own analysis of this process on nineteenth-century novels, but the model applies with some exactitude to the ways that Tristram, as narrator of himself, manipulates his imagined readers. The storyteller in *Tom Jones* calls attention to his function as Providence-surrogate; Tristram insists on the fallible humanity he shares with his readers. He knows them because he knows himself, knows how to work on their desires because he knows his own. Their desires have little power over him precisely because he acknowledges them so fully.

Inasmuch as *Tristram Shandy* tells the story defined by its problematic plot, it tells of its protagonist's tortuous yet typical consciousness. The story of the novel's telling is the story of the mind, of "human nature." More specifically, the novel's running commentary on the difficulties of plot emphasizes possibilities already apparent in *The Female Quixote*. To construct a plot constitutes a moral endeavor, Tristram tells us. To falsify experience by the imposition of rules and logic violates the storyteller's central obligation of truth. He reveals the forms of his desire in his narrative's intricate and self-cancelling shapes; the most important truths he has to tell—more important than any of the data that nominally comprise his story of his family and his life—are of his own inconsistent wishes and will. The impossibility of imparting to his life a retro-spective unity that helps him "to achieve, even at a late hour, some reconciliation with the past" (Wollheim 315)—that impossibility constitutes Tristram's tragedy.

Fielding's narrator, in his obsession with the marvel of his "De-sign," bears little obvious resemblance to Sterne's, forever plagued by his inability to achieve design and perplexed by the relation be-tween life and story. But both, talking about plot, convey belief in the profound meaning of formal arrangements. The narrative or-der of *Tom Jones*, the storyteller says, affirms the moral order: it tells the truth. (We shall see in the next chapter how complicated the relationship of narrative to moral meaning proves in practice.) The apparent narrative chaos of *Tristram Shandy* tells its truth about the human mind. Samuel Johnson thought that Sterne's novel had failed to last because it was "odd"; the integrity of its oddness and of its narrator's reflections about that oddness has come to seem its excellence. Plot implies not only an arrangement of episodes, both narrators suggest, but a fundamental structure of meaning.

Utterances about plot reveal outlines of possibility; only by investi-gating the operations of specific plots will we see what kinds of substance plots have, what meanings they convey. Commentary by eighteenth-century critics who did not themselves write novels, however, may help to form our expectations. Such commentary recurs insistently to three issues: truth and verisimilitude, morality, and (increasingly as the century went on) emotional power. The three concerns often relate closely.

James Beattie, in 1783, summarized the position about truth in relation to fiction that critics appear generally to have agreed on. (Part of this passage was quoted previously in the Preamble.)

The love of Truth is natural to man; and adherence to it, his indispensable duty. But to frame a fabulous narrative, for the purpose of instruction or of harmless amusement, is no breach of veracity, unless one were to ob-trude it on the world for truth. The fabulist and the novel-writer deceive nobody; because, though they study to make their inventions probable, they do not even pretend that they are true: at least, what they may pre-tend in this way is considered only as words of course, to which nobody pays any regard . . .

It is owing, no doubt, to the weakness of human nature, that fable should ever have been found a necessary, or a convenient, vehicle for truth. (505)

The end justifies the means, in this view: if novelists have a moral purpose, or even the aim of innocent entertainment, they may indulge the weakness of human nature by inventing fictions. Beattie uses the word *truth*, confusingly, in two different senses. On the one hand, "fabulous narratives" are acceptable only if they do not claim truth for themselves. On the other, such narratives become justifiable as "vehicles for truth." Truth means accurate representation of actual happenings; in this signification, it has little connection with fiction. But it also means, as it does for Johnson, valid moral doctrine, which fiction has the power to promulgate.

This terminological confusion hints at the difficulty and ambiguity of verisimilitude in fiction. Clara Reeve comes closer to stating the problem:

The Novel gives a familiar relation of such things, as pass every day before our eyes, such as may happen to our friend, or to ourselves; and the perfection of it, is to represent every scene, in so easy and natural a manner, and to make them appear so probable, as to deceive us into a persuasion (at least while we are reading) that all is real, until we are affected by the joys or distresses, of the persons in the story, as if they were our own. (1: 111)

All very well, as an ideal. In practice, the capacity of the novel to deceive its readers into temporary conviction "that all is real" creates not only a source of emotional energy but a ground for serious moral difficulties.

(It is worth noting Todorov's explanation of the twentieth-century preference for long books over short texts: "not because length is taken as a criterion of value, but because there is no time, in reading a short work, to forget it is only 'literature' and not 'life'" [*Poetics* 143]. We retain our forebears' desire that literature deceive us; but literary critics still worry about its propriety.)

Reeve herself goes on to point out fiction's moral dangers, in discussing the evils of the circulating library.

The seeds of vice and folly are sown in the heart,—the passions are awakened,—false expectations are raised.—A young woman is taught to expect adventures and intrigues,—she expects to be addressed in the style of these books, with the language of flattery and adulation.—If a plain man addresses her in rational terms and pays her the greatest of compliments,—that of desiring to spend his life with her,—that is not sufficient, her vanity is disappointed, she expects to meet a Hero in Romance. (2: 78)

This evocation of a generalized equivalent for Lennox's Arabella epitomizes the danger of allowing temporary conviction to extend itself beyond the text.

The same imagined female figure appears in many critical discussions. Her delusion, as other commentators point out, might lead her to neglect ordinary duties, to make herself socially useless. Novel-readers could exhaust their sensibility in emotion directed toward imaginary characters and abandon their moral obligations toward actual human beings. Henry Mackenzie, himself the author of a well-known sentimental novel, worries about this point: "In the enthusiasm of sentiment there is much the same danger as in the enthusiasm of religion, of substituting certain impulses and feelings of what may be called a visionary kind, in the place of real practical duties, which, in morals, as in theology, we might not improperly denominate good works" (330). Henry James Pye, at the end of the century, in the course of a commentary on Aristotle, puts the position more straightforwardly:

> May not the young woman, who is for ever weeping over the distresses of a Clarissa, or a Sydney Biddulph [sic], and tracing the affecting scenes, and wonderful revolutions, to be found in the adventures of a Cecilia, or an Emmeline, have her feelings something deadened to the less interesting distresses of ordinary life. (148)

Pye does not end his query with a question mark: there is really no question about it. Such observations as this suggest a concern lest the forms of social love turn into the substance of self-love. Fiction can provide its readers the illusion of concern with other people, but those figments of the writer's imagination only encourage the reader's inward life, his or her (and of course the "young woman" reader inhabits the imagination of most critics) self-absorption.

The threat of self-absorption implies a range of difficulties inherent in the linking of truth with desire. In Johnson's uncharacteristically optimistic fable, fiction has its essence, truth, made more attractive when clothed with desire. But even the most cursory exploration of desire's actual dimensions raises questions about how well truth can survive its disguises. If, to pursue Pye's example, "desire" takes the form of yearning for emotional outlet, whatever doctrine a fiction offers will not penetrate the mind of a reader who uses novels as pretext for feeling. The space between "moral" and "tendency" that Godwin would locate allows room for a reader's selfish redirection of meaning. Knowing fictions to be fictions— and Beattie suggests the meretriciousness of a writer's pretending persuasively that they are something else, although of course many eighteenth-century novelists at least nominally declared the factuality of their fictions—the hypothetical reader need not take them seriously except as devices for self-stimulation. Even novels of ex-

acting verisimilitude may function as means of emotional indulgence. To force readers to make a connection between the truths
of fiction and those of the world they inhabit often proves, Pye
suggests (Bertolt Brecht, among others, would amplify his insight
long afterwards), beyond a novelist's power.

Yet sensibility itself implies a kind of morality for many eighteenth-century thinkers. The idea that someone might altogether
lack sensibility horrifies critics more than does the notion of misdirected sensibility. A minor writer named Martin Sherlock, useful
for my purposes because he confines himself almost entirely to reiterating his period's commonplaces, puts the point vividly. "With
what cold indifference do many people see their fellow-creatures
in distress, and read Clarissa, without shedding a tear! Clarissa,
because they know it is not true; and human beings in misery, because, though it *is* true, what is that to them?" (1: 30–31). It would
be wicked to weep only for Clarissa rather than for the worthy
poor, but worse not to weep even for Clarissa. Sherlock implies a
moral danger in dismissing fiction because it is "untrue." As Reeve
puts it, "There needs no other proof of a bad and corrupted heart,
then its being insensible to the distresses, and incapable to the rewards of virtue.—I should want no other criterion of a *good* or *bad*
heart, than the manner in which a young person was affected, by
reading *Pamela*" (1:135). John Moore, suggesting a logical foundation for this kind of argument, attributes the fundamental pleasure of novel-reading to recognition of one's common humanity.
"Nothing can be so interesting to men as man." He demands a kind
of local verisimilitude: "The modern romances [i.e., novels] are or
ought to be a representation of life and manners in the country
where the scene is placed" (*A View* 62). Only thus, presumably, can
"men" recognize the authenticity of fictional rendition.

Emotional power measures fiction's worth. Lord Kames uses
drama and poetry as his types of "fiction," but his explicit observation that in some respects the distinction between fiction and history does not matter announces radical critical possibilities for
understanding the novel. "In judging beforehand of man, so remarkably addicted to truth and reality, one should little dream that
fiction can have any effect upon him," Kames comments (51), going
on to elaborate his theory of "ideal presence": the capacity to see
absent or unreal phenomena with absolute conviction, as though
they were literally present.

If, in reading, ideal presence be the means by which our passions are
moved, it makes no difference whether the subject be a fable or a true

history: when ideal presence is complete, we perceive every object as in our sight; and the mind, totally occupied with an interesting event, finds no leisure for reflection. This reasoning is confirmed by constant and universal experience. (53–54)

Kames's theoretical argument puts in more abstract and generalized terms Reeve's observation about fiction's power to deceive us into conviction of its reality and to make us participate in the concerns of imagined characters as though they were our own. As Eric Rothstein points out, this notion of ideal presence articulates implications of views suggested by many critics before Kames. In Rothstein's summary,

the logical end of mimesis is full illusion: the best work of art will call least attention to itself and will most enforce on the viewers the sensuous presence of its content. . . . Although few eighteenth-century critics applied this rule single-mindedly, most of them made it one central thrust of their aesthetics, with various reservations and counterbalances. ("'Ideal Presence'" 309)

Rothstein also notes the degree to which Kames's theory, by implying the reader's imaginative participation in the work of the text, entails the uncontrollability of the fictional work. "Any theory of ideal presence must accept imaginative expansion of the text. No poetic description, after all, can be as detailed as a present object in its particularity and within its context. The reader's imagination supplies what the poet can not, and different readers are likely to be . . . far apart" (312). In Kames's view, according to Rothstein, the reader's "imaginative expansion . . . should . . . strengthen that sympathy between poet/speaker and reader which is basic to eighteenth-century aesthetics" (331).

Kames's theory of ideal presence works toward suggesting that the truth of imaginative literature is necessarily that of desire. In the relation between reader and text that he posits, the reader "finds no leisure for reflection," caught in the immediacy of an imagined situation. This immediacy, Kames says, provides "the means by which our passions are moved." Conceivably, the reader's passions and the author's will duplicate one another in response to textual evocations. But, as Rothstein's elucidation emphasizes, passions are in their nature unpredictable. Individual emotional needs differ. The reader's desire will shape the text's meaning, as the author's desire has constructed it in the first place. The sympathy between writer and reader depends on their identification as beings of passion. The authenticity of fiction—its "truth"—derives from this identification.

Critics less theoretically inclined than Kames, less concerned to figure out how fiction acts on the emotions, agree that it does so. An imitation of Dr. Johnson, in a collection of essays by John and Anna Laetitia Aikin (better-known by her married name of *Barbauld*), chooses fiction as its subject. "But let it be remembered," the essay ("On Romance") concludes, "that we are more attracted by those scenes which interest our passions, or gratify our curiosity, than those which delight our fancy: and so far from being indifferent to the miseries of others, we are, at the time, totally regardless of our own" (45). Works of fiction, in fact, "teach us to think, by inuring us to feel" (46). This idea has far-reaching implications. If reason and feeling cooperate rather than compete, if feeling logically precedes and facilitates thought in the operations of fiction on its readers, then novels and romances threaten the established pre-eminence of the rational. The Aikin essays recur frequently to questions about the nature and value of the sensibility aroused by fiction. Why is it, "On Objects of Terror" inquires, that we get pleasure from experiencing fear in our reading? Perhaps the pleasure derives not from fear but from the necessary power of plot.

The pain of suspense, and the irresistible desire of satisfying curiosity, when once raised, will account for our eagerness to go quite through an adventure, though we suffer actual pain during the whole course of it. We rather chuse to suffer the smart pang of a violent emotion than the uneasy craving of an unsatisfied desire. (123)

The "desire," in this instance, is precisely the one Peter Brooks identifies as dominating readers: the desire to get to the end, to achieve resolution.

When critics focus on the experience of reading, as Kames does and as the Aikins do in the examples thus far quoted, they tend to assign high value to emotion. When they concern themselves, more abstractly, with fiction's moral effects, the novel's emotional power troubles them. We have already seen instances of critics' moral reservations about fiction's capacity to generate emotion; others abound. Dour Vicesimus Knox, for example, suggests that sentimental fiction is as dangerous as licentious fiction can be. "It has given an amiable name to vice, and has obliquely excused the extravagance of the passions, by representing them as the effect of lovely sensibility" (305). The pleasure produced by novels constitutes their danger: "the mind, once accustomed to [novels], cannot submit to the painful task of serious study. Authentic history becomes insipid" (306). An anonymous writer to the *Gentleman's Magazine* sums up one case against the novel:

> Novels not only enervate the mind, by superinducing an affectation of sentimental feeling; they not only render it incapable of acting with fortitude and propriety in cases of REAL distress, which short experience of life will shew to be more abundant than to need the addition of imaginary evils; but they have a tendency still more fatal, they bring young readers acquainted with the worst part of the female sex, habituate them to loose principles and immodest practices, and thus send them into the world debauched, at least in heart, at an age which should be adorned with simplicity and innocence. ("Sentiments" 367)

Implicitly, once more, the novel's capacity to create "ideal presence" constitutes its potential for evil. If desire is truth, other truths yet remain. Moral rectitude typically opposes passion. Given the notion that "simplicity and innocence"—i.e., moral and psychological ignorance—should characterize young women, they must be protected from a literature of desire.

The Aikins, in the course of several pages of "An Enquiry into Those Kinds of Distress Which Excite Agreeable Sensations," avoid an exclusively moralistic tone in favor of thoughtful discussion of how good feelings induced by fiction may corrupt the mind. "Nothing is more dangerous," they write, "than to let virtuous impressions of any kind pass through the mind without producing their proper effect" (211). Such emotions as compassion and moral approbation, "if they do not lead to action, grow less and less vivid every time they recur, till at length the mind grows absolutely callous" (212). This again sounds Brechtian. It may remind us of the similar argument offered in our own time about television: that the spectacle of bodies in Viet Nam, or of imaginary and real violence on the streets of the United States, repeated before our eyes night after night, induces moral and emotional insensibility.

The Aikins's second concern calls attention to obfuscations of social class in certain kinds of eighteenth-century English fiction. "Another reason why plays and romances do not improve our humanity is, that they lead us to require a certain elegance of manners and delicacy of virtue which is not often found with poverty, ignorance, and meanness" (212). People with vulgar accents may not appeal to a reader's sense of pity, and "we must not fancy ourselves charitable, when we are only pleasing our imagination" (213). We please our imaginations specifically by denying such realities of experience as the British class system. Fiction still in the 1770s made

poverty emotionally appealing by ignoring its specific manifestations. Thus the illusion of life fiction provides becomes actively misleading. In this way too, novels may diminish their readers' capacity
to live their own lives responsibly.

René Wellek quotes Richard Hurd as calling novels "hasty, imperfect, and abortive poems" (Wellek 122). But other eighteenth-
century critics, as my sampling shows, tried to find language for
discussing novels fruitfully in the novels' own terms. The critics'
moral misgivings coexist with—to some extent depend upon—
their awareness of the emotional energy novels contain and generate. Although only the Aikins write specifically about plot as
source of that energy, most of the critical utterances I have quoted
imply that the intersection of plot and character centrally concerns
them. But plot, some critics suggested, is the fundamental interest
of readers. In a 1751 letter to Samuel Richardson (then projecting
Sir Charles Grandison), Philip Skelton writes,

Above all, consider the bulk of your readers, how grossly attached they are
to facts, and adventures, and be sure to enliven the performance with
plenty of subordinate events, all conspiring, and leading to the grand
event or catastrophe. The main stem of your story may now and then
branch into episodes; but take care that every twig grow as naturally out
of the tree, and bear as much fruit, as in *Clarissa*. (Skelton 170)

The gross attachment of readers to facts and adventures had long
been assumed. Skelton's letter suggests that he finds in this attachment the fundamental ground of their interest in fiction.

Mary de la Rivière Manley, writing early in the eighteenth century, herself a prolific composer of *romans à clef*, like the Aikins
associated plot with the reader's desire.

An Acute Historian ought to observe the same Method at the Ending as at
the Beginning of his Story, for he may at first expose Maxims relating but
a few Feats, but when the End draws nigher, the Curiosity of the Reader
is augmented, and he finds in him a Secret Impatience of desiring to see
the Discovery of the Action; an Historian that amuses himself by Moraliz-
ing or Describing, discourages an Impatient Reader, who is in haste to see
the End of Intrigues. . . .
    'Tis an indispensible Necessity to end a Story to satisfie the Disquiets of
the Reader, who is engag'd to the Fortunes of those People whose Adventures are described to him; 'tis depriving him of a most delicate Pleasure,
when he is hindred from seeing the Event of an Intrigue, which has caused
some Emotion in him, whose Discovery he expects, be it either Happy or
Unhappy. (Manley 38)

Considering the problems of novelists rather than of readers, Manley concentrates on the writer's obligation to gratify the reader's

desire—the obligation that aroused apparent anxiety in the narrators of *Tom Jones* and *Tristram Shandy*. Her comments suggest in a different way from Lord Kames and the Aikins the degree to which fiction can generate emotion that becomes a controlling force for readers. Although she takes a pragmatic attitude toward the phenomenon, she evokes a disturbing sense of how forcefully desire animated by plot can generate in a reader a will for the resolution of that plot.

One final extended critical comment: John Dennis, always interested in literature's emotional effects, uses the novelist's power over plot to account for the special pleasure fiction provides.

Nothing is more plain than that even in an Historical Relation some Parts of it, and some Events, please more than others. And therefore a Man of Judgment, who sees why they do so, may in forming a Fable, and disposing an Action, please more than an Historian can do. For the just Fiction of a Fable moves us more than an Historical Relation can do, for the two following Reasons: First, by reason of the Communication and mutual Dependence of its Parts. For if Passion springs from Motion, then the Obstruction of that Motion or a counter Motion must obstruct and check the Passion: And therefore an Historian and a Writer of Historical Plays passing from Events of one nature to Events of another nature without a due Preparation, must of necessity stifle and confound one Passion by another. The second Reason why the Fiction of a Fable pleases us more, than an Historical Relation can do, is, because in an Historical Relation we seldom are acquainted with the true Causes of Events, whereas in a feign'd Action which is duly constituted, that is, which has a just beginning, those Causes always appear. (Dennis 2: 5–6)

Dennis's implicit translation of *Action*, in the Aristotelian sense, into *Motion* calls attention to plot's dynamic function. Associating motion with emotion ("Passion"), he specifies the connection between plot and the reader's response to fiction. By the end of the century, Pye could allege the superiority of *Tom Jones* to *Tristram Shandy* on the basis of the preeminence of plot in the earlier work. In Sterne, he says, manners hold the first place; Fielding makes them "secondary to the action, though arising immediately, and necessarily, from it." Only "where our passions are engaged by incident" does Pye find novelistic excellence (165). And plot determines incident.

Dennis and, less emphatically, Pye reveal a level of critical awareness absent from most of the commentators I have quoted. Whether or not critics explicitly discuss "ideal presence" or its equivalent, most seem themselves confused about fiction's distance from literal experience. Expressions of concern about the effect on young women's behavior of reading novels, for instance, often sound as though the writers fear the literal presence of loose women in their daughters' bedrooms. The insistence, in *Tom Jones*, that knowledge of "human nature" dictates the novel's happenings, like Tristram's declarations that he writes just what comes into his head, emphasizes the novel's claims to create an illusion of life. Such an illusion has little to do with verisimilitude; indeed, the devices that sustain it often oppose verisimilitude. To think adequately about the implications of plot in the eighteenth-century novel, then, requires thinking about what Pye calls "incident" and how it engages our passions.

Paul Ricoeur, in the course of an illuminating discussion of verisimilitude, speculates about the

reason for [the] reduction of the concept of plot to that of mere story-line—or schema or summary of the incidents. If the plot, once reduced to this skeleton, could appear to be an external constraint, even an artificial and finally an arbitrary one, it is because, since the birth of the novel through the end of its golden age in the nineteenth century, a more urgent problem than that of the art of composition occupied the foreground: the problem of verisimilitude. The substitution of one problem for the other was facilitated by the fact that the conquest of verisimilitude took place under the banner of the struggle against 'conventions,' especially against what plot was supposed to be, on the basis of epic, tragedy, and comedy in their ancient, Elizabethan, and 'classical' (in the French sense of this term) forms. To struggle against these conventions and for verisimilitude constituted one and the same battle. (10–11)

This historical summary provides a useful context for considering the situation closer to that undefinable moment that announced "the birth of the novel." When Fielding wrote, even when Sterne followed him, conventions of plot derived from epic and drama governed most novelistic practice. (Pye's Aristotelian criticism considers epic, drama, and novel interchangeably, as though generic distinctions had no meaning.) "The problem of verisimilitude" existed only in rudimentary form, reflected in the claim that happenings in novels exceeded in probability those recorded in romance. Ricoeur suggests that the notion of plot as "external constraint" developed only in response to the growing obsession with literal realism. By implication, a more organic concept of plot operated, paradoxically, at the very time when manifestly "artificial" notions of form controlled the shape of most novels. Fielding's "perfect plot" presents itself ostentatiously as contrivance. If plot follows, as the narrator claims, the laws of "human nature," it more manifestly follows the will of its deviser. P. N. Furbank remarks that "the marriage-novel (from Fielding to Forster) is a particularly strong discouragement . . . to any lingering tendency to think of novels as replicas of life—in that their form, a set of events all tending towards a marriage, so little suggests a 'slice of life' and so loudly announces a purpose" (36). The plot of *Tom Jones* fairly brims with purpose: not only to reinforce the social order, but also, as Ralph Rader, Leopold Damrosch, and Martin Battestin have demonstrated, to assert and embody the operations of cosmic order.

Yet eighteenth-century readers took plot more seriously than we do, not as didactic form but as passionate content. To quote Kames's account of "ideal presence" once more: "the mind, totally occupied with an interesting event, finds no leisure for reflection" (54). The interesting events constructed by eighteenth-century novels apparently could register on their readers' emotions as immediate happenings, almost as direct experience. Highly contrived plots evidently facilitated rather than impeded the willing suspension of disbelief. We cannot hope to recapture the emotional situation of Fielding's contemporary readers in order to understand the kind of immediacy the artifice of plot conveyed to them, but it may be worth speculating about possible correlation between the ideological freight carried by eighteenth-century plots and their direct emotional effects.

Michael McKeon's one-sentence summary of the purpose of ideology describes equally well the purpose of the novel. "The purpose of ideology," McKeon writes, "is to mediate apparently intractable human problems so as to make them not simple but intelligible, to provide an explanation of reality whose plausibility will depend upon the degree to which it appears to do justice to the reality it explains" (223). To think of early novels as providing not a rendition but an explanation of reality helps to elucidate their contemporary power. James Beattie, in 1783, observed that "The rise and progress of the MODERN ROMANCE, or POETICAL PROSE FABLE [by which he means such novels as *Tom Jones*], is connected with many topicks of importance, which would throw (if fully illustrated) great light upon the history and politicks, the manners, and the literature, of these latter ages" (518). Unfortunately, he does not elucidate how novels throw light on public affairs or what light they shed.

One kind of light novels cast upon "history and politicks" emerges from their assumptions about relations among people, the assumptions on which fiction depends. Beliefs about the operations of power, the structures of hierarchy, the nature of intimacy, of causality, and of character, govern arrangements of incidents among imagined as among actual human beings. These often unexamined but always essential assumptions and beliefs emerge vividly in structures of plot that reveal possibilities of causality available to a given novelist. Plot declares how and why things happen. In satisfying the reader's (and the novelist's) sense of order, plot demonstrates the potency of desire for order. Within the context of its fiction, it alleges order's truth. In this sense, the fiction of coherent plot always serves conservative ends.

Inasmuch as it offers explanations of reality, plot insists on its own power. Novelists may claim, like the narrator of *Tom Jones*, to gain their authority and that of their plots from the "Book of Nature." They thus implicitly define truth as external to their own psyches and as operating by immutable laws, cosmic rather than social, although the fundamental principle they uphold may be that of social obligation. At the other extreme is the kind of writer represented by Tristram Shandy, whose truth is personal, idiosyncratic, and closely linked to desire. In the view of the world he promulgates, he effectively denies social meaning. He also denies the possibility of coherent order in experience or in narrative. The truth of his plot, or antiplot, is that of desire: not at all what Shaftesbury meant by "poetical and moral truth." To the degree that fiction commits itself to the preeminence of desire as governing principle, it challenges established political orders. On the other hand, it affirms a powerful ideology of individualism—also part of western political mythology.

The "truth" of transcendent moral doctrine and that of individual sensibility rarely coincide, although a novel may make its plot out of both. The invention of good stories and the furthering of good character in the imagined reader do not necessarily prove compatible aims. Nor is the definition of "good stories" (to say nothing of "good character") by any means clear. Are good stories those that entertain you? that do you good? that represent an ideal of goodness? The relation between compelling narrative and "poetical and moral truth" remains obscure. In the continuing multivocal argument about human behavior and possibility, plot contributes theses and evidence of many kinds. Plot makes and conveys meaning. The varieties of plot, even within the eighteenth century, encourage questions about the kinds of meaning it makes.

3

OF PLOTS AND POWER:
RICHARDSON AND FIELDING

Speculations about the dynamic of power in plots of eighteenth-century fiction might begin with the century's most famous pornographic novel. Toward the end of *Fanny Hill*, the protagonist, after several years and many sexual adventures, finds herself in bed once more with the man who deprived her of her virginity. She speaks ecstatically of "the pressure of that peculiar sceptre-member which commands us all: but especially my darling, elect from the face of the whole earth" (Cleland 215). The ambiguity of her syntax allows the possibility that the "sceptre-member" commands even its possessor, but Fanny presumably intends to say that her lover, "elect from the face of the whole earth," boasts the most commanding member of all.

Whether Charles controls his sexual organ or it governs him, the attribution of peculiar power to the phallus seems unsurprising in a novel which, as many commentators have noted, dwells obsessively on the size and force of male genitals, fostering an eighteenth-century sexual myth. (As a 1709 commentator, John Marten, put it, speaking before the publication of Cleland's novel about women in general, the penis "is a Part in great Esteem among the Women; for if by any accident they see it, so as not to be seen or known they see it, it instantly inflames their Hearts with a Passion not presently assuaged" [qu. Boucé 32].) But *Fanny Hill* also considers possibilities of female sexual power. At one point, Fanny seeks revenge on a lover who has betrayed her with a servant girl by going to bed herself with a young footman who proves to have a "machine" (Fanny's most persistent locution for the male organ) of enormous size. Fanny worries lest his penetration stretch her to a degree that will make her infidelity obvious to her keeper, but her worry proves unfounded. She feels great satisfaction, reflecting that she is "palpably mistress of any size of man" (102). The word *mistress* reverberates in both its meanings, but primarily Fanny here glories in her own sense of command. As she observes later, "There is, in short, in the men, when once they are caught, by the eye especially, a fund of cullibility that their lordly wisdom little dreams of, and in virtue of which the most sagacious of them are seen so often our dupes" (155).

Male power, these examples suggest, derives from the phallus; female power, from female beauty and the female capacity for trickery. One might speculate that the notion of a female physiological and psychological talent for deceit belongs to the same male fantasy that glorifies the phallus: wishes and fears, after all, are opposite sides of a single coin. But I do not propose at the moment to expand such speculation or to offer detailed analysis of *Fanny Hill*, in psychological or in literary terms. Rather, I would suggest that this work, with its crude and overt statements of theme, sketches a paradigm for the early eighteenth-century novel. *Fanny Hill* probably appeared in 1749, late in the dazzling decade that also saw the publication of important novels by Richardson, Fielding, and Smollett. Its plot expresses and confirms its sexual ideology: sexual relations are power relations in which men, with the advantage of social and physical force, oppose women, whose resources depend mainly on indirection and on socially confirmed male fantasies about the female nature. Either man or woman may choose to submit rather than to combat, and society provides many disguises for the struggle. Nonetheless, the contest for dominance remains the fundamental fact of relations between the sexes.

This scheme emerges with great clarity in the obsessively repetitive structure of *Fanny Hill*, less inescapably in more intricately crafted fictions. But the same preoccupation with the vicissitudes of phallic power informs major novels of the 1740s and 1750s and determines the shape of their plots. Lennard Davis, following Adorno and Horkheimer in his belief that the new emphasis on "selfhood" in the eighteenth century implies the acknowledgement of power as central in human exchange, claims that novelistic plots invariably express power relations, "through the systematic enmeshing of the self into the totality of system" (202). The "system" controlling the imagined worlds evoked by Fielding and Richardson indeed depends on the assumed centrality of power. That assumption weakens as the century continues; by the 1790s, I shall argue in later chapters, novelists sought ways to refute it.

To their contemporaries, to themselves, to succeeding generations of critics, Richardson and Fielding, writing at the same historical moment, appeared as rivals, exemplifying opposed assumptions about the nature of the novel and about human psychology. Without denying common wisdom on this point, I wish to focus rather on what Richardson and Fielding have in common.

Despite their different notions of plot and of character, both organize fictions as representations of power struggles, particularly sexual power struggles. Often, for both writers, the making of fictions figures explicitly as a locus of competition. I shall support these contentions by beginning with an overview of some shapes of conflict in *Joseph Andrews* and *Clarissa*, then concentrating in more detail on operations of power and attitudes toward fiction in *Clarissa* and *Tom Jones*.

Early in *Clarissa*, we learn that Lovelace "troubles not his head with Politics, though nobody knows the interests of Princes and Courts better than he is said to do" (Richardson, *Clarissa* 1: 74; 1: 50);[1] on the other hand, in his private correspondence "he is as secret and careful as if it were of a treasonable nature" (1:73; 1:50). His treason operates in the private rather than the public sphere. He prides himself on the gift for plotting that will destroy him, a gift he uses with special delight in his relations with the other sex. Clarissa's friend Anna Howe, suspicious of Lovelace although vividly aware of his glamor, shares Lovelace's conviction that men and women vie constantly for dominance. She imagines how, after marriage, her husband "*ascends*, and how I *descend*, in the matrimonial wheel, never to take my turn again, but by fits and starts, like the feeble struggles of a sinking State for its dying Liberty" (2: 148; 1: 340). Like Lovelace, Anna understands politics as the science of power. Clarissa, on the other hand, who believes that all the world was originally one family—and ironically ignores the possibilities for conflict implicit in *that* metaphor—would prefer to avoid power struggles but finds herself precipitated into them. Through much of Richardson's novel, sexual issues serve mainly to dramatize conflicts over power.

The literal penis hardly figures in this erotic text; the metaphoric phallus, symbol of male force, dominates. Neither Lovelace nor anyone else alludes to his "sceptre-member." Clarissa's rape occurs off-stage; drugged into unconsciousness for the occasion, she cannot recall its details. Unlike Fanny Hill, Clarissa acknowledges no interest in the sexual. She claims her willingness to submit to a husband, for reasons having to do with religion, not sex. Male power, in her apparent view, rests on social and theological foundations.[2] She thus in effect denies what Fanny so cheerfully posits: the inherent force of male sexuality. Once seduced by Charles, with her own enthusiastic connivance, Fanny remains his forever, her abundant other sexual liaisons incidental and irrelevant. Clarissa, on the other hand, becomes impregnable after her rape. Far from making her yield to Lovelace, his violation of her hardens her will against him. Her chastity matters to her; his sexuality does not. She defeats him partly by refusing to grant his sexual power.

Dominance constitutes a mode of relationship. Lovelace knows no other. He imagines himself as Julius Caesar and as emperor both of an adoring and subjugated Clarissa and of his male companions.[3] Unable to grasp other possibilities even when his friend Belford suggests them, unwilling to accept evidence of Clarissa's capacity to devote herself to him as a loving and helpful companion, Lovelace, doomed by his pathology, falls victim to a duel with rapiers, emblem of his phallic insistence. Clarissa's brother James, the novel's other conspicuous phallic aggressor, ends in isolation, condemned by the rest of the family for his agency in ostracizing Clarissa, suffering an unhappy marriage, calling himself "THE MOST MISERABLE OF BEINGS" (8: 283; 4: 535). Yet the view of the world implicit in the attitudes of these two insistent males shapes Richardson's novel, despite the fact that Clarissa remains its most compelling character, and despite the fact that she triumphs in the end (although only when safely dead).

Once Lovelace has raped her, Clarissa, whose early life has passed in loving relationship to others, retreats into preoccupation with perfecting her self and her story. She subordinates her will to God's, as she comprehends it (I shall return to the complicated question of Clarissa's theology), but she refuses relationship with Lovelace, who is now irrelevant to her concerns. Everyone else becomes increasingly irrelevant as well. At first she yearns for support from her old friends, longs for reconciliation with her family, and regrets her solitude. As she becomes increasingly absorbed in her preparations for death, she needs others less. She makes use of Belford and values the benevolence of new acquaintances, but essentially she stands alone. Thus she reduces Lovelace to helplessness, his letters testifying to her dominance. He has nothing to give her, nothing with which to tempt her, no valid ground for his pleas. She refuses to accept his authority, his money, his sexuality, or his version of her story. His consequent helplessness partly elucidates the grounds of his original power: his belief that he had something to bestow.

In the beginning, Lovelace could give Clarissa at least the illusion of help in her familial imprisonment; he could give flattery and apparent devotion; and he kept in reserve the ultimate gift of his sexual potency. His fantasies of adoring women betray his conviction that once he has breached their chastity, they will yearn for what only he can offer them. The familiar connection of sex and money in eighteenth-century novels conveys their shared identity not only as forms of power but as opportunities for generosity. Moll Flanders reports that her first lover offers her fine words and money, alternate sorts of currency; love and money substitute for one another with bewildering rapidity in her adventures. Less economically oriented heroines encounter the same equivalence. When economic power does not correspond to phallic potency, it atones for potency's absence. Clarissa's toadlike suitor, Solmes, must offer rich financial settlements to compensate for his lack of other attractions, and comparable compensatory arrangements occur in other contexts. Thus Fanny Hill makes up for the possible wound to her lover's phallic pride implicit in her career as a whore by endowing him with her wealth; Pamela's Mr. B asserts his manhood, both before and after his marriage, by emphasizing how much money he has. Lovelace, after his erotic failure, insists on his economic potency, trying to bribe Clarissa into marriage. Both money and phallic force constitute *something to give*, and both have power only if desired or accepted. Clarissa's refusals unman Lovelace, just as Pamela's premarital refusals reduce Mr. B to helpless pleading. After Pamela's marriage, on the other hand, her husband reasserts his dominance: she has now accepted his sexual, social, and economic gifts. As Anna Howe vividly knows, only so long as a woman declines what is offered can she retain control. Her refusals nullify man's gifts.

Even acts of benevolence readily associate themselves with power. And even Richardson, with his subtle grasp of female psychology, his high valuing of the feminine, his avowed identification with his heroine, constructs novelistic plots that corroborate the conviction shared by wicked Lovelace and reformable Mr. B: power relations define significant action in the world. Some men and many women among Richardson's characters deny this fact; they participate nonetheless in its manifestations. Power makes plot—Lovelace's kind of plot, but also Richardson's, Defoe's, Fielding's, and the early Smollett's: these novelists consistently incorporate their characters into a discourse of power.

Joseph Andrews, in which the most attractive characters exemplify the stereotypically "feminine" values of chastity and charity, presents a complicated case in point. Its prevailingly comic narrative tone denies the cogency of the violence that marks many of the novel's episodes, yet the vision of an ugly and destructive social universe compels Fielding's imagination. A merciless struggle for dominance preoccupies most of the book's characters. Joseph and his Fanny Goodwill and Parson Adams escape its consequences only by acquiring sufficient wealth or status to become less easy targets.

The power-hungry indulge in sexually motivated depredations. From Mrs. Slipslop, compared to a "hungry tygress" and a "voracious pike" in her attitude toward Joseph, to effeminate Beau Didapper, men and women seek to "conquer" or to "vanquish" one another. Those who attempt to make an amorous meal of Joseph include not only Lady Booby and Mrs. Slipslop, but servants and their mistresses at inns throughout his journey. Threats to Fanny come from all sides. Even Parson Adams, accidentally in bed with Mrs. Slipslop, finds his bedmate moving toward him in a sexually threatening fashion. The interpolated stories of the jilt Leonora and of Mr. Wilson's early career dwell on sexual exploitation. In the general brutality of the depicted social world, the openness and crudeness with which men and women attempt to use one another epitomize the prevailing spirit of interpersonal relations. There is little question of giving: only of taking. Sexual taking constitutes the principal form of self-aggrandizement.

If new financial resources for the protagonists finally stabilize the plot, the power of money here too provides a metaphor for sexual force, as the account of Leonora's father emphasizes:

He pass'd in the World's Language as an exceeding good Father, being not only so rapacious as to rob and plunder all Mankind to the utmost of his power, but even to deny himself the Conveniencies and almost Necessaries of Life; which his Neighbours attributed to a desire of raising immense Fortunes for his Children: but in fact it was not so, he heaped up Money for its own sake only, and looked on his Children as his Rivals, who were to enjoy his beloved Mistress, when he was incapable of possessing her. (127; bk. 2, ch. 6)

Leonora's father proves more successful at his enterprise than Mrs. Slipslop does at hers, but his lust for money and hers for sexual gratification comprise equivalent appetites. Indeed, Mrs. Slipslop falls readily into financial metaphors for her sexual wishes: feeling she owes herself a "Debt of Pleasure" (32; bk. 1, ch. 6), she proposes to convert Joseph into a species of currency.

From one point of view, all the aggressive energy in *Joseph Andrews* is only a joke. We know that no serious consequences will mar the comedy.[4] Parson Adams's son will return from the dead as soon as his father has had time to reveal the inconsistency between his principles and his practice; Fanny will remain inviolate for Joseph to enjoy at the final curtain. Rape does not exist in the text—only its threat, always nullified. The night of bed switching epitomizes the farcical mode of treating desire. First Beau Didapper seeks Fanny's bed, with the intent of rape, but finds himself mistakenly in Mrs. Slipslop's. When Parson Adams comes to her rescue in the dark, he allows Didapper to escape, thinking him a woman, and buffets Mrs. Slipslop under the impression that she is the rapist. Once Adams understands the cast of characters, Mrs. Slipslop approaches him with sexual intent. He flees to what he supposes his own bed and ends up in Fanny's. When he explains himself, however, all difficulty vanishes. The ready crediting of verbal elucidation suggests that no real sexual problems exist in this novel, only their appearance, to be dissipated by explanation or, in the worst cases, by Joseph and Adams with their sticks.

Beau Didapper, the last of Fanny's assailants, has a face of womanish smoothness, a conspicuous lack of male strength, and very moderate passions, despite his nefarious intent. He feels content to substitute sexual reputation for sexual action. His sexual ambiguity, emphasized toward the narrative's end, reminds the reader once more of the novel's central joke: the reversal of conventional sexual attitudes in men and women. Bridget Allworthy and Lady Bellaston in *Tom Jones*, sexually aggressive women, adopt standard female modes of behavior, indirect modes, in achieving their desires. In *Joseph Andrews*, on the other hand, Lady Booby, Slipslop, and Betty at the inn all attack the hero with traditionally male directness, forcing him to defend his virtue as a woman might have to. Their sexual aggression is a joke specifically because it belongs to women, not imagined to present real threats to men any more than sexually ambiguous men really menace women.

Nonetheless, *Joseph Andrews*, like *Clarissa*, shows individual fates working themselves out through operations of power and assumes a society organized on the basis of power. Without the assumption of male sexual aggression, the fantasy of female aggression would have no comic force. Without the idea that a man who sets out to kiss a woman's breasts should accomplish his purpose, Beau Didapper's insufficiency would be meaningless. Without the conviction that a young woman inevitably encounters a series of attackers (the conviction on which countless eighteenth-century novels construct themselves), Fanny's repeated dangers would seem merely arbitrary. The frequent episodes of sexual aggression in *Joseph Andrews* represent the irresponsibility and lack of control that mark power-oriented societies. The interpolated stories of Leonora and Mr. Wilson dramatize painful and lasting consequences of sexual misbehavior, reminding the reader that the lack of serious consequence in Fanny's near misses depends on the control of a comic narrator, not on mimetic accuracy. Although Fielding's comedy criticizes sexual brutality and lack of charity, it assumes the universal struggle for dominance that implies the prevalence of such qualities. The text invites contempt for Beau Didapper in his unmanliness. "His Face was thin and pale: The Shape of his Body and Legs none of the best; for he had very narrow Shoulders, and no Calf; and his Gait might more properly be called hopping than walking. The Qualifications of his Mind were well adapted to his Person" (312; bk. 4, ch. 9). The text appears to deduce his moral inadequacy from his effeminacy. The novelistic narrator does not approve of rape, but he does not admire a man physically incapable of it. He thinks it funny that a woman should lust openly after a man because he shares a set of established assumptions about how women normally behave.

When Joseph and Fanny enter, at the novel's end, into a perfect marriage, their parentage and their financial security firmly established, one hears the echo of fairytale. In *Joseph Andrews* as in *Clarissa*, relations between the sexes *not* based on considerations of power appear to belong to the realm of fantasy. Anna Howe manipulating and scorning her compliant lover has the energy of conviction—authorial conviction as well as her own. Married to Hickman, in a relation of ideal equality, she sounds like a contrivance rather than a character: "there is but *one will* between them; and that is generally *his* or *hers*, as either speaks first, upon any subject, be it what it will" (*Clarissa* 8: 301; 4: 548). Similarly, the Wilsons in *Joseph Andrews* epitomize the novel's vision of perfect marriage, in contrast to the unions of henpecking wives with cowed husbands or of domineering husbands with submissive wives that the travelers typically encounter. But Wilson's account of himself resembles parable more than recollection:

We are seldom asunder during the residue of the Day; for when the Weather will not permit them to accompany me here, I am usually within with [my wife and children]; for I am neither ashamed of conversing with my Wife, nor of playing with my Children: to say the Truth, I do not perceive that Inferiority of Understanding which the Levity of Rakes, the Dulness of Men of Business, or the Austerity of the Learned would persuade us of in Women. (226; bk. 3, ch. 4)

(Later, Mr. Wilson takes care to point out that his wife is also a good housewife.) One may applaud Wilson's enlightened views of women, but his evocation of marital harmony carries less conviction than does the travelers' repeated experience of human efforts to control or dominate one another. Whether men or women win in these struggles, the construction of relationship as combat affirms a stereotypically "masculine" view of the world.

Fanny and Joseph embody sexual passion controlled by reason and principle and consequently leading to flawless pleasure when licensed and indulged. This ideal creates the happy ending for Fielding's comic fiction, but it does not create the plot. The happenings that generate the interest, the comedy, the vitality of the novel emerge from tensions inherent in the desire for power, the desire—not essentially sexual—that makes the threat of rape the novel's recurrent theme. Joseph, like Clarissa, remains relatively innocent of intent to participate in the struggle for control that surrounds him, but neither can eschew the contest on which their creators' idea of society is predicated.

Lovelace's *plots* and Clarissa's *story* supply the implements of power by which Richardson's characters wage their sexual battle. Plots, which imply more forceful intent than do stories, might seem at the outset the more powerful weapon. But I have already indicated my conviction that Clarissa emerges as winner in the struggle Richardson narrates; the nature of her chosen story contributes to her victory.

Lovelace's elaborately emphasized role as plotter, in both the literary and the political sense of the term, expresses his insistent maleness. As Anna's first letter hints and Clarissa's subsequent communications confirm, Clarissa initially concerns herself with issues of self-control and with the impression she creates in others. Lovelace, in contrast, from the beginning wants to enforce himself on the world, to dominate and control others. Clarissa's initial position is relatively passive: she thinks about what others think of her rather than about what she does to others. As Jonathan Loesberg puts it, "she desires a pure passivity that will not taint her with action" (44). Lovelace, on the other hand, is insistently, sometimes almost psychotically, active. The novel's two central characters thus conform to masculine and feminine stereotypes. As they more fully define their gender positions, this sense of difference intensifies—although one also comes to recognize qualities they share. "She will be *more* than woman, . . . or I *less* than man," Lovelace proclaims, "if I succeed not" (3: 95; 2: 42). By constructing his plots, he projects his power into the future, declaring his omnipotent control of what will happen. Clarissa, in contrast, concerned with the story that will survive after her, accepts as given (although not always as acceptable) what has already happened, wishing to control its interpretation.

Internal as well as external effects of Lovelace's plotting make the activity essential to him. The act of plotting both generates and demonstrates imaginative energy. Some of the passages Richardson introduced specifically to convince his readers of Lovelace's villainy exemplify this point with particular clarity: for instance, the "plot" (4: 270; 2: 420) to rape Clarissa, Anna, the maidservant, and Anna's mother and to throw Anna's lover, Hickman, overboard from the ship where these activities are to take place.[5] Although Lovelace boasts, near the beginning of the letter elaborating this scheme, that "with me, in a piece of mischief, Execution, with its swiftest feet, is seldom three paces behind Projection" (4: 269; 2: 419), in fact his detailed plans come to nothing at all. Indeed, the exuberance of invention with which he specifies them suggests that for Lovelace plotting is its own reward. Glorying in imaginative mastery, he need not proceed to "Execution." As Carol Kay observes, "Even the plotting letters to Belford could be interpreted as the extravagance of wit rather [than] the signs of an irreparably perverted heart" (175–76).

Plot making offers Lovelace other specific satisfactions, most of them manifest in this scheme of shipboard rape. First of all, plotting itself is power. The letter about his extravagant plans begins, "And now, that my Beloved seems secure in my net . . . " (4: 268; 2: 418). Feeling triumphant over his apparent control of Clarissa, he wishes to extend his mastery. His imagination, in his imagining of it, controls even the weather. Like Johnson's mad astronomer, he believes—or pretends to believe: the line between delusion and pretence blurs—he can summon storms at will: "I know it will be hard weather: I *know* it will" (4: 271; 2: 420). A denial of uncontrollable causality, an assertion of the omnipotence of his own will, plotting reassures Lovelace of his triumphant masculine force.

All of this sounds close to madness. Lovelace does not, however, appear mad at this point in the narrative. The playfulness of his extravagance rescues him, lending him a kind of appeal that one feels almost ashamed to confess. The fantasy of quadruple rape leads Lovelace to imagine the scene of his subsequent trial for rape—not a further plot, this, but a fanciful meditation on the consequences of plotting. Like Polly's imagining, in *The Beggar's Opera*, of Macheath's hanging, Lovelace's vision of his own trial converts ignominy into splendor. The courtroom becomes in his fantasy a stage for his grandest and most grandiose performance. What he can imagine in advance, he seems to believe, can do him no harm.

"You delight in crooked ways," Clarissa tells Lovelace impatiently (3: 121; 2: 196). She considers such a statement strong condemnation. With emphasis on the verb rather than the adjective, though, the characterization also suggests Lovelace's attractiveness in his capacity for enjoying his own mental operations. Anna Howe's responses to Lovelace more manifestly than Clarissa's reveal the sexual allure of the man's ingenuities of wit.

Plotting as power, as imagination, as escape from and denial of reality, as play, as pleasure, as erotic attraction: all of these aspects of Lovelace's plotting analogize the novelist's function. Loesberg comments astutely on Lovelace's predilection for narrative (45); Melinda Rabb observes that "Lovelace speaks not only for creativity, but also for the problems of creativity: his inventions both define and undo him; his contrivances make him the self-creating artist/author of his own demise" (66). The "problems" Lovelace encounters as a direct result of his creativity stem from plot's tendency to become an end in itself. He enjoys the process more than the fruition of seduction, he acknowledges. Similarly—identically—he delights in the play of his imagination quite without regard for the end in view. If plotting is Lovelace's preeminent source of power, it turns out to be power not altogether under his control. Considerably before the rape, he finds reason to reflect on this fact. "My Invention is my curse," he tells Belford (4: 329; 2: 460). Meditating ruefully on the failure of his elaborate plot to frighten Clarissa into his arms by raising the alarm of fire, he summarizes, "This was my Mine, my Plot!—And this was all I made of it!" (4: 397; 2: 506). He experiences the futility of plotting so intensely that he actually contemplates giving it up, only to draw back from the idea because his capacity to plot constitutes his very identity. "If I give up my contrivances, my joy in stratagem, and plot, and invention, I shall be but a common man" (5: 312; 3: 229). Intolerable! But Lovelace's experience of the disproportion between cause and effect in his machinations only intensifies, until the rape itself, that culmination of plots, leaves him almost devoid of language, as of satisfaction.

Plotting—literary plotting and Lovelace's variety—involves manipulation of desire. Lovelace's plotting, like the Female Quixote's more innocent version of the same activity, expresses his desire: not for sexual pleasure (that point becomes increasingly obvious) but, like Lennox's Arabella, though more perversely, for self-assertion. He plays on Clarissa's desire for reconciliation with her family, on the whores' desires for self-justification, on his agents' desire for financial gain, on a widow's desire for sexual titillation, unerringly aware of other people's human wishes in all their vanity. Yet his inability to do anything *but* plot becomes increasingly apparent. When Belford reports Belton's misery and approaching death, Lovelace can only respond by constructing a scheme to drown Belton's mistress and her sons, a response that denies the weight of actuality and dramatizes the limitations of the plotter's resources. As Lovelace's power wanes, the novel appears to raise serious questions about the value of plotting.

I shall return to the implications of this development in relation to fiction. First, it will be worth considering another aspect of fiction: *story* as opposed to *plot*. That subject focuses attention on Clarissa, concerned from the beginning with telling and with constructing her story, triumphant in her ultimate control of the story.

Terry Castle and William Warner, from opposed points of view, have analyzed the competition of narratives in *Clarissa* and called attention to the importance of interpretation as novelistic substance. Clarissa as self-interpreter and as promulgator of her own story has become a familiar figure in literary criticism. I want to concentrate on a single aspect of the heroine's role as story-maker: her use of the Christian story for paradoxical self-assertion. Christianity of course functions in Richardson's fiction as far more than a narrative device (see Damrosch; Doody, *A Natural Passion*), but the novel also brilliantly employs religious conviction as a strategy for characterization—indeed, as a strategy for achieving power. As Carol Kay points out, "Instead of harmonizing society as in *Pamela*, in *Clarissa* moral language . . . add[s] fuel to competitions in power" (163).

Unlike her precursor Pamela, Clarissa neither invokes Christian authority nor relies on Christian comfort as she initially struggles for minimal autonomy against the impositions of father and brother. The heroine early finds herself forced into severe doctrinal selectivity. Her father claims Godlike authority yet abrogates paternal responsibility, failing in attentiveness and in moral awareness. "Honor thy father and thy mother" therefore takes second place for Clarissa to a notion of "steadiness" inculcated by her religious mentor, Dr. Lewen.

Steadiness of mind (a quality which the ill-bred and censorious deny to any of our Sex) when we are absolutely convinced of being in the right [Otherwise it is not *steadiness*, but *obstinacy*], and when it is exerted in *material* cases, is a quality which, as my good Dr. Lewen was wont to say, brings great credit to the possessor of it; at the same time that it usually, when *tried* and *known*, raises *such* above the attempts of the meanly machinating. (1: 136; 1: 93)

Clarissa does not yet doubt her own rightness or her capacity to rise above her enemies. But her parentheses call attention to her uneasiness about the story she is in the process of constructing, a story which, in her version as in Anna Howe's, will emphasize Clarissa's virtue. Although she believes in the possibility of getting "great credit" for her steadiness, she knows how gender stereotypes may control interpretations of her actions. And she imagines the specific reading of her character ("not *steadiness* but *obstinacy*") that will help articulate the family conflicts generating the novel's complex narrative. Indeed, she tacitly realizes her violation of an absolute moral imperative in her failure to yield to her father, despite his wrongness. The "pride" she will later declare her besetting sin urges her on, but her awareness of interpretive ambiguity already troubles her.

Clarissa realizes that to follow Dr. Lewen's recommendation of "steadiness" may bring her only unhappiness, "since what I call *steadiness*," she explains,

is deemed stubbornness, obstinacy, prepossession, by those who have a right to put what interpretation they please upon my conduct.

So, my dear, were we perfect (which no one *can* be) we could not be happy in this life, unless those with whom we have to deal (those more especially who have any controul upon us) were governed by the same principles. But then does not the good Doctor's conclusion recur,—That we have nothing to do but to chuse what is right; to be steady in the pursuit of it; and to leave the issue to Providence? (1: 137; 1: 94)

Parenthood creates the right of interpretation, in Clarissa's view, but other people's readings of her hardly matter. "Providence," at this point in the narrative, sanctions a simple order of events and of story: "we have nothing to do but. . . . " The young woman, more concerned about approaching perfection than about achieving happiness, appears confident of standing higher than her parents in the moral hierarchy (not perfect, but adhering to proper principles). As often, she here tells a microcosmic version of her entire story: her unyielding steadiness, interpreted as obstinacy, will make her unhappy because other members of her family lack her principles; her theological self-justification will support her in her choice; she refuses to acknowledge concern about outcomes, all acceptable because necessarily providential. Inflexible moral logic creates her orderly syntax of necessity. Possible unhappiness has a rationally comprehensible cause, suggested by *since*; a connective of causality (*So*) leads to the hypothesis of perfection which produces a necessary effect, given imperfection elsewhere; the final rhetorical question declares the inevitable conclusion. Clarissa sounds a little smug, a little blind, unaware of terrible experiential possibilities. But she also sounds *right*: the Christian premise generates its own inexorable logic.

Like the reader, Clarissa comes to know logic's insufficiencies. Her obligations to others conflict with her responsibility to God. More and more clearly, events force her to understand the painfulness of choice: choice, it sometimes seems, about whom to hurt. The individual's relation to Providence becomes murky. What if, by trying to avoid trouble between James Harlowe and Lovelace, Clarissa intercepts "the designs of Providence" (2: 255; 1: 413)? She has earlier assumed that Providence will ratify her virtue. Gradually she lowers her sights: enough if she can be "*justly* acquitted of wilful and premeditated faults. The will of Providence be resigned to in the rest: As *that* leads, let me patiently, and unrepiningly, follow! I shall not live always!—May but my *closing* scene be happy!" (2: 264; 1: 420). This depressed utterance foreshadows not only the conclusion of Clarissa's earthly career but the degree to which events focus her attention on death rather than life. Although Providence remains the figure for cosmic order, Clarissa no longer feels confident of her relation to its operations; her anxiety about her own "presumption" and her desire to "follow" contrast with her earlier certainties.

If while she remains in her father's house Clarissa's religious allusions become increasingly depressed and confused, though her faith remains strong, after she leaves home her theological references at first dwindle further. Struggling to work out her own fate, she explores the limits of self-reliance, never abandoning Christian conviction but telling her story, for a time, by means of other allusions. Lovelace lavishes on her the language of divinity ("angel," "divine") while he plots her debasement and she struggles to discern her proper course through his mazes. She describes herself as "one who ever endeavoured to shun intricate paths" (4: 209; 2: 378), in contrast to Lovelace's delight in crooked ways, but no other paths reveal themselves. After she has eloped but before the rape, Clarissa cannot even define the shape of her own narrative. Is she involved in a love story or a tale of seduction and betrayal? Will she or will she not, can she or can she not, choose marriage as its ending? Does she fill the role of heroine or of victim? Asking

such questions, she implicitly wonders about the position and possibilities of a female self in a Christian universe.

Her mistake, Clarissa concludes, consisted in self-dependence;
she considers herself a "presumptuous creature" for relying on her
"own knowledge of the right path" (4:38; 2: 263). On the other
hand, when challenged she continues to declare her self-reliance,
reinterpreted as indirect dependence on God. Her hesitations
about marriage, she explains to Anna Howe, come from her heart,
from "Principles that *are* in my mind; that I *found* there; implanted,
no doubt, by the first gracious Planter: Which therefore *impel* me,
as I may say, to act up to them" (4: 102–3; 2: 306). Although she
acknowledges in the succeeding paragraph that "The heart is very
deceitful," she here declares her confidence in the divine origin of
her moral convictions. Yet self is the grand misleader, Clarissa concludes, commenting on her secret vaunting of her "good inclinations"; self

is at the bottom of all we do, and of all we wish. . . . Is it not enough to
make the unhappy creature look into herself, and endeavour to detect
herself, who, from such a high Reputation, left to proud and presumptuous Self, should, by one thoughtless step, be brought to the dreadful situation I am in? (4: 210; 2: 379)

But she will not allow herself to repine; she will rely on her divine
Father.

Clarissa's mistake, not yet punished by rape, has brought her to
desperate self-denial, to a vocabulary of abnegation. The story she
tells is undeniably Clarissa's story, but who, now, is Clarissa? A
woman whose heart impels her unerringly toward rectitude, or an
"unhappy creature [i.e., created being]" helpless to find the good?
A self focused on virtue, or a "proud and presumptuous self?"
These fundamental interpretive questions lie at the heart of Clarissa's difficulties about her narrative: not merely the familiar problem, Who am I?, but the equally fundamental one, How, and what,
do I *mean*? The same question, in the third person, troubles Lovelace, who by his plotting tries to resolve the problem of Clarissa.
Does she possess the same meaning as his fantasies of the female
nature? If he can believe in some alternative version of female
meaning, he thinks he can write Clarissa's story with a happy ending. As for Clarissa herself, almost 250 pages before the rape (in
the Everyman edition) she has reached an apparent nadir of selfhood. Unable to assert value in herself, she employs Christian
rhetoric to deny that her story has a heroine.

This denial continues to the novel's end. More and more distinctly, Clarissa defines herself as a soul seeking salvation—a definition given urgency by the rape. After the rape, her increasingly insistent Christian interpretation of self and world serves a new narrative purpose. The violation which utterly changes Clarissa's life also redirects her rhetoric and, paradoxically, allows her most grandiose claims. Leopold Damrosch invites us to "admire the subtlety with which the struggle between self-assertion and ethical convention is embodied in the imaginations of the characters themselves" (220). More subtle still is the gradual *identification* of self-assertion and ethics that takes place in Clarissa.

Immediately after the rape, Clarissa's fragmentary utterances on paper recur obsessively to the problem of self while rejecting the language of religion. She denies her continued identity, she declares herself ignorant of her own name. Her parable of the lady with the young lion or bear or tiger concludes that "what *she* did was *out* of nature, *out* of character, at least" (5: 329; 3: 206); succeeding fragments reiterate the self-humbling inherent in her suffering: "I was too secure in the knowlege I thought I had of my own heart" (5: 330; 3: 207). If she no longer knows who she is, she has no doubt about Lovelace: "O Lovelace, you are Satan himself" (5: 335; 3: 210). God appears in these meditations only as a conventional allusion to forgiveness or punishment; Clarissa can feel herself in no vital relation to her Creator.

Yet only the utterly destructive experience of rape enables her fully to assert herself. Clarissa sees her escape from Lovelace as a "triumph" (although she attributes her success to "grace") which she wishes to magnify: "The man whom once I could have loved, I have been enabled to despise: And shall not *Charity* complete my triumph? And shall I not *enjoy* it?" (7: 232; 4: 186). Belford and Lovelace confirm the view that Clarissa has triumphed, even before her death. Lovelace, eerily echoing the vocabulary his victim employed immediately after the rape, loses his sense of identity and can consolidate no other form of power: "O Belford! Belford! I am still, I am still, most miserably absent from myself! Shall never, never more be what I was!" (8: 140; 4: 439). By refusing to make claims, Clarissa has won. Playing out the full theological and social implications of her self-acceptance as *nothing*, replacing worldly hopes with heavenly ones, she adopts the language of religion to convey rage and outrage and to assert the power allowed her, a power intimately allied with death.

Clarissa's new self-definition is not only unworldly but emphatically unsexual. Belford, praising her angelic nature, declares it impossible "to have the least thought of sex"—that is, of her existence specifically as a woman—when with her (4: 248). By converting herself to an asexual angel, the woman conveys that life as a woman has been made impossible for her. She denies her own physicality, making herself pure spirit, concentrating her physical concerns on arrangements for a coffin to contain her body, that entity she has declared insignificant and transformed into a profound symbol. Her physicality has enabled her violation; her determined spirituality encapsulates her rage at violation.

Clarissa's ever more concerted self-narration as all spirit in effect appropriates her society's professions of Christianity. As many commentators have noted, the Harlowe family epitomizes capitalist society.[6] The family aggrandizement that troubles Clarissa centers on money; the male Harlowes speak obsessively of the financial. But this society believes and declares itself Christian. Clarissa's strategy (identical in many respects with her conviction) derives force from its exploitation of the social gap between profession and practice. As Margaret Anne Doody points out:

In *Clarissa* as in the heroic tragedies the sexual battle is a spiritual combat, and the terms "soul" and "will" are constantly invoked. Such a combat would not be necessary if social, moral, and sexual life had not degenerated, because of the depravity of human nature, into a struggle for power. Clarissa's world, which has long given up Christianity without knowing it, is the world as described by Hobbes. (*A Natural Passion* 123)

Their refusal to *know* their deviance from the Christianity they profess gives special energy to the contesters for power who surround Clarissa. Even Lovelace professes Christianity, in an offhand fashion; so do the heartless Harlowes; so, even, does Mrs. Sinclair, far from atheistic, who wishes no parson at her deathbed because of her agonizing fear. Everyone claims to believe; no one takes seriously belief's implications.

Clarissa adopts as her own the Christian story of humiliation, sacrifice, and transcendence. What her community accepts as a vague and on the whole comforting symbolic structure, Clarissa relentlessly literalizes. At the same time, she dramatizes in her own person the precise implications of what Lovelace has done to her. As she observes in her will, he has once in a manner seen her dead; she will turn metaphor into fact. He has destroyed her bodily integrity; she will discard her body. He vacillates between thinking that rape hardly matters (its effects can be repaired by marriage) and believing that it matters enormously (i.e., it will definitively subordinate Clarissa). Clarissa demonstrates the truth of both judgments: rape cannot matter, since it affects only her body; on the other hand, it matters so much that she must die. The young woman's increasing power derives from her overwhelming assertion of unity between her story and her life. She acts what she professes, thus reproaching all who do not; she obsessively tells and writes the story given authority by her action and suffering, thus making her presence and its meaning inescapable. While abrogating the luxury, and the futility, of verbal reproach, she makes herself a reproach to endemic hypocrisy as well as to more active sins.

Although Clarissa recognizes the sinfulness of despair, her initial turn toward Christian narrative derives from something close to that emotion. Previous narrative possibilities have disappeared for her. She can neither tell nor enact her society's preferred fable for young women, the tale of contented compliance with male wills; nor can she play out the structure of romance; nor is the story of repentance and reconciliation available to her in her lifetime. As her "mad" fragments reveal, narrative coherence has vanished with the rape. She eludes the tragedy of incoherence (one form of Lovelace's fate) and rediscovers herself by carrying self-subordination to its logical extreme, absorbing herself in a larger story.

A single instance—the important letter in which Clarissa expresses her hope of meeting Lovelace again after her return to her father's house—may suggest how powerfully the heroine appropriates the Christian story. (That this transparent allegory confuses and deludes both Lovelace and its other readers emphasizes the underlying religious alienation of the society.) Obsessively concerned with her relationship to her own literal family, Clarissa longs for parental blessing; her father's curse preys on her mind. For the date of her death on her coffin she substitutes the date on which she left her father's house. Her earlier insistence on defining the world by its origins in "one family" suggests a strategy: by metaphorical transformation she can enlarge her family of origin. She claims the Smiths and her doctor and Widow Lovick as surrogate parents, she incorporates Belford into a symbolic family structure, she makes her will an act of unification. Her most fundamental enlargement and substitution, however, insists on the equation of God and father.

"Sir,—I have good news to tell you," Clarissa writes Lovelace.

I am setting out with all diligence for my Father's House. I am bid to hope that he will receive his poor penitent with a goodness peculiar to himself; for I am overjoyed with the assurance of a thorough Reconciliation, thro' the interposition of a dear, blessed friend, whom I always loved and honoured (7: 189–90; 4: 157)

The allegory, based precisely on Biblical promises, also stays close to immediate emotional and physical actualities: hence its ready misreadings. Reminding the reader how Clarissa's hopes have failed her, the transposition into divine terms expresses her sole remaining possibility for emotional stability.

But it also both expresses and defends against self-assertion and aggression. In its transparent Christian meaning, it subordinates all earthly concerns to the task of salvation. "I am so taken up with my preparation for this joyful and long-wished-for journey, that I cannot spare one moment for any other business, having several matters of the last importance to settle first" (7: 190; 4: 157). Preoccupied with her death and her eternal welfare, Clarissa announces her negligence of worldly matters, thus defending against any imputation of self-concern. Not her mortal *self* but her undying *soul* preoccupies her.

But "this truly divine Lady," to quote Lovelace (7: 190; 4: 157), employs her "divinity" for her own purposes. Her desperate need, she feels, justifies her use of Christian revelation as deception; the reader may recall Dr. Johnson's dictum that there is always something Clarissa prefers to the truth. Yet her allegory tells the vital truth of her anger and her will to triumph. In her postmortem elucidation to Lovelace, she reminds him of his inadequacies and of her superiority: "indeed, Sir, I have long been greatly above you: For from my heart I have despised you, and all your ways, ever since I saw what manner of man you were" (8: 137; 4: 437). She quotes Biblical "threatenings" about "the wicked man," recalling the diction of her written "meditations," which often adopt the Bible's aggressive language to characterize those who have failed or denied her.

God is always on Clarissa's side, a student of mine once commented. The remark calls attention to the heroine's self-aggrandizing uses of piety. To quote the Bible to Lovelace in an effort to reform him constitutes unexceptionable Christian behavior. To add, "I have long been greatly above you" reminds readers from Lovelace onwards that Clarissa has by no means disappeared as a "self." On the contrary, she has discovered her self in denying it, as she has discovered a way to declare her ascendancy in the battle of the sexes.

Clarissa preempts power by stating the actualities behind Lovelace's professions and manipulations. She wishes, she says, "to awaken you out of your sensual dream" (8: 138; 4: 437); her posthumous letter of clarification insists on what lies at the dream's heart. A "gay, cruel, fluttering, unhappy man!", Lovelace has in his "barbarous and perfidious treatment" of Clarissa hazarded his immortal soul, using "the name of Gallantry or Intrigue" to disguise his baseness (8: 135, 136; 4: 435). Clarissa claims to deal in facts rather than names; her linguistic deception reveals truth. Although she is not at the outset a plotter, Lovelace has forced her to plot: invariably for the purpose of escaping from him. This particular plot of deception has worked as well as any of Lovelace's. Her trickery equals his, and she, unlike him, presumably achieves what she wants, in heaven if not on earth.

The "father's house" letter implicitly reproaches Clarissa's family as well as her violator. Penitence helps her not at all with her unforgiving earthly parent; the interposition of dear friends proves fruitless. The divine Father hypothesized in Clarissa's text will, she believes, prove *just*, as the earthly father has not. For her, the language of Christian forgiveness belongs to the realm of fact, asserting compensatory order and enforcing her superiority to her family as well as her capacity to rise above Lovelace. Her ability to sustain simultaneous consciousness of utterly separate planes of being informs her rhetorical strategy. Thus she writes Lovelace,

You have *only* robbed me of what once were my favourite expectations. . . . You have *only* been the cause that I have been cut off in the bloom of youth. . . . I will *only* say that, in all probability, every hour I had lived with [such a man as you] might have brought with it some new trouble. (8: 137; 4: 434; my italics)

Only stresses Clarissa's repudiation of earthly standards: neither what Lovelace has done nor what she can say about him matters from an otherworldly viewpoint. From the point of view of readers more committed to the life of the world (including Lovelace), *only* emphasizes the horror of what has happened. Envious Bella has insisted that Clarissa's brilliant letters consist *only* of rhetoric, that the young woman possesses persuasive skills rather than genuine emotions. But Clarissa has earned her linguistic doubleness. Her attention directed to heaven, she literally believes what she says. Inasmuch as she still belongs to the world, however, her language also supplies a rhetoric of superiority, reorganizing the family's lost order with herself as triumphant exemplar. To achieve such triumph, she must die. Death gives her language and her self the authority they could not fully claim in life.

For Richardson to formulate his tale of amorous betrayal as a blatant struggle for power may appear "natural," inevitable, inherent, as Lennard Davis suggests, in the genre of novel. Perhaps one may find striking or surprising the degree to which the novelist

underlines power conflicts by repetition: the struggle for dominance within the Harlowe family (son versus father, husband versus wife, sister versus sister), the struggle between Anna and
Hickman, between Anna and her mother, between Lovelace and
the whores, between Lovelace and his male companions, all emphasized by the pair of duels that frame the action, help the reader
to understand the dynamic between Clarissa and Lovelace. Later
in the century, as we shall see, novelists tried to avoid or at least to
mystify the relation between power and plot—a fact that calls into
question the "naturalness" of Richardson's scheme, making it seem
more emphatically an ideological choice.

The terms I have used to examine the battle for control between
Lovelace and Clarissa, *story* and *plot*, suggest another perspective
on Richardson's novelistic practice. What does it mean for the novelist to give "story" victory in the conflict of story and plot? "Story,"
as Clarissa uses the word, primarily implies interpretation of past
events. Clarissa's way of creating and enforcing her own story, as
we have seen, involves assimilating it to the authoritative—the
true—preexistent narrative of Christianity. "Plot," for Lovelace,
suggests the imposition of personal will on happenings in the
world. Hubristically, he conceives of plotting as capable of forestall-
ing even death, as a way of fulfilling the desire of the self. Clarissa's
victory over Lovelace, then, affirms Richardson's narrative method.
Like Clarissa, the novelist claims his primary commitment to truth.
Writing in the third person, in a "Postscript" to the novel, he describes himself as having "imagined, that . . . in an age given up to
diversion and entertainment, he could *steal in*, as may be said, and
investigate the great doctrines of Christianity under the fashionable guise of an amusement" (8: 308; 4: 553). He argues for the
moral necessity of his fiction's structuring; he tries desperately, as
Warner has richly demonstrated, to enforce his interpretation on
his readers. Implicitly he rejects the notion of self-willed plot. The
arrangements of action in *Clarissa*, he would have it, derive from
moral necessity, not from aesthetic artifice.

Generations of readers have in fact responded to the aesthetic
artifice of *Clarissa*. The lengths to which Richardson went to deny
its importance, like his desperate (and unsuccessful) efforts to
make Lovelace unattractive, suggest the intensity with which the
very idea of plot, understood as artifice, as pleasure, and as instrument of control, appeals to writers and to readers. It is difficult to
understand why Melissa Rabb finds *Clarissa* underplotted (61). If
plot consists in "the temporal synthesis of the heterogeneous" (Ricoeur 158), Richardson's novel displays extraordinary power in in-

corporating into a temporal scheme minutiae of thought, feeling, and action, composing out of such minutiae a unity of plot. Not only the horror of the unnarrated rape but the fully narrated retrospective details of Clarissa's daily record keeping. Only by rereading does one begin to grasp what tiny facts may constitute an event in this narrative, and how the weaving together of event composes the totality of plot.

Richardson radically re-imagines the uses of desire and the nature of truth. "Richardson prided himself on being a moral and religious writer," Anna Barbauld points out;

and, as Addison did before him, he professed to take under his particular protection that sex which is supposed to be most open to good or evil impressions; whose inexperience most requires cautionary precepts, and whose sensibilities it is most important to secure against a wrong direction. (Richardson, *Correspondence* xxii)

One wonders about the weight of *professed* in that sentence. As a moral guide for females, the author of *Clarissa* leads in odd directions. His novel may demonstrate the dangers of disobeying one's parents, but it shows more compellingly the devious ways in which pious submission can generate secular power.

Soon after Sophia Western and Harriet Fitzpatrick, in *Tom Jones*, arrive at the Upton Inn, a "noble Peer" intrudes upon them. This peer, "a very particular Friend" of Mrs. Fitzpatrick, turns out to have played a role, although an occluded one, in the elaborate self-justifying story she has just told Sophia.

To say Truth, it was by his Assistance that she had been enabled to escape from her Husband; for this Nobleman had the same gallant Disposition with those renowned Knights, of whom we read in heroic Story, and had delivered many an imprisoned Nymph from Durance. He was indeed as bitter an Enemy to the savage Authority too often exercised by Husbands and Fathers, over the young and lovely of the other Sex, as ever Knight Errant was to the barbarous Power of Enchanters: nay, to say Truth, I have often suspected that those very Enchanters with which Romance every where abounds, were in Reality no other than the Husbands of those Days; and Matrimony itself was perhaps the enchanted Castle in which the Nymphs were said to be confined. (607; bk. 11, ch. 8)

The narrator's allusion to "the savage Authority too often exercised by Husbands and Fathers" reminds us of one form assumed by the battle of the sexes in *Tom Jones*. Squire Western's determination to exercise tyrannical power over his daughter helps to precipitate Sophia's flight and thus to initiate central actions of the plot; Blifil's desire to assume the role of tyrannical husband justifies

Sophia's repugnance and also shapes the plot. Moreover, the arch invitation to read romance allegorically (emphasized by the crucial reiterated formulation, "to say Truth") calls attention to another important element of Fielding's plot: the competition of narratives that, in *Tom Jones* as in *Clarissa*, helps to determine meaning. I want to examine both the power struggles of the fictional world and the attitudes toward fiction conveyed by the narrative itself (as opposed to the narratorial interpolations touched on in the last chapter). I shall begin by looking at the two longest interpolated stories in the text, those of the Man on the Hill and Mrs. Fitzpatrick, before examining more obvious manifestations of the contest for control that generates the plot.

The long autobiographical narrative by the Man on the Hill invites reading as an allegory of possibility.[7] The old man specifies his youthful character in terms directly applicable to Tom: "I was high-mettled, had a violent Flow of animal Spirits, was a little ambitious, and extremely amorous" (453; bk. 8, ch. 11). Like Tom, he loves a woman; like Tom, he proves loyal to his friends. The didactic purpose of his account, in Fielding's scheme of things, thus seems all too apparent—and not very interesting. Tom sees the point and makes the appropriate judgment: misanthropy is not the only response to misfortune; people are more interesting than the old man suggests; we must remember our Christian obligation to love our neighbor.

But the reader may learn more than Tom does from this tale in its telling. Partridge interrupts the narrative repeatedly, to offer his responses or his requests for further information. When the old man tells of his trial for a theft he has actually committed, at which his accuser's failure to appear results in the culprit's unanticipated liberty, Partridge accounts for the accuser's absence by suggesting that "he did not care to have your Blood upon his Hands" (457; bk. 8, ch. 11). Although Tom laughs at him, Partridge insists on telling his own illustrative story, of a drunk villager who struggles with a ghost after he has acted as witness in a capital case. A calf with a white face is found dead in the lane the morning after; the skeptical believe that "the Battle was between *Frank* and that, as if a Calf would set upon a Man" (460; bk. 8, ch. 11). Neither Tom nor the old man comments about this narrative; it simply remains embedded in the larger story.

With its alternative hypotheses of ghost and calf, Partridge's story in itself concerns the problem of interpretation. In its context, it reminds the reader emphatically of the degree to which hearers construct the stories they hear. The autobiography of the Man of the Hill also explicitly raises questions of interpretation. The teller's mother, devoted to her elder son, interprets all her younger son's actions to his disadvantage. The apothecary who brings the news of the Duke of Monmouth's rebellion, the Man on the Hill tells his listeners, "would swallow almost any thing as a Truth, a Humour which many made use of to impose on him" (476; bk. 8, ch. 14). By implication, such gullibility is reprehensible. Soon afterwards, Tom tells the old man of the current Jacobite uprising. He responds, "I cannot be so imposed upon as to credit so foolish a Tale" (478; bk. 8, ch. 14). Skepticism, it seems, can be as misleading as gullibility. Neither Tom nor Partridge, for different reasons, hears in the old man's tale the meaning he presumes it to have. When Tom ventures to offer his own interpretation of it, the old man responds "so warmly" (486; bk. 8, ch. 15) that Tom refrains from further argument.

Mrs. Fitzpatrick's explanatory account of how she comes to be at the Upton inn has an equally obvious didactic purpose in Fielding's scheme and an equally conspicuous narrative interruption to its telling. No correspondence of personality in this case links the teller to the hearer; on the contrary, Mrs. Fitzpatrick makes a point of the contrast in their natures, reminding Sophia that they used to be called "Miss *Graveairs*, and Miss *Giddy*" (581; bk. 11, ch. 4). Sophia herself, however, sees the possibility of equivalence in their fates, as her responses to the narrator's comments about men indicate. She takes the story she hears as an instructive fable about marriage. In the larger structure of the novel, this story too indicates dark possibilities for the character not sufficiently guided by prudence.

The landlord of the inn creates the interruption to Mrs. Fitzgerald's account. Although he, unlike Partridge, feels no conscious desire to tell a story, the story created by his fancy emerges in his reactions to Sophia. Convinced that Sophia is in fact the Young Pretender's mistress, Jenny Cameron, he alludes obscurely to the arrival of the French. In response to Sophia's questions, he then constructs a retrospective narrative of what happened at her arrival ("I knew your Ladyship the Moment you came into the House: I said it was your Honour, before I lifted you from your Horse, and I shall carry the Bruises I got in your Ladyship's Service to the Grave . . ." [592; bk. 11, ch. 6].) When Sophia's maid, Honour, more clearly reports the advent of the French, to her mistress's manifest relief (Sophia fears only her father), the landlord continues his process of reinterpretation and narrative construction. Like Partridge's intrusion into the story of the Man on the Hill, the landlord's intervention calls attention to the self-serving nature of narrative. Wish creates story.

The nature of the desire shaping Mrs. Fitzpatrick's story oddly parallels that of the Man on the Hill. Both narrators present themselves as victims. The Man on the Hill takes responsibility for his youthful sins, although in reporting them he emphasizes the guilt of the richer man who led him astray. But the betrayals he experiences lead him to believe in universal human malignancy. Tom delicately suggests that his choice of companions may have contributed to his disillusion and that one must bear responsibility for choices. The Man on the Hill will not listen to such doctrine. Mrs. Fitzgerald shows even less inclination to blame herself for her imprudent marriage. She explains "I believe, I should not have erred so grosly in my Choice, if I had relied on my own Judgment; but I trusted totally to the Opinion of others, and very foolishly took the Merit of a Man for granted, whom I saw so universally well received by the Women" (586; bk. 11, ch. 4). Although she acknowledges in passing her own folly, she emphasizes more strongly the responsibility of the other women who approved her husband. In reporting later events of her life, she suppresses all data that might arouse Sophia's disapproval, telling a strangely truncated story. (As does Sophia herself, who omits all mention of Tom in her own autobiographical report.)

The didactic point is clear enough: both Tom and Sophia must understand the need to assume responsibility for oneself, the fundamental ground of prudence and of self-knowledge. More interesting, because less predictable, is the suggestion that self-justification motivates narrative. Self-justification becomes urgent, given the competitive environment Mrs. Fitzgerald and the Man on the Hill (like Tom and Sophia) inhabit. In this fictional universe, as in that of *Clarissa*, struggles for power inform action. Tom and Sophia, largely unconscious of such matters, must learn this truth among others. The Man on the Hill opens his story with the competition for maternal favor between him and his brother. Then he tells of Sir George Gresham, who lures his companions into financial excess, "by which he accomplished the Ruin of many, whom he afterwards laughed at as Fools and Coxcombs, for vying, as he called it, with a Man of his Fortune" (455; bk. 8, ch. 11). Sir George manufactures a simulacrum of a competitive situation in order to triumph in it. The gamblers whom the Man on the Hill subsequently encounters engage in open attempts to dominate and control others, but also in covert competition among themselves. Most of what happens to the storyteller, in fact, can be interpreted as evidence of humankind's heartless contest for dominance, the cause of his misanthropy. Mrs. Fitzgerald, unlike the Man on the Hill, offers no embracing moral judgments, but her story too reports competitive struggle. "I was pleased with my Conquest," she explains—*conquest* being a characteristic locution for a woman's attracting the affections of a man. "To rival my Aunt delighted me; to rival so many other Women charmed me" (584; bk. 11, ch. 4). So her troubles begin, to develop into the familiar Fieldingesque contest for power with a husband who fears domination by a woman.

In the competitive world of *Tom Jones*, stories become an instrument for asserting control. Stories, but not plots. Plots, in the sense that interests me, imply a dynamic. They involve a movement of mind, an action of desire. Plots keep changing. Lovelace's exuberant, self-perpetuating inventiveness calls attention to the fluidity inherent in the idea of plot, which thrusts itself forward into the future. In *Tom Jones*, the plotters are the bad guys—young Blifil and his father before him; less elaborately, Thwackum and Square. They think about the future at the cost of full awareness of the present; they utterly lack Lovelace's capacity for exhilaration. The only joyous plotter here is the narrator who controls all that happens and who frequently calls attention to the richness of future possibility.

Stories, as interpretations of past events, have, individually, more stability than plots. On the other hand, many different stories can form around any given sequence of events. *Tom Jones* supplies a bewildering abundance of interpretive narratives for virtually every happening, virtually every person. I am hardly the first to notice this phenomenon. Maurice Johnson and Susan P. McNamara, among others, have called attention to the ubiquity of storytellers in Fielding's narrative. As McNamara puts it, "The world represented within this narrative exists as it is by virtue of the same process to which the narrator and his fellow passengers devote their energy—fiction-making" (397). Ronald Paulson examines in provocative detail the process by which events large and small, national and personal, become "mythologized" within the text; he finds in that process an important subject of narrative as well as a narrative method (Paulson, "Fielding"). Paul Hunter notes that "Along with the action of Fielding's plot and the continuous byplay the narrator initiates with the reader, the interpolations enrich the consciousness of response" (160). Agreeing with all these interpretations, I would add that the consciousness of response, like the processes of mythologizing and fiction making, contribute to the dynamic of power that shapes the plot of *Tom Jones.*

Despite general critical agreement about the masterful (if somewhat ostentatious) artifice of Fielding's plot, commentators have conspicuously failed to agree on the purpose of this grand design. To inculcate the value of prudence, to question the penetrability of motive, to celebrate love, to draw the reader into the moral complexities of life and of fiction—these are only a few available hypotheses. In adding one more to the list, I am less concerned to offer a definitive account of *Tom Jones* than to suggest what the assumptions of its plot have in common with those governing *Clarissa* and other novels of the mid-eighteenth century. Writing about *Little Dorritt,* Peter Garrett suggests that the aesthetic pattern of plot can be "a form of knowledge. It results from an attempt to discover a hidden pattern that both unifies the novel's form and expresses its significance" (31). The word *attempt* suggests a kind of conscious purpose that I would not in this instance attribute to Fielding. The "hidden pattern" of *Tom Jones,* I propose, like that of *Joseph Andrews, Fanny Hill,* and *Clarissa,* consists in alignments of force that call attention to competitive structures governing the imagined social universe. These alignments indeed constitute a form of knowledge about a world in which power derives most obviously from possession of money, social authority, and erotic energy (the three often contending for preeminence), but in which the narrator's power of plotting emerges as triumphant.

It hardly needs demonstrating that Tom encounters and inadvertently participates in struggles of power wherever he goes. The conflict with Ensign Northerton, motivated on the ensign's part by the most gratuitous kind of masculine competitiveness, epitomizes the possibilities of arbitrary conflict. Husbands and wives invariably compete for authority. Wives in these competitions, from Mrs. Partridge onwards, typically win, partly, it often seems, because their erotic energy exceeds their husbands' (although they often accuse their spouses—sometimes correctly—of sexual misbehavior). Paradise Hall itself supplies a scene for struggle, Thwackum and Square competing for Bridget's favors, Captain Blifil domineering his wife, and everyone trying to manipulate Allworthy, whose social, moral, and financial authority, however, remain preeminent. Blifil engages in a secret effort to triumph over Tom. Squire Western and his sister vie for control over Sophia. By the time Tom reaches London, his involvement in a dog-eat-dog society has become apparent. Men compete for women, women for men; fathers browbeat daughters and sons alike; the upper classes oppress the lower; everyone wants money as the most obvious instrument of control. Only Tom's long-preserved moral innocence protects him from awareness. Even Sophia appears to grasp reality more fully than he does.

The narrative's comic energy and the narrator's comic control help to prevent this scheme of things from impressing the reader as ferocious or even gloomy. Yet sinister implications occasionally penetrate the comic surface, as in the true story of the murderer Fisher introduced in one of the narrator's discourses on writing (402–3; bk. 8, ch. 1) and, more importantly, in the account of Tom's liaison with Lady Bellaston. "Few English novelists share Fielding's sane, generous viewpoint about human sexuality," Steven Cohan writes (51), echoing John Middleton Murry. Well, maybe. But Lady Bellaston supplies a whiff of corruption.

As apologists for Tom and for Fielding have long noted, a mistaken principle of honor and a genuine sentiment of gratitude motivate Tom in responding to Lady Ballaston's manipulative sexual advances and in sustaining the affair as long as he does. Because the lady gives him money, which he needs, and fine clothes, Tom feels obligated to offer her what she wants, until Sophia reappears in his life. Then he finds a consultant who can tell him how to rid himself of a mistress who has become a burden.

Lady Bellaston, dedicated to her pleasures and to her independence (Tom gets rid of her, of course, by proposing marriage), might have been presented sympathetically, but Fielding does not present her so. On the contrary, he even gives her bad breath. Here as in *Joseph Andrews* women consistently figure as sexual aggressors. The text treats Lady Bellaston more contemptuously than it treats Molly Seagrim or Mrs. Water, previous seducers of Tom, perhaps because she, with money, cleverness, and social position, constitutes a more genuine threat than they do to the established order. The idea of female power is even more dangerous than that of female sexuality. Lady Bellaston, like Fanny Hill, is a mistress in two senses of that word. She must be rejected for her desire to control others, attested by her manipulation of Sophia as well as of Tom.

But it must be said that Tom fully participates in whatever corruption Lady Bellaston embodies, and this fact qualifies the "healthiness" of depicted sexuality in the novel. If the lady employs her wealth and status to buy him, he allows himself to be bought. If she uses him for her purposes, he uses her for his. Neither "innocence" nor "gratitude" justifies such behavior. The alacrity with which Tom jettisons Lady Bellaston when she becomes a serious inconvenience suggests that gratitude vanishes before self-interest. The particular form of self-interest—Tom's continuing desire for Sophia—is one in which most novel-readers will invest.[8] Tom's interest is the interest of the novel. Identifying with it, we justify his behavior. But in the total scheme of *Tom Jones*, such behavior indicates that even a generous, good-hearted, feckless innocent finds it necessary to operate in terms of structures of control. Tom resolves to leave Lady Bellaston after Nightingale has convinced him that ending the relationship would amount to "turning himself out of her *Service*, in which Light he now saw his Affair with her" (819; bk. 15, ch. 9). The perception that he has subordinated himself into the role of servant stands behind the letter to Lady Bellaston in which Tom claims it his "sole Ambition . . . to have the Glory of laying my Liberty at your Feet": he will subordinate himself utterly to her. It ends with the request that she "generously bestow on me a legal Right of calling you mine for ever" (820; bk. 15, ch. 9): he will be legal master. Lady Bellaston understands the proposal as a threat to her autonomy and an effort to gain possession of her wealth. She has known all along about the dialectic of master (or mistress) and servant, controller and controllee. Now Tom knows about it too. The erotic connection cannot survive that knowledge.

The contest for hegemony plays itself out not only in the lives of lovers, family members, masters and servants, hosts and guests, soldiers and officers, squires and poachers—not only in the lives, but also in the talk. The proliferating fictons or "myths" that surround the characters (Allworthy as lecher or as tyrant, Sophia as Jenny Cameron, Blifil as disciple of Thwackum or of Square, Tom as Jacobite or as madman, and so on) dramatize the same contest. People endlessly invent and/or tell stories, explanatory fictions, and try to impose them on one another. The battle of interpretations, which is also one of narratives, organizes the plot. Blifil's story of Tom (a story long and carefully developed) causes Allworthy to banish his foster son; the new stories of Tom that Allworthy hears in London generate reconciliation. Mrs. Fitzgerald tells Sophia a story designed to encourage sympathy; Sophia tells Mrs. Fitzgerald a story intended to obscure the true cause of her own flight. Partridge tells himself a story of Tom that causes him to join forces with the young man. Tom tells himself one story after another, influenced by each new situation, each new companion. Thus everyone seeks his or her advantage, seeks to "win" in a struggle not necessarily perceived or understood, except presumably by the narrator. Tom needs to become his own author (see Kraft 37); he can only do so by evading other people's attempts to

rewrite him. The politics of fiction making and telling duplicates
the other political patterns that lend density to this novel.[9] More
clearly than the politics of nations, the power exchanges of individual persons betray, in Fielding's imagining, the intricate disguises of a universal desire for control: of language and meaning,
and of other people.

Homer Brown's brilliant exposition of narrative patterns in *Tom
Jones* calls attention to how the text moves by a series of spin-
offs and swerves, "the ever deflected lateral movement of the
narration" (219). He also discusses the rather troubling sense a
reader gets

> that Fielding's novels are constructed, on some level, as classical orations
> in which examples serve technically as proofs for argument. Incidents or
> characters often seem present in the narrative more to serve the needs of
> the underlying argument than for any plot necessity, although they can
> serve that purpose also. (216)

The novel's reliance on ostentatious patterns of identity and contrast, its abundant deflections, its recurrent air of constructing
an argument rather than a fiction: such elements call attention to
what the narrator frequently asserts, his triumphant power to dis-
pose events and characters—and ideas—as he will. The narrator's
conspicuous presence, his conspicuous demands on the reader,
dramatize what the novel repeatedly demonstrates in local instances, the fact that the imposition of verbal forms on another is
the very ground of power.

Not phallic power, exactly: we have come a long way from Fanny
Hill's lover. But the arrangements of power within the fiction, the
arrangement by which Sophia is bestowed as reward on enlightened Tom, speak of a society in which males are assumed to have
official dominance. Women have their own forms of power, as they
do in *Fanny Hill*. But the mantle of authority rests primarily on
men. And authority belongs, finally, to authors, who may construct
"morals" for their fictions that obscure the operations of power, but
who, in the mid-eighteenth century, consistently created fictions
whose "tendency" exposes power's omnipresence.

4

THE IDEAL WOMAN AND
THE PLOT OF POWER

"If characters exist for novels," Martin Price writes, "they exist only as much as and in the way that the novel needs them" (*Forms of Life* 37). The needs of novels have curious configurations. I want to speculate about what needs are answered by a tiny subspecies of character in eighteenth-century English fictions: the ideal woman, as evoked by the male imagination. She does not loom large in most novels by men. Although Smollett, for instance, like such minor novelists as Henry Brooke and Henry Mackenzie, rewards his heroes with the love of a good woman, the woman herself exerts little force in his plot or in the imagined life of his fiction. Even Sophia Western, an exceptionally active female, as she dwindles toward wifehood becomes a less compelling figure. Her status as an energetic and self-respecting woman becomes less important than her symbolic virtue and even more remotely symbolic "wisdom" as appropriate complements to a reformed Tom Jones. April London points out that in all of Fielding's fiction, "virtuous women are given power in order that they may renounce it by the willing ceding of their property, metaphorically and literally considered, to the control of their male partners" (331). Like Fanny Goodwill, Sophia loses force in the ceding.

Clarissa might seem to exemplify an eighteenth-century ideal, but in fact she is too fully imagined to preserve that status. Richardson wanted her to have faults, to avoid the superhuman: as he says in his preface to the second edition, she is perfect but not impeccable. He provided her with such meticulously understood conflicts, such complexities of self-will, that she lives in the reader's mind not as ideal but as a genuine "form of life." Pamela, on the other hand, exists for her creator, if not for every reader, as paragon. The "editor's" concluding comments point out that her character exemplifies twelve specified virtues or sets of virtues: "so many signal instances of the excellency of her mind, which may make her character worthy of the imitation of her sex" (Richardson, *Pamela* 533). Fielding's narrator in *Amelia*, similarly, frequently

85

characterizes his heroine as "the best of Wives" (e.g., 533): another ideal. And John Cleland's Fanny Hill represents the erotic version of the ideal woman. This chapter will investigate how such figures function in the dynamics of the plot of power.

Before thinking about good women, we might begin by thinking about bad ones: women straightforwardly condemned by the texts they inhabit.

In *Fanny Hill*, there is but one: Fanny's landlady, Mrs. Jones, eager to sell her even during the paradisaical period she spends with her first lover, Charles. *Wicked* women, of course, abound: women motivated by self-interest, like Mrs. Brown, the first madam Fanny encounters; for that matter, like Fanny herself. Women committed to sexual indulgence, women willing to do almost anything for the sake of excitement, women conspicuously uninterested in the idea of chastity—women who violate in various ways accepted social standards appear throughout Cleland's novel. Yet only a single female among the many women represented proves willfully destructive: *bad*. *Pamela*, despite its limited cast of characters, contains, in Mrs. Jewkes, a terrifying figure of evil who apparently reforms quite effortlessly toward the novel's end. *Amelia* embodies several forms of badness in women, nor does any of Fielding's bad women move far toward virtue. To think about how such characters work helps to clarify the plots they inhabit.

Fanny Hill, constructed in terms of a lucid if not altogether orthodox moral scheme, provides the simplest version of evil. Heterosexual desire supplies the standard of good in this pornographic novel; economic interest isolated from such desire contains the potential for evil. Although Fanny herself and those she admires maintain a fervent concern for the financial, they value the erotic more highly. At the other extreme, Charles's father, punishing the young man for his putative economic control over his grandmother, devises an economic pretext for sending him to the South Seas. Mrs. Jones quickly takes advantage of this situation. Providing "cruel and interested care" when Fanny miscarries (76), she restores her victim to health, demands money from her, threatens debtors' prison, and presents her to a "very honourable gentleman," advising her to "make your market while you may" (78). Fanny never modifies her tone of resentment and disapproval toward this woman. In fact, though, Mrs. Jones introduces Fanny to full consciousness of precisely the nexus of eros and cash that will organize her life until Charles's return. Eros means pleasure, of course, but also profit; the bad woman is bad not because of her interest in money, but because of her lack of direct interest in sex. (In this respect she differs from the much less harshly treated madam who tries to sell Fanny's virginity—a woman who hires a trooper for her private sexual gratification.)

Richardson's Mrs. Jewkes, unlike Mrs. Jones, manifests little explicit concern for money but quite a lot of sexual feeling. In a novel that, unlike Cleland's, assumes and entirely condones the primacy of economic power and suppresses even while exploiting female sexuality, she is accordingly condemned. Far more forcefully than Mr. B, she embodies Pamela's sexual nightmare. Unlike Mr. B, she remains unresponsive alike to Pamela's charms and her virtue. Nor does Pamela ever find means to divert her from her purposes, for Mrs. Jewkes operates always on the principle of loyalty to her master. Good servant that she is, she will mindlessly do whatever she believes him to want. Pamela feels, and convinces most readers, that Mrs. Jewkes enjoys her roles as jailer and as bawd. She pins one arm while Mr. B pins the other in the climactic scene where Mr. B, having disguised himself in Fieldingesque fashion as a woman, actually enters Pamela's bed. Mrs. Jewkes urges him on, like the whores in *Clarissa*, suggesting that the loss of virginity is no such great matter, and that Pamela will be fully compliant by the morning after.

Although her master's presumed wishes always authorize her conduct, Mrs. Jewkes's aggression exceeds situational demands. Pamela suspects her of lesbian impulses: she seems rather too fond of kissing her victim. She also seems, and looks, masculine. "She has a hoarse, man-like voice, and is as thick as she is long; and yet looks so deadly strong, that I am afraid she would dash me at her foot in an instant, if I was to vex her.—So that with a heart more ugly than her face, she frightens me sadly" (116). Her lack of stereotypically feminine characteristics, until her abject compliance at the end, makes her inaccessible to the kinds of persuasion Pamela can imagine. She prides herself on the implacability she consistently demonstrates.

Mrs. Jewkes functions both as agent and as object of power. Her explicit formulation of her responsibility makes her position clear.

Why, look ye, madam, said she, I have a great notion of doing my duty to my master; and therefore you may depend upon it, if I can do *that*, and serve *you*, I will; but you must think, if *your* desire, and *his* will, come to clash once, I shall do as he bids me, let it be what it will. (110)

His will, Pamela's desire. Mrs. Jewkes understands Mr. B as compact of focused will and imagines Pamela as possessed by futile desire. The narrative will evolve from conflicts between will and desire on both sides of the struggle for control, but Mrs. Jewkes, firmly oriented toward the locus of power, cannot conceive of divided will in her master. Because he is a master, he should get what he wants; because he can will what he desires and expect to have his will, he is a master. When Pamela becomes mistress of the household servants, rules change. Now her desire and his will, his desire and her will, her will and his—all officially coincide. Mrs. Jewkes changes accordingly. "She is very civil to me now," Pamela says, the day before her wedding, "and her former wickedness I will forgive, for the sake of the happy fruits that have attended it" (355). The next day, Mrs. Jewkes still demonstrates vestiges of depravity. "The poor woman has so little purity of heart," Pamela explains, that even when she says good and appropriate things, they carry no weight (357). Five days after the marriage, "her talk and actions are entirely different from what they used to be, quite circumspect and decent; and I should have thought her virtuous, and even pious, had I never known her in another light" (399). Pamela draws a conclusion about domestic power: "By this we may see, my dear father and mother, of what force example is, and what is in the power of the heads of families to do" (399).

Presumably Mrs. Jewkes's impurity of heart has not changed with the change of heart in her master. She now *appears* virtuous and pious, but Pamela knows better, having seen her in another guise which, in Pamela's view, testified to the state of Mrs. Jewkes's heart. Her circumspect and decent aspect bears no relation to her heart—such is Pamela's belief—yet Pamela applauds. The power of the heads of families allows them to control appearances rather than hearts in their domestics. It is, in other words, the power to encourage hypocrisy.

I do not belong to the party that sees Pamela herself as a hypocrite. Still, the loud announcement, by way of Mrs. Jewkes's "reform," that outsides need bear no relation to insides hints that the "bad woman" and the "good woman" of this novel bear a troubling similarity to one another. Pamela too has served as a domestic in Mr. B's household; she too has perceived the example of the would-be profligate master. Her conduct has responded to his just as Mrs. Jewkes's has. Are we to see her only as an effect, the cause being, always, the head of the family, the center of domestic power?

The question of how we should understand Mrs. Jewkes likewise remains unresolved. What has happened to the horror of her sexuality and of her aggression? All disguised, all subdued . . . but there, beneath the surface of circumspection and decency, violence, lasciviousness, rage, and unscrupulousness presumably remain. Beneath the good woman lurks a bad one. Richardson fully evokes the terror for Pamela of the unwomanly, unreachable, violent creature whose perfect obedience to her master authorizes her brutality. He does not dwell on the potential terror of her "reform."

In *Amelia*, no one reforms except, nominally and implausibly, Booth himself and, conveniently, Robinson (on what he thinks is his deathbed). We leave Blear-eyed Moll in Newgate when Captain Booth achieves freedom. Although she inhabits the scene only briefly, she survives in the imagination with remarkable force, permanently appalling. Mrs. James remains shallow and hypocritical from beginning to end; only her self-presentation alters. Mrs. Ellison, pimping for the Noble Lord, has brought destruction to Mrs. Bennet. She is quite prepared to do the same for Amelia. Miss Mathews seduces Captain Booth in the novel's first chapters; she wishes only for the chance to do so again. Richardson does not appear to take full responsibility for the implications of Mrs. Jewkes; similarly, Fielding's narrator avoids dwelling on the meaning of his many embodiments (male and female) of social corruption. As many commentators have noted, he has difficulty reconciling the plot of public corruption with that of private virtue and struggle. Part of the problem is that corruption frequently permeates the private sphere as well.

It feels a bit unnerving that the novelist who imagines Amelia can also imagine Blear-eyed Moll, physically monstrous, almost phantasmically powerful, capable of inciting and of committing violence. "The phenomenon of Blear-eyed Moll and that of Amelia simply cannot connect," Claude Rawson writes at the end of a brilliant treatment of *Amelia*: ". . . a world in which both exist can only be acknowledged, not 'explained'" (96–97). I would hypothesize, on the contrary, that the two "phenomena" imply one another, since the imagining of perfect goodness involves repressed knowledge of the potential for badness, and the repressed, inevitably, returns. Women in their graciousness may choose to subordinate themselves to men; men lovingly imagine the implications of such a choice. But women also embody the hidden potential for irrational, unpredictable, dangerous aggression. This is the point, I suspect, of the faint hinted analogy between Pamela and Mrs. Jewkes.

The fusion of the erotic and the economic that resolves the plot of *Fanny Hill* also resolves the problem of female evil. Fanny, prosperous and protected, no longer feels vulnerable. Mrs. Jones and her like presumably continue to exist in the world, but they do not matter any more. *Pamela*, where the potential presence of bad women has more troubling implications because of the disguising force of hypocrisy, must work out its plot by energetic reaffirmation of socially ordained power relations. Husbands rule wives, masters rule servants; the good master will ensure good conduct if not good feeling in his subordinates, so one need not worry about Mrs. Jewkes and her kind. *Amelia*, where bad women variously manifest economic, social, and erotic motivation, can find no comforting solution to the threat they represent. Reasserting the moral control of the good woman provides a precarious and localized reorganization of power relationships. The implications of such reorganization will emerge more fully as we examine the figure of the female paragon at the center of each plot.

Pamela allows the reader little doubt about the extent of her virtues and her talents. She reports abundant testimony of others about her beauty, her deftness at carving, her cleverness as poet and as narrator of herself, her wondrous goodness. Her protestations of her own virtue become only more emphatic as her story continues. For narrative purposes, her virtue, beauty, and social skills are essential. They add up to that "femininity" on which Margaret Anne Doody comments, the femininity that provides Pamela's instrument in the power struggle. Doody writes that Pamela

is unaware of the force of femininity which is her weapon—the power not only of her youth and beauty but also of her very female cast of mind—because, like most women, she sees the masculine as the powerful. Eventually, it is the force of femininity which defeats Mr. B., or, alternatively, brings him to victory by making him acknowledge the softer side of his nature. (*A Natural Passion* 49)

Without the specific manifestations of Pamela's femininity, the marriage that appears to threaten the social status quo could not be narrated.

I have analyzed elsewhere (Spacks, *Adolescent* 24–30) the movements of power in *Pamela*: the heroine's development—if it can be called that—from psychological ascendancy while she plays the role of young, poor, naive servant to willing submission when she rises to the place of rich, socially secure wife and mistress of the household. Her "victory" remains pyschologically ambiguous. Her initial power over Mr. B does not derive from her goodness, but her goodness makes it tolerable for a conservative readership. The novel does not explicitly make that point, but it dwells in extraordinary detail on the facts of power relations. The second letter from Pamela's parents spells out the situation between Pamela and Mr. B as a potential power conflict. The girl's mother and father worry about the hazards their daughter faces from "a designing young gentleman, if he should prove so, who has so much *power* to oblige, and has a kind of *authority* to command, as your master" (13). Mr. B's power, in their view, derives from his capacity both to give ("oblige") and to command. Pamela, however, appears to have no trouble resisting either kind of force.

Both stem from Mr. B's social position. The novel makes even a twentieth-century reader vividly experience the magnitude of the power inherent in social status, first of all by reference to such crude facts as a master's capacity to abduct a servant without obstacle. Pamela's father proves helpless to intervene; neighbors of Mr. B's own class think the issue much ado about nothing; a clergyman who tries to help becomes himself a victim of social hierarchy. Richardson fairly rubs our noses in it. More subtle aspects of the narrative, such as the nature of various dependents' compliance with Mr. B, underline the fundamental social reality. Mrs. Jewkes suggests that class makes legality. "Look ye, said she, he is my master; and if he bids me do any thing that I *can* do, I think I *ought* to do it; and let him, who has his power to command me, look to the *lawfulness* of it" (111). But the novel, through its characters, also repeatedly, if somewhat uncertainly, redefines the terms of power. Pamela explicitly claims the soul of a princess; she asserts, and possesses, the power of resistance. In a particularly interesting dialectical moment, Mr. B, under the spell of Pamela's written records of events, suggests that the struggle between the two of them turns on *plots*. Demanding to see more of Pamela's narrative, he concludes, "there is such a pretty air of romance, as you relate them, in *your* plots and *my* plots, that I shall be better directed in what manner to wind up the catastrophe of the pretty novel" (242). Pamela's relating of events—that is, to preserve the terms I have been using, her *story*—incorporates his plots and hers and can determine meaning and outcome. The word *plots*, as Mr. B uses it, poises between its literary and its political sense. Pamela literally writes the story, yet her master tries to arrogate the position of novelist. Her plots and his vie, in his view of things, but her "romantic" understanding of the import of plots may control their outcome.

Mr. B's statement, positive in form though tentative in content, since he has not yet seen the narrative brought up to date, suggests that he tacitly acknowledges the same priority of story over plot that Richardson would work out more elaborately in *Clarissa*.

But much of the novel indeed consists in plots and counterplots, with the word *plot* ringing through the text as emphatically as it would in *Clarissa*. Despite the social power that gives Mr. B an obvious advantage as plotter, Pamela holds her own. In the course of saying so—and she is capable of Lovelacean exultation about her powers ("How nobly my plot succeeds!" [134])—she, like her opponent, often wavers between the literary and non-literary meanings of plot. When, for instance, Mrs. Jewkes tells Pamela that Mr. B will force her to marry Colbrand and then buy her from the Swiss man on her wedding day, she reflects, "this, to be sure, is horrid romancing! Yet, abominable as it is, it may possibly serve to introduce some plot now hatching!" (188). She means that she believes Mrs. Jewkes has invented the story she tells, yet it might nonetheless provide a clue to Mr. B's actual plans and projects. Mrs. Jewkes's story, or romance, like Pamela's own, may possess more meaning than its teller knows. Pamela thinks the story is fiction; Mr. B's plots are truth. But the two interpenetrate. The plots intended as strategies of sexual politics figure also as elements of narrative. When Mr. B refers to Pamela's "treasonable papers," justifying the epithet by the explanation, "for you are a great plotter" (238), he still seems to mean something literary as well as something political.

The text elaborately proclaims the importance of Pamela's "story," meaning not the sequence of events that has befallen her so much as "the light [she] put[s] them in" (250–51). She wins friends and influences people by what Mr. B refers to, shortly before their marriage, as her "wondrous story" (317), sign of her virtue and accomplishment and even of her erotic attractiveness. All plotting stops, once Mr. B yields to that story's power. Pamela, rescued into rank and wealth, no longer needs to plot; nor does Mr. B, once the object of his desire yields to his mastery as husband. Now *stories* begin to multiply: Mr. B's narratives of phallic prowess in duel and seduction (both stories provoked by his sister's hints of his wickedness); the later, fuller story of Sally Godfrey. Pamela's story of virtue and success circulates. The most dramatic postmarital event, Pamela's confrontation with her husband's sister Lady Davers, occurs because two women accept conflicting versions of the same story. Lady Davers believes Pamela to figure in a narrative of seduction and betrayal; Pamela knows her story has already had its happy ending. Putting things in different lights generates intense conflict.

The importance of story in this novel, epitomized by the narrative created by Pamela's letters, emerges also in Mr. B's efforts to triumph over his maidservant. As Michael McKeon points out, "the squire has his own fictions to propound" (360). McKeon comments on one of the scenes in which rape appears imminent, "B. reveals that his dominant motives are not strictly sexual but political, and that he takes power to consist in the ability to make others accept one's version of events as authoritative" (359). By this standard, Pamela wins. Her version justifies her nature. It becomes her husband's version too.

By reading, retrospectively, Pamela's letters, Mr. B (and others) can discover the extraordinary stability of her character. Mr. B changes his ideas about things: his mother's maidservant at first appears to him an object of seduction, then an object of marriage. The clergyman Williams is first to be punished, then to be rewarded for trying to help Pamela. Mr. B will abandon his sister forever, only to embrace her moments later. He has moody and violent aspects. Not so Pamela. Although she gradually allows herself to know the nature of her desire, her assumptions about herself and about the social order do not significantly change. She reiterates endlessly, in the letters, what she believes, and she continues to believe in chastity and other forms of conventional virtue, in her right to respect from herself and from others, and in the obligations of obedience but also of self-reliance. She discovers her desire, and she discovers her own powers more fully than she has known them before, but she remains unchanging in her goodness. Mr. B does not reward her for goodness alone, but Richardson comes close to doing exactly that. Pamela constitutes a powerful fantasy of female possibility. By her absolute stability, she counters the implicit threat of Mrs. Jewkes, the threat of hypocrisy. Pamela, always the same, cannot, need not, resort to appearing as her master would have her: she simply *is*.

Hence her power, the kind of power she will retain after marriage—although certainly her resources are greatly truncated once Mr. B has her firmly in his possession. Roy Roussel, one of the most interesting recent commentators on *Pamela*, considers the action of the novel from Mr. B's point of view and develops a good deal of sympathy for a man who, in Roussel's reading, wants Pamela to understand his sincerity and to believe that he says exactly what he feels (77). Roussel understands *Pamela*, as I do, as plotted through a dynamic of power. The situation that keeps the lovers apart for so long, he explains, is not

the result of a conflict of personal qualities. It is a function of the conventional structuring of their relationship, which marks B's sincerity with the sign of the master so that Pamela can read in it only the fact of his power, and marks Pamela's reserve with the sign of social propriety so that B sees in it only the reflection and condemnation of his own lack of control. (78)

This careful formulation avoids suggesting that social power has reality apart from a single individual's perceptions of it. Accordingly, Roussel goes on to applaud B's view of marriage, which centers, he believes, on love. B, Roussel explains, "wants love to act as a unifying element which makes the issues of power and the differences between husband and wife or master and servant irrelevant" (84). And he achieves approximately this: "their marriage allows Pamela and B to establish an equality within difference" (86).

But this is a marriage in which Pamela early writes down forty-eight rules of conduct promulgated by her husband—although, to be sure, with hints of reservations along the way. Pamela continues to think of her husband as her master, to defer to him in every possible way. Her only clearly defined power is that of distributing some of his money. Roussel's fantasy of equality may duplicate B's, or even perhaps Richardson's. But B (and even perhaps Richardson) only mystifies realities of socially-ordained power that in fact govern virtually every depicted detail of the marriage.

I do not mean to imply that Pamela finds herself deprived of all power—only that power remains a covert issue of the relationship. B himself, his rhetoric calling attention to the social system that preserves female subordination by glossing it in exalted terms, metaphorizes the marriage as Pamela's victory: "You . . . have nobly overcome: and who shall grudge you the reward of the hard-bought victory?" (354). (He goes on immediately, however, to announce, "This affair is so much the act of my own will, that I glory in being capable of distinguishing so much excellence": his victory too, converted by his formulation into a product of will rather than desire.) In a prayer shortly after her marriage, Pamela evokes a more provocative figure. She asks God to enlarge her will, so that she can dispense to others a portion of the happiness she has received from Providence.

Then shall I not stand a *single* mark of thy goodness to a poor worthless creature, that in herself is of so small account in the scale of beings, a mere cipher on the wrong side of a figure; but shall be placed on the right side;

and, though nothing worth in myself, shall give signification by my *place*, and multiply the blessings I owe to thy goodness. (383)

"On the right side," Pamela becomes a symbol of multiplication: of power. The manifest logic of the metaphor might suggest that she *gains* significance by her "*place*," but she finds it important to claim, rather, a new capacity to *give* signification. Such giving is specifically B's form of power—he has bestowed new meaning on his wife. Now Pamela claims corresponding capacity.

Clarissa uses the same figure of herself as cipher, to different purpose. Writing to Anna Howe, about Lovelace, she observes, "I am but a *cypher*, to give *him* significance, and *myself* pain" (4: 40; 2: 264). In her depressed view, the nothingness of the cipher defines it; what she gives to Lovelace, she lacks herself. Pamela, despite her rhetorical self-description as a "poor worthless creature," feels the magnitude of possibility in her new position. The marriage provides her with new resources which she experiences as power.

If this is Richardson's vision of balanced marriage, its balance consists in its apparent realignment of power. Pamela, the representation of virtuous stability, will supply moral ballast for her more erratic husband. He can flirt with other women (as, in *Pamela II*, he will), yet Pamela's force—product partly of his fantasy—will always draw him back.

As a figure of female changelessness, Fanny Hill of course displays virtues altogether different from Pamela's, playing out the implications of love of pleasure as female motive. She is, after her fashion, as much a paragon as is Richardson's heroine, an equal-but-opposite product of male fantasy. Her career demonstrates her absolute consistency. Orphaned at fourteen, she goes to London to seek her fortune, drawn not by perceived economic need but by a friend's account of urban diversions, "the detail of all which," Fanny adds, "perfectly turned the little head of me" (17). So motivated, she need not fear the conventional fate of innocent country maidens; quickly taught to associate pleasure with eros, Fanny eagerly awaits a seducer.

Cleland's imagining of his protagonist's character, despite the conventional pornographic sentimentalism with which it suppresses the potential for sordid or tragic outcomes, has its own integrity: Fanny's persistent cheerfulness reflects her commitment to self-gratification. Previously deprived by her rural environment of what she can understand as genuine experience, she welcomes the whores' efforts to educate her. Within a day or so, she feels convinced that sexual activity promises the greatest available pleasure. Pleasure, however, hardly associates itself with the repellent man to whom the madam sells her. Fanny fights off his efforts at rape, avoids the immediate repetition of those efforts by falling ill, and definitively escapes the would-be rapist when he is arrested for commercial fraud. She then chooses her own seducer, Charles, a handsome young man with whom she elopes from the whorehouse and embarks on her progress of pleasure.

A cruel father separates Charles from Fanny. Roy Roussel suggests that the plot move which invokes "paternal and economic authority" to separate the lovers "simply enacts the real relationship between personal intention and conventional meaning" in the earlier conversations through which Charles has begun to "educate" Fanny. In these conversations, contrary to his conscious intention, Charles reasserts "the conventional masculine power to define the feminine" (61). Convention of one kind or another rules this text. When economic necessity drives Fanny to prostitution, she literalizes the familiar eighteenth-century convention of women as objects of exchange. Reporting her second sexual adventure, she stresses her passivity. "I sat stockstill; and now looking on myself as bought by the payment that had been transacted before me, I did not care what became of my wretched body; and wanting life, spirits, or courage to oppose the least struggle, . . . I suffered, tamely, whatever the gentleman pleased" (80). (Here as elsewhere in the novel, one may wonder whether some irony clings to the word *gentleman*.) This episode ends in Fanny's "merely animal" pleasure, which she compares unfavorably with "the enjoyments of a mutual love passion" (85). Animal satisfactions, however, come to seem increasingly satisfactory. Never again merely passive, she appears to take control of her own destiny (always within a totally assumed context of male domination) and to use her body, her main resource, to achieve physical, economic, and psychological gratification. The text emphasizes as Fanny's three principal forms of pleasure the direct delights of sexuality, the more devious satisfactions of voyeurism, and the lasting fulfillment of financial gain; she abundantly experiences all three.

Cleland subsumes Fanny's three forms of pleasure under the embracing satisfaction of self-development. Her voyeurism, for instance, expresses her desire to enlarge her knowledge of her world. She happily watches heterosexual encounters of various kinds (for example, between a prostitute and a fantastically endowed idiot boy); she feels enlightenment and disgust when witnessing the activities of a pair of homosexual men. In her own sexual performances too she looks for new experience, willingly submitting to a sadomasochist's flagellations because she wants to know what it feels like to be a willing victim. She takes advice about investing her money. And finally she allies herself with an elderly man possessed of great "power of pleasing." He touches Fanny's heart by appealing to her understanding. "From him it was I first learned," Fanny explains, " . . . and not without infinite pleasure, that I had such a portion of me worth bestowing some regard on" (206). This mentor trains Fanny's mind and makes her his heir. Fanny's relations with him, as Nancy Miller points out (*The Heroine's Text* 62) thus reiterate her experience with the beloved Charles, who had earlier instructed Fanny "in a great many points of life that I was, in consequence of my no-education, perfectly ignorant of" (73): self-improvement has always helped to define pleasure for Fanny. At the old man's convenient death, eight months after the beginning of their liaison, she finds herself prosperous, cultivated, and more self-satisfied than ever.

J. H. Plumb, in his introduction to *Fanny Hill*, describes Fanny as "a male dream, with little contact with the reality of feminine passion" (xiii). Not only the guiltless and ardent sexuality Plumb cites, but Fanny's independence, her concern with self-development, her concentration on pleasure also help define her as a "male dream." Her delineation as a self-sufficient and cheerful woman who sooner or later gets what she wants (and who usually wants what she gets) justifies the fundamental sexual fantasy of the "ideal erotic companion" (another of Plumb's phrases). In this particular piece of male imagining, the woman who fulfills every man's dream also fulfills herself; Fanny's gratification inevitably coincides with male satisfaction.

But the most important element in the fantasy is the fact that Fanny, despite all her "education," all her self-development, never changes: that is, the more she changes, the more she remains the same. To locate her ruling passion in love of pleasure calls attention to this fact. Men provide more pleasure as sexual partners than do women; love offers more satisfaction than can lust; the joys of virtue excel those of vice; and so on. But the text subsumes all of Fanny's valued experience under the single criterion of pleasure. This fiction allows its protagonist only the voice that might plausibly belong to an icon of lust, the voice of a guilt-free woman who implicitly obviates the guilt of all men. The character's independence and assertiveness increase the titillation of her absolute subordination to the beloved man. And all of her "self-development" reiterates her dedication to the single criterion of pleasure. No one would have the slightest difficulty deciding what Fanny wants.

Although Fanny tells her own story, the reader encounters her more as object than as subject: as a collection of qualities whose changeless sum equals the gratification of male need, the alleviation of male anxiety. Nancy Miller suggests that

> the erotics erected by female impersonation is a mirroring not of female desire but of a phallic pride of place, a wish-fulfillment that ultimately translates into structures of masculine dominance and authority. . . . [T]he recollecting masculine 'I' disguised in *Fanny Hill* through the memory of sexual history becomes or borrows the body of the Other the better to assure the transcendence of the Same. ("'I's' in Drag" 54–55)

Agreeing that power is always at issue in this novel, which obsessively reasserts "masculine dominance and authority," and agreeing that the act of "female impersonation" partakes of this reassertion, I would suggest that the character of Fanny comforts the male imagination in another way as well. Fanny projects the longing for a comprehensible and manageable Other. Her eagerness to cooperate, after her marriage, in the orthodox structures of male socialization and male dominion belongs to the same constellation of traits that accounts for her horror at male homosexuality and her pleasure in pleasing. In every possible sense of the phrase, Fanny is "a man's woman."

Her changelessness makes her a reassuring figure, from the male point of view. Yet because *Fanny Hill* participates so fully in an erotics of power as well as of sex, the novel hints at anxiety about the possible instability of even that male power on which bourgeois society rests. Robert Markley summarizes the novel as "an extended fantasy of masculine power and prerogatives that defines 'sexuality' socially and ideologically rather than individually; it explores, with some sophistication, the dynamics of sexual—and linguistic—power in eighteenth-century society" ("Language" 344). Like other wish-fulfillment fantasies, this one has its dark side. Fanny's capacity for deceit, touched on in the last chapter, implies it. This heroine will never turn into a Mrs. Jones, any more than Pamela will become a Mrs. Jewkes: her absolute consistency guarantees that her interest in money, substantial though it is, will only serve as a means to fulfill her ultimate desire for pleasure. But the fantasy of Fanny includes her ability to deceive when deception seems warranted. Her commitment to pleasure implies that the man she marries must remain a dependable source of pleasure.

Otherwise she may deceive him. Hence the novel's flirtation with sentimentalism (see Braudy 12, Copeland) and romance ("The virgin heart of the romantic love plot of the novel seems sealed off from the 'vale' or 'mine' or 'avenue' that we have seen penetrated time and again in the classification of the erotic" [Ragussis 97]). "Love" must finally sanction the distribution of power in order to make Fanny's dependability dependable from a male point of view.

Fielding's Amelia seems as implausible a sister for Fanny Hill as one could find. She too, however, clearly embodies an eighteenth-century feminine ideal, as well as—perhaps it amounts to the same thing—another fantasy of male fulfillment. Amelia does not appear as a character until book II of Fielding's novel. The action of book I takes place mainly in the prison where Captain William Booth finds himself unjustly incarcerated. This section of the fiction establishes the narrator's important social and literary attitudes, including his conviction that the female world divides into bad women and good women, the former disconcertingly abundant. Prison supplies examples of both. Bad women are aggressive: Blear-eyed Moll, physically loathsome, leveling curses at Booth and threatening to "lay hold" of him, attacking (with several companions) a male homosexual so violently that they "would probably have put an End to him, had he not been rescued out of their Hands by Authority" (33; bk. 1, ch. 4); Miss Mathews, imprisoned for the murder of her lover and pursuing with determination her purpose of seducing Booth. Good women are sacrificial victims: the "little Creature sitting by herself in a Corner and crying bitterly" (33; bk. 1, ch. 4); the "young Woman in Rags sitting on the Ground, and supporting the Head of an old Man in her Lap, who appeared to be giving up the Ghost" (33–34; bk. 1, ch. 4), a type of the virtuous female utterly devoted to a man.

Miss Mathews tells Booth her story of female rivalry, jealousy, and violence, and then asks to hear the narrative of his marriage. Thus we first encounter the figure of Amelia, her character mediated by her husband's understanding of it. Booth has only praise for his wife. He tells first of the accident by which "her lovely Nose was beat all to pieces" (66; bk. 2, ch. 1), extolling Amelia's "Magnanimity of Mind" in submitting "with Patience and Resignation . . . to the Loss of exquisite Beauty, in other Words, to the Loss of Fortune, Power, Glory; every Thing which human Nature is apt to court and rejoice in!" (67; bk 2, ch. 1). Despite its faintly comic overtones, this scene outlines boundaries of female possibility. Beauty constitutes and limits female power, dependent on male response. "Fortune, Power, Glory," conventionally male values, are assumed as ultimately desirable for women too. Patience and res- ignation define female virtue.

Booth's narrative, with its stress on Amelia's virtue and devotion, concludes with his going to bed with Miss Mathews, an episode veiled by the narrator in its details but emphasized in its meaning: "To say the Truth, we are much more concerned for the Behaviour of the Gentleman, than of the Lady, not only for his Sake, but for the Sake of the best Woman in the World, whom we should be sorry to consider as yoked to a Man of no Worth nor Honour" (154; bk. 4, ch. 1). Laws outside the storyteller's control appear to dictate Booth's sexual lapse. These laws belong, as the narrator makes clear, partly to male human nature, but they reflect also the pressures of social actualities on individual capacities. The male reader is invited to consider Booth's sin venial; yet the narrator has raised a malevolent alternate possibility. Perhaps, after all, saintly Amelia is yoked—bound like a laboring animal—to a man of no worth or honor. Perhaps the social system that condemns Booth to prison has definitively corrupted him. Although, like Fielding's earlier novels, *Amelia* works its way to a happy ending, it acknowledges other possibilities by its hints about the often unmerited fates of the prison population and by its occasional dark suggestions about Booth's character.

In this novel, Eric Rothstein maintains, "the energy of plot . . . is diverted to the examination of character" (*Systems* 160). Yet despite its emphasis on character, *Amelia* is heavily, and rather confusingly, plotted. As Ronald Paulson puts it,

> on the one hand, there is the public plot which displays the evils of contemporary society on as many fronts as possible. On the other is the private plot, concerned with the individual Booth, his betrayal of Amelia, his personal flaws, and his eventual reformation; it shows a Christian individual overcoming adversity not by changing circumstances but by rising above them and coming to terms with himself. The public and private themes fail to mesh; indeed, they seem to conflict. (*Satire* 163)

Many commentators have perceived this discrepancy. Moreover, Paulson's summary perhaps inadvertently reveals another perplexing aspect of Fielding's plot. Although the novel's title gives primacy to Amelia, its "private" action is mainly "concerned with the individual Booth." Of Amelia herself, it is possible for Maurice Johnson to claim that "It is her wayward husband who allows her to seem interesting" (155). Yet this "uninteresting" good woman becomes an iconic figure tacitly assumed to compensate for social corruption and to make private life possible in a decadent but still providentially governed environment.

Both Amelia and her husband suffer as a result of society's assumed corruptions. To summarize a few events following the prison scene may recall the complexities of Fielding's plotting. Booth, imprisoned and released in a recurrent pattern, powerless to obtain money by his own efforts, must woo others for help. Repeatedly he makes mistakes, results of weakness or naiveté, which cost money. He gambles away the family's entire store; he gives all he has in a futile effort to gain patronage. Miss Mathews tries to blackmail him into resuming their sexual connection. She writes an anonymous letter to Amelia, telling of Booth's fall from grace; Amelia silently forgives her husband. Meanwhile, Amelia faces repeated assaults on her virtue. Afraid that Booth's anger will impel him to risk his life in a duel, she refrains from telling him of her trials, some of which come from a man he considers his friend. Although she repeatedly defends herself successfully, only providential intervention can save her from the lord who, with the worst of intentions, almost lures her to a masquerade. Finally, when the couple possess no financial resources at all, Booth, once more imprisoned, is converted to Christianity and an unexpected inheritance promptly follows. Like Fanny Hill, Amelia lives happily ever after.

She has earned happiness by continuing simply to be "the best Woman in the World." Booth, as hard beset as she, as helpless against social actuality, has behaved more variously. Sometimes he acts virtuously in a traditionally "feminine" mode, as when he comforts and helps his wife during childbirth. Sometimes he enacts male virtue, serving courageously as a military officer. And sometimes, of course, he demonstrates his moral inadequacy. By turns weak and strong, foolish and wise, self-indulgent and devoted to his family, he undergoes a process of growth through which he acquires fuller knowledge of his wife's excellence and his own weaknesses, as well as of the truths of Christianity which he had earlier rejected in favor of a superficial and fashionable belief in Fortune and in the dominance of human passions.

Leopold Damrosch argues that Fielding, on a deep level, "was committed to the idea of the moral personality as a continuous state of being rather than acting" (271). Thus Tom Jones's goodness inheres in his nature, although his behavior deviates from virtuous norms; and Booth too, we can assume, remains "good"—his tears attest it—despite his dubious actions. Accepting this point, one must still note the distinction between Booth and his wife in rela-

tion to essence and action. Amelia's "continuous state of being" determines the nature of all her behavior; her husband, like Tom
Jones, can be allowed a split between "being" and "acting."

A comment on the Marquis de Sade's outrageously persecuted
virtuous character Justine may help to illuminate Fielding's way of
conceiving Amelia. Of Justine, Angela Carter writes,

> her innocence invalidates experience and turns it into events, things hap-
> pen to her but do not change her. This is the common experience of most
> women's lives, conducted always in the invisible presence of others who
> extract the meaning of her experience for themselves and thereby dimin-
> ish all meaning. (51)

Things happen to Amelia as well without changing her. She becomes increasingly aware of evil: at least twice she tells her children
that the world is full of wicked people, and once she goes so far as
to announce that their father is a wicked man—a statement that
she quickly repudiates in action, since without her steady devotion
to Booth she would lose the primary motive of her existence. Billy
Booth appropriates the meaning of Amelia's struggles. She works
both to repel the sexual advances of Booth's friend Colonel James
and to keep her husband from knowing what's happening. Her
confidant, Dr. Harrison, tells Booth the truth; the outraged husband responds with a diatribe about his honor, imagining himself
mocked as cuckold and dupe. Amelia responds that she would
make any sacrifice to preserve his honor. Although Booth comments offhandedly that he does not doubt *her* honor, he in effect
declares Amelia's integrity and her feelings irrelevant, absorbing
her struggle into his own drama. His posturing about himself as
cuckold and dupe has no bearing on the situation: Amelia has
steadily protected him from cuckoldry. By denying Amelia's centrality in her own experience, Booth insists that she must understand herself only as an adjunct, never as significant actor. He
insists on his own role as center of the story, whatever the story
may be. He acts, for good or for evil; Amelia's efforts only help or
hinder him. Her experience can hardly change her because her
husband—incomparably the most important person in her
life—will not acknowledge it as experience.

My purpose is not to demonstrate moral inadequacy either in
Booth or in Fielding, but to use *Amelia* as a way to explore more
extensively male imaginings of women and to demonstrate their
centrality in the construction of novelistic plot. Such imaginings do
not necessarily deny woman meaning or power because they appear to deny her experience. Amelia is a genuine and an active

heroine. "O my *Amelia*," Booth cries on one occasion, "how much are you my Superior in every Perfection! How wise, how great, how noble are your Sentiments! Why can I not imitate what I so much admire? Why can I not look with your Constancy, on those dear little Pledges of our Loves?" (162; bk. 4, ch. 3). Amelia's "Sentiments" and her "Constancy" define a state of being that constitutes authentic superiority, to her husband and to all the novel's other characters except for Dr. Harrison, the good clergyman who acts as moral mentor to the Booths.

In his "Essay on the Knowledge of the Characters of Men," probably written around 1739–40, Fielding expounds views on human nature compatible with those implicit in *Amelia*. Here, too, human nature means *male* human nature; the essayist says so explicitly. "I do by no means hint at the various Laughs, Titters, Tehes, &c. of the Fair Sex, with whom indeed this Essay has not any thing to do; the Knowledge of the Characters of Women being foreign to my intended Purpose; as it is in Fact a Science, to which I make not the least Pretension" (*Miscellanies* 160). This ritual disclaimer of course need imply no real sense of ignorance. Conventional utterances of this sort—ancestors of Freud's remark about women as the Dark Continent—may express contempt (i.e., women aren't worth knowing about) or dismissal (I have better things to do with my time than trying to figure out women) or anger (women just don't make sense), or, for that matter, awe; but male claims not to understand women always convey belief in some absolute difference between the sexes. Female laughter must mean something quite different from male laughter; the Dark Continent will hardly resemble the continent of Europe. Amelia in her transcendent virtue conveys the same sense of utter difference from the male as that hinted by Fielding's condescension toward "the various Laughs, Titters, Tehes . . . of the Fair Sex."

Utter and *absolute*, modifying *difference*, are the words that matter here. To experience as *absolute* the differences dividing men and women makes male comprehension of the female impossible or, alternately, very simple indeed. Men, as men know, experience complex, ambivalent, contradictory emotions and behave in complex, ambivalent, contradictory ways. But some men on occasion imagine women as existing in a condition approaching stasis. Thus Fielding, characterizing his heroine by her total dedication to her husband, frees her from profound conflict. As Robert Alter observes, when Booth inquires, "art thou rather an angel in human form?", "the reader may be tempted to answer the rhetorical question with an irony that Fielding never intended" (*Fielding* 162). One can become impatient with perfection. No hidden inclination toward her would-be seducers weakens Amelia's will; however burdensome her yoke, she never wishes it away. She is, of course, not *quite* perfect. She manifests traces of vanity; once she teases her husband to reveal something he wishes not to tell her. But her self-approving glances in the mirror seem theatrical devices for proving her humanity; they emanate from no aspect of her nature that deeply affects her actions.

What not only affects but determines her actions is her unfailing devotion to Booth: her only means for shaping the plot. The novel offers no reflection on this phenomenon, which simply constitutes a fact, implying no internal complexity. Fielding would not describe Amelia's devotion as a "ruling passion," an aspect of character the narrator associates with Booth's mistaken secularism. Like other forms of secularism, belief in the power of a ruling passion provides a way to make excuses for oneself; those who accept the possibility of such passion, the text suggests, rationalize weakness of will and deviate from prudence.

No one could accuse Amelia of imprudence. She consults Dr. Harrison for guidance; she painstakingly assesses moral risk and gain. But her prudential calculations operate always in the context of her total marital allegiance. Fielding does not consider her passion for Booth "a predominant Passion" in the reprehensible sense because its object conforms to the highest moral expectations for women. Raphael, in *Paradise Lost*, rebukes Adam's tendency to ignore essential hierarchy by placing Eve higher than himself; the angel recommends "self-esteem" as remedy. A woman's adoration of a man, on the other hand, defines the shape of female prudence and affirms the natural order of things.

Amelia in her adoration conforms to a moral order at least slightly different from Booth's. Loving and admiring his spouse, he yet can forget her on occasion: to go to bed with Miss Mathews, to gamble away his family's money, or simply to function effectively as a soldier. He changes from day to day, from hour to hour, and he grows in self-knowledge and responsibility over the course of the novel. "To retrieve the ill Consequences of a foolish Conduct, and by struggling manfully with Distress to subdue it, is one of the noblest Efforts of Wisdom and Virtue" (16; bk. 1, ch. 1). This pronouncement by the narrator summarizes the novel's action, inasmuch as it concerns Booth, and it indicates the reasons for taking him seriously.

But the novel's title accords primacy to Mrs. Booth, who, having done nothing foolish herself, struggles womanfully with distress, who resists and represses and refrains, but whose action is all responsive rather than initiatory. The image of her deciding not to have a glass of wine in order to save sixpence for her family epitomizes her character. We must take *her* seriously because she exemplifies noble womanhood: non-aggressive, sacrificial, subordinating herself to another whom she also helps and inspires. Providing the still point in a turning world, she makes Booth's development possible.

Amelia's "changelessness" centers her power. It is of course not literally true that she never changes. She too has varying moods, and she too grows—but only to become more unmistakably what she was from the beginning. Her "Constancy" extends to all aspects of her being. Just as her unfailing devotion to her husband differentiates her from the traditional "light woman," marked by inconstancy, her utter stability separates her from women in general and declares her specialness. Fielding's characterization of Amelia refutes Virgil's familiar judgment of female volatility ("Woman's a various and a changeful thing"—a formulation several times alluded to in the novel) with an individual case, reminding us of the example's rarity: Amelia, like Fanny Hill, is an ideal. But female changelessness is only the other side of female changefulness; it equally denies the possibility of rich and complicated moral development in women. Not coincidentally, it implies for women a limited role in the dynamics of fictional plot.

Amelia makes one aware of that fact as Pamela and Fanny Hill, more openly self-dependent characters, do not. Yet all three in their changelessness possess restricted forms of agency. Like every eighteenth-century woman, real or imagined, they function within a system of causality in which men make the rules. Fanny Hill and Pamela subvert the male system yet finally serve it. Amelia accepts the given order within the family and knows her powerlessness in the larger world. Despite their energetic responses to provocation, the essential predictability of fictional female paragons demands that the excitement of plot derive from other sources. Women respond rather than initiate. Even Fanny, with her independent career, reacts always to the needs of male desire.

Amelia in her fidelity and changelessness has a mythic aura, as though she existed outside of time. And of course myth is the subject here: a myth of womanhood, complicated and ambiguous as most myths are, capable of including Fanny Hill and Pamela and Amelia, a myth of mysterious power. Amelia, subordinate not only to her husband but to Dr. Harrison, insisting on her own intellectual inadequacy, constitutes the psychic as well as moral center of

Fielding's novel, if not the source of action. She possesses the force of her ethical urgency and of her absolute emotional commitment but most of all that of her unalterable being. The more she and the men emphasize her secondary status, the more emphatically she emerges as primary. Amelia's relative helplessness to effect change, like her vanity and her tearfulness, belongs to the realm of social actuality; the story of her unarticulated power to draw her husband to the good records another level of perception.

Similarly, *Fanny Hill* depicts its protagonist as blindly pursuing a sordid career, yet maintaining a personal integrity that magically calls back her first lover and raises her to prosperity. Socially victimized, Fanny still triumphs, her power, like Cinderella's, implicit in her degradation. And the fable of *Pamela*, while acknowledging realities of class structure, claims the possibility of social transformation by the steadily virtuous female.

If the ideal woman in her erotic and her moral aspect alike reveals the same transcendent stability, she also demonstrates a quality more obviously flattering to the male ego: perfect compliance. (Pamela, of course, refuses to comply until love and legality sanction submission; then she becomes gratifyingly subordinate.) This characteristic does not conform to the demands of social realism any more than her changelessness does. The real whore does not so happily answer every male need; the real wife sometimes contradicts her husband. When Amelia disobeys a man—for example, by avoiding the masquerade—she does so only to meet her husband's deeper needs; after Fanny betrays her keeper, she continues to satisfy his sexual desires. The vision of a woman powerfully, continuously herself, yet unfailingly attuned to male desire, implies a potent wish-fulfillment fantasy. Like Fanny and, finally, Pamela, Amelia finds self-realization in gratifying a man. What do women want?—Freud's famous question. Ideal women want whatever men want them to want. The naughty woman differs from her virtuous counterpart in the number of men each chooses to satisfy and in the ways she is willing to provide satisfaction.

Amelia and her husband diverge from the protagonists of *Pamela* and *Fanny Hill* in their relation to plot and story. Neither proves an accomplished plotter in the sense that Lovelace or Pamela exemplifies. Neither, in other words, claims to assume control over future events, planning a trajectory for self or others to follow. The best Amelia can do is to plan to cook her husband's favorite dinner (predictably, he misses it). The plot to avoid the masquerade originates with Mrs. Atkinson, not with Amelia. Amelia will pawn her clothes or her miniature when financial disaster strikes, but never does she foresee, or even believe herself to foresee, coming events; she therefore cannot imagine shaping them. When confronted by a sexual threat in Colonel James, she must turn to Dr. Harrison for help. (He, of course, displays little more competence than she as a plotter.) Booth resembles his wife in this respect. The closest he comes to a plot involves his unsuccessful bribe in the hope of preferment, and that idea too originates elsewhere. He makes plans to deceive his wife by concealing his adultery with Miss Mathews; as it turns out, Amelia already knows.

The failure of all efforts by virtuous characters to exert control over future events emphasizes the state of indeterminacy Fielding has imagined as that of human existence. As Robert Uphaus observes, "*Clarissa* unflinchingly represents secular life as a condition of indeterminacy, whereas *Amelia*, even in the light of such indeterminacy, longs for a solution to this condition" (71). No solution, however, emerges.

Around the Booths, plotters abound. Sexual plotting seems the principal activity of every man but Colonel Bath, whose straightforward interest in the sword substitutes for others' more devious concern with the phallus. Bad women like Mrs. Ellison and Mrs. Trent abet and participate in such plotting. Even "good" women like Mrs. Atkinson plot for their own advantage: Mrs. Atkinson uses her disguise as Amelia to get a commission for her husband. Miss Mathews plots on her own behalf.

Nor are Mr. and Mrs. Booth effective makers of stories, verbal formulations that interpret past events. In the opening Newgate sequence, Booth tells Miss Mathews the story of his marriage with fluency and force, although not with perfect coherence. She tells him, yet more effectively, her story of female envy and rage. This storytelling results in adultery. As Joseph Boone points out, "the art of telling becomes, for both Miss Matthews and Booth, an elaborate act of erotic enticement and deferral" (120). Miss Mathews has constructed this new definition of narrative; Booth cannot evade it. Thereafter, he never achieves much narrative success. If he makes up a story, as about what has happened when a strange man invades their apartment and ransacks their belongings, events will rapidly prove him wrong. If he tells his wife that Atkinson has married Mrs. Ellison, it will turn out that Atkinson has married someone else. Most of the Booths' attempts to explain what has taken place founder on their insufficient knowledge or their limited analytic capacity.

Mrs. Bennet's story of sexual betrayal fills a Providential place in Fielding's narrative, since the Noble Lord thriftily plans to make

the same plot that seduced her work to entrap Amelia; by telling
the story Mrs. Bennet rescues a potential victim. More typically,
stories (miniature stories) serve plotters' purposes. Stories deceive
Dr. Harrison, who believes what the neighbors report about the
Booths. A story that his wife has become ill in a toymaker's shop
lures Booth to imprisonment. The conventional stories servants tell
about their masters (he's still in bed, he's gone out) epitomize the
prevailing theme of stories as means for misleading.

On the other hand, the making and revealing of stories constitutes the means of salvation in the novel. John Bender calls attention to the analogy between the narrator and Dr. Harrison, both
working

> to set things straight through narrative construction, that is, through in-
> quiry into the 'several small and almost imperceptible links in every chain
> of events by which all the great actions of the world are produced' . . . ,
> and through the silent manipulations of those events into meaningful,
> causally coherent sequences. (186)

I shall argue that neither inquiry nor manipulation proves altogether successful in *Amelia*. Yet the effort to make sense out of
experience by discovering causality and by imposing coherence,
however inadequate, represents the only hope for escape from the
impositions of others.

Their roles as objects of manipulation by other people's stories
and plots call attention to the Booths' peculiar place in Fielding's
plot. Billy Booth has a position in the world: he gambles, fights
duels, participates in battles, projects appeals to the mighty. In
comparison, as I have already suggested, Amelia only responds to
stimuli, never declaring a positive will of her own unfocused on
husband or children. But the male-female contrast proves less distinct than one might anticipate, because Booth too finds himself
forced toward a position of passivity. Given the world's vast corruption, given the presence of plotters about him, given his lack of
financial resource, he has virtually no place in the games of power.
He can exercise no force at all, except through verbal explosions at
home. Increasingly, he too finds himself only able to respond, not
to initiate. Although the domestic balance of power receives strong
verbal reassertion at the novel's end, with Amelia explaining that
she is the best of wives only because her husband has made her
the happiest of women, the resolution depends on removing the
Booths from all operations of social power. In addition to a happy
family, Tom and Sophia have the role in a community that Amelia
and Billy apparently lack. Mr. and Mrs. Booth can administer their

respective forms of domestic power, but the larger world has defeated them.

Amelia as the figure of changeless virtue is especially important in Fielding's plot because of this novel's dark social vision. Fielding's difficulties in reconciling the narrative of a worthy couple's marital career with the theme of social criticism permeate the text. The novel varies wildly in tone; the plot fails to tie up loose ends. No narrator boasts here about how cleverly he has managed the crossings of characters at Upton; on the contrary, the narrator's control often seems precarious. Roger D. Sell has argued that "the essential design is to involve us in Booth and Amelia's heuristic adventure, their attempts at probable explanations of other people's behaviour" (57). The theory helps to rescue Fielding's novel from the charge of incoherence, but it does not account for the narratorial outbursts of indignation or for tonal inconsistencies. Most relatively successful attempts to explain the structure of *Amelia* rely on thematic concerns (see Knight, "Narrative Structure of *Amelia*"; McCrea; Mulford). Martin Battestin, who calls *Amelia* "Fielding's most disconcerting novel" ("Problem" 613), maintains that a "crisis of belief may be seen to define the problem of *Amelia*, reflected not only in the hero's hard progress from doubt to faith, but in Fielding's strange new conception of his art" (615). Battestin himself has done much to illuminate that conception; I propose that the moral changelessness of Amelia as a character serves an essential purpose in the novelist's working out of his new vision of narrative art and of social life. To return to Martin Price's formulation: the novel *needs* her.

To say why will require a detour. Unlike Lovelace or Mr. B or Pamela, plotters in *Amelia* do not provide verbal formulations of what they are up to. Plotting moves far from its literary meaning. Correspondingly, the novelist himself seems to have trouble with plot, not because of any difficulty with language, but because of difficulties in conceiving causality. In the famous passage about life as an art, the narrator claims the relation of novelistic practice to this most fundamental of art forms.

As Histories of this Kind, therefore, may properly be called Models of HUMAN LIFE; so by observing minutely the several Incidents which tend to the Catastrophe or Completion of the whole, and the minute Causes whence those Incidents are produced, we shall best be instructed in this most useful of all Arts, which I call the ART OF LIFE. (17; bk. 1, ch. 1)

He thus announces an intention of attending to causality in all its details. Later he echoes the formulation in declaring the reader's interest in causal sequence: "there is no Exercise of the Mind of a sensible Reader more pleasant than the tracing the several small and almost imperceptible Links in every Chain of Events by which all the great Actions of the World are produced" (496; bk. 12, ch. 1y). But not only does the text fail to reveal the causes of certain effects (e.g., who wrote the letter informing Amelia of her husband's illness in Gibraltar), the effort to trace links often has disconcerting results. In fact, Amelia, in all her virtue, indirectly causes many of Booth's disasters. Men lust after her and plot her seduction; Booth's troubles follow as a consequence. Moreover, many specified causes of significant effects are morally shocking: the nobleman who will not help Booth because Dr. Harrison refuses to support his candidate in an election, the gambler who gives Booth money as part of pimping for the Noble Lord. Although such forms of causality may be predictable to someone who understands the ways of a corrupt world, they baffle the novel's virtuous characters. And they appall the narrator. The social world he describes is not chaotic, exactly, for it operates mostly by discernible causality. Yet it remains unpredictable to those who cannot fully imagine the operations of corruption. What will Justice Thrasher do next? The answer depends on the location of his self-interest, and how can anyone foresee that?

In this world, Amelia alone provides a principle of stability; yet she fails to interest many readers. Discussion of *Amelia* typically focuses on Booth. But the existence of a stable character matters enormously in the text. Even Dr. Harrison can prove erratic, capable, like Squire Allworthy, of being misled. Amelia, however, participates in a crucial nexus of forces: femininity / goodness / Providence. Never unpredictable—the interests of her husband and children always guide her, regardless of what stories she hears—she functions always on the side of Right.

The problem Fielding has established in this novel—how can individuals live in a corrupt world?—defies rational resolution. The figure of Amelia provides an answer that satisfies desire if not the demands of realism. In her, causality becomes comprehensible. The entirely good individual can live in a corrupt world by being entirely good. Wishfully, the fiction writer can construct for her a providential rescue. Amelia never acts on her own behalf, only in response to needs of her family, and she becomes the agent of salvation for all. If she has inadvertently caused Booth trouble, in the world of social corruption, she as inadvertently generates his rescue. Her noble pawning of the miniature stimulates Robinson's repentance and leads to the recovery of the lost inheritance that solves the family's problems. Femininity / goodness / Providence opposes masculinity / power / society. To each his or her own sphere. The novel needs Amelia to rescue it from despair.

All three of these novels require the changeless woman at their centers; *Amelia* makes the need particularly manifest and particularly urgent. The myth of womanhood variously embodied in Pamela, Fanny Hill, and Amelia serves important literary and psychological purposes. In a thoughtful essay written more than a decade ago, Marlene LeGates examines the provenance of "the image of the chaste maiden and obedient wife" that flourished in eighteenth-century fiction (23). She concludes that "Traditional controls not only contribute to our heroines' virtue; they are in turn strengthened by it. While the woman is allowed moral superiority, it cannot become uncontrolled individualism; her virtue must be subordinate ultimately to male authority" (30). The point holds as well for Fanny Hill as for Pamela and Amelia: her "virtue" (her capacity for full commitment to pleasure) eventuates in her compliance to a single man.

But despite the ostentatious obedience of good women in eighteenth-century fiction, it would be far too simplistic to claim that the myth of eighteenth-century womanhood is one of passivity. Myths do not work that simply. English social actualities largely enforced female passivity; but myth reflects more than social actuality. Myths declare wishes and reveal fears; the fantasized compliant woman expresses fear of alternative possibility. Anna Laetitia Barbauld observes of Richardson, "He seemed to think women had a great deal to hide" (Richardson, *Correspondence* 1: cl). Clarissa and Pamela, many readers have felt, hide a great deal even from themselves. But even if Pamela's virtue comprises surface rather than substance, it resolves the problem, from a male point of view, of female threat. As long as women commit themselves to keeping it hidden—whatever the particular threatening "it" may be—they do not endanger men. So, persistently, men fantasize. Women in their graciousness may choose to subordinate themselves to men; men lovingly imagine the implications of such a choice. Still perhaps they suspect that women also embody the potential for irrational, unpredictable, dangerous aggression.

Amelia's moral energy and Pamela's correspond to Fanny Hill's splendid vitality. The eighteenth-century myth of femininity tacitly acknowledges the female force that it converts into subordination. The aggressiveness of Blear-eyed Moll and of the equally sinister Miss Mathews, like Mrs. Jewkes's erotically tinged sadism, suggests the dimensions of a power that Amelia and Pamela transform into love and Fanny into pleasure seeking. Moreover, the myth of the feminine implies a corresponding myth of manhood, of men as full of desire and implicitly of guilt, both of which women alleviate by willing submission.

Finally, and most importantly for my purposes, the idea of the changeless woman may alleviate anxieties generated by what I have been calling the plot of power. As we shall see, later eighteenth-century experimentation with plot often undermined the fundamental structures of power. The figure of the utterly stable female contains in itself the potential for such undermining, as Amelia demonstrates, with her apparent incapacity to engage in power games. To be sure, she is assigned power by her husband. Indeed, her role reveals that the existence of power may depend more on assignment by others than on claims by the self. Changelessness may subsist as power in the male imagination, but the fantasized human capacity for absolute constancy also hints at the possibility—the further fantasy—of a non-competitive social universe. On the other hand, by locating that capacity in women, male writers envision a yet more reassuring possibility: that women will not compete with men, as Fanny apparently does not vie with her husband or Amelia with hers or even Pamela with hers. They do not work out the implications of this faint vision; that task remained for their successors.

My three texts, I believe, call attention to forms of imagining extending beyond themselves, yet I can only speculate about how large a claim such isolated instances permit. Few other eighteenth-century novels by male writers construct female paragons. But male writers who concentrate on women with the capacity for change corroborate some implications of the kind of plot I have been discussing. Roxana, for instance, like Fanny Hill both enormously successful and insistently female, obviously changes in the course of the novel that contains her. She resembles, in this respect, Richardson's Clarissa, the century's most fully developed fictional "good woman," who also alters some of her basic assumptions as a result of a devastating series of events. The plots of *Clarissa* and *Roxana* support—from the other side, as it were—my view that much was at stake for eighteenth-century male imaginations in dreaming of women as changeless.

Robinson Crusoe realizes that he should not have disobeyed his father and that he should believe in Providence; he then lives happily ever after. Tom Jones realizes that he cannot tumble into bed with any woman who appeals to him and still have Sophia; he reforms and wins the woman he loves. Roderick Random, after a misspent youth, settles into respectability, given the love of a good woman. One can multiply examples of male novelistic protagonists whose errors demand little more than self-acknowledgement to allow their careers happy endings. For Roxana and Clarissa, on the other hand, self-awareness (admittedly not *full* awareness in Roxana's case) does not permit them earthly happiness. Experience both generates their knowledge and punishes them for it—or, to put it more accurately, the plots that shape their fates tacitly insist that female capacity for change, unlike its male counterpart, generates suffering. The imagined stability of women makes them potentially comprehensible; the imagined volatility of women makes them hardly worth trying to understand. But the woman who grows, develops, changes as men do, who claims agency as men do, denies fundamental difference. As a fictional character, such a woman, taking on a form of being generally reserved for men, endangers herself and implicitly endangers men.

5

THE SENTIMENTAL NOVEL AND
THE CHALLENGE TO POWER

In some respects, *Amelia* exemplifies the plot of power at its most emphatic. The Booths inhabit a society which allows men only two roles: agent or victim of power. (Dr. Harrison, who appears to function outside this scheme, actually only redefines its terms.) Women possess slightly more freedom, able at times to act independently of the power scheme, but more often dramatizing—as both Amelia and Mrs. Atkinson vividly do—dynamics of dominance or submission. It seems, from this point of view, hardly accidental that Booth is a soldier or that he finds himself forced to fight a duel, the prototypical contest of power for men as the defense of chastity is for women. The recovered inheritance that gives the Booths social status at the novel's end allots them corresponding power. The fiction as a whole has educated the reader to understand the inevitable connection of money and power, as well as the absolute necessity of acquiring sufficient force to avoid victimization.

But *Amelia* can also be read as Fielding's attempt to accomplish something new: not to duplicate Richardson's achievement in *Clarissa*, but to evolve new principles for structuring plots. The glorification of Amelia as character, expressed in outbursts by the narrator and by Booth, suggests fresh possibilities. Unlike Pamela and Clarissa, Amelia engages in no contest for control. Obsessively concerned with her family's welfare, she assesses possible courses of action in relation to their effect on husband and children. She also values the ties of friendship and her quasi-filial relationship with Dr. Harrison. As I observed in the last chapter, Amelia keeps bad things from happening but she directly accomplishes good principally by providential intervention: when she pawns the miniature. New possibilities of plot would inhere in such a character if her creator could imagine ways in which she too might cause significant happenings. Fielding does not go so far. His successors did.

This chapter will examine experimental fictions of the 1760s and 1770s, works which raise questions about the fundamental nature of plot. Two kinds of shift will concern me: the move away from plots resting on causality and even on sequence, implying rejection of overt stress on power—or at least on power of orthodox sorts; and the less radical movement toward plots based on dynamics of affiliation rather than of power. The two categories overlap, but works challenging systems of causality include Sterne's fiction and such novels as *The Man of Feeling* and *The Fool of Quality*; the group of novels concerned with affiliation contains many works by women, including most notably *Evelina* and Frances Sheridan's harrowing *Memoirs of Miss Sidney Bidulph*. Both categories consist mainly of novels we now perceive as "sentimental." My enterprise, therefore, will necessarily involve an attempt to think about values inherent in sentimentalism. Why, at a certain moment in history, did serious novelists typically resort to it? I start with the hypothesis that the sentimental implies meanings—positive values, sources of appeal—now largely lost to us.

It is far easier to criticize the moral and political inadequacies of sentimental thought and the fiction reflecting it than to empathize with our predecessors who wrote and read such fiction with enthusiasm. Philip Fisher offers a useful reminder of sentimentalism's historical importance:

> from roughly 1740 to 1860 sentimentality was a crucial tactic of politically radical representation throughout western culture. Until it was replaced by the strategies of literary naturalism, class struggle, anger, and counterforce in the last third of the 19th century, the liberal humanism of sentimentality was the primary radical methodology within culture. (92)

Twentieth-century critiques typically ignore this historical insight. Thus Robert Markley, for instance, argues from the point of view of a postmodern Marxist that sentimental narrative "implicitly assumes and explicitly asserts the values of a middle-class culture intent on demonstrating the naturalness and benevolence of its moral authority" (Markley, "Sentimentality" 210). The sentimental novelist, Markley continues, "attempts both to assert the 'timeless' nature of a specific historical and cultural construction of virtue and to suppress his reader's recognition of the social and economic inequalities upon which this discourse of seemingly transcendent virtue is based" (211). Given the contradictions inherent in such an enterprise, signs of strain inevitably emerge; indeed, "ethical and theological quandaries . . . define the sentimental novel" (221). Markley condescends to Shaftesbury as politically naive (215) and implicitly rebukes Sterne and Mackenzie because "they can drama-

tize their heroes' benevolence but cannot convince either themselves or their readers that good nature is sufficient to correct the
ways of a corrupt and unjust world" (230).

Agreeing about the conspicuous presence of "ethical and theological quandaries" in eighteenth-century sentimental fiction, I yet
think it a mistake to assume that writers of the past failed to know
what they were doing—although most modern readers assume just
that. *A Sentimental Journey* retains uneasy canonical status and *Evelina* has recently acquired it, but most of the novelists treated in this
chapter no longer find readers even in university classrooms. Their
exclusion from the canon probably results specifically from their
sentimentalism, more readily rejected or patronized than comprehended. I propose that Sterne and Mackenzie may not wish to convince anyone that good nature solves the problems of a corrupt
world but rather to suggest the contrary, and that the quandaries
Markley accurately notes in fact constitute the central concern of
certain sentimental novels, the focus of their "politically radical
representation." Plot supplies an index to psychological and moral
issues latent in a body of fiction usually dismissed as irrelevant to
late twentieth-century concerns.

Something strange happened to plot in the 1760s—something
foreshadowing late twentieth-century developments in fiction. Lionel Trilling, speaking of the twentieth-century sense of "the inau-
thenticity of narrative," points out that narrative now may appear
unsatisfactory because of "its assumption that life is susceptible of
comprehension and thus of management" (135). Novels of the
1740s and 1750s, by and large, employed plots heavily reliant on
providential intervention and resolution (see Battestin, *Providence*;
Damrosch; Hunter; Rader; Williams). Even *Clarissa*, with its disastrous earthly outcome, implies the presence of heavenly management that brings the wicked to appropriate ends and rewards the
good in an afterlife. More typical dénouements conformed to the
famous observation in *The Importance of Being Earnest*: "The good
ended happily, and the bad unhappily. That is what Fiction
means." Rewards and punishments are appropriately, often ingeniously, distributed. Thus in *The Vicar of Wakefield*, a work of the
1760s rich in sentiment, Olivia, the lovely young woman who has
stooped to folly, recoups her honor by discovering the reality of
what her seducer thought a sham wedding, but her "reward" consists in a worthless husband; her wiser sister Sophia achieves love
and marriage with a far richer man. Similar patterns govern many
novels.

Providential means and ends in fiction conformed to broadly

similar models for at least two centuries. What of the power that wills them? Edmund Burke's *Enquiry into . . . the Sublime and Beautiful* (1757) suggests possible answers. Interested primarily in emotional response to aesthetic stimuli, Burke divides the aesthetic universe into the opposed categories of his title. The beautiful, associated with women (who provide abundant examples of beauty's characteristics—smallness, delicacy, curving lines, and so on), constitutes a mode of attraction, "a social quality," because beautiful people and animals "inspire us with sentiments of tenderness and affection . . . ; we like to have them near us, and we enter willingly into a kind of relation with them." Why should matters be thus designed? Burke cannot decide; he concludes that providence must have had "a view to some great end, though we cannot perceive distinctly what it is, as his wisdom is not our wisdom, nor our ways his ways" (42–43).

Inscrutability, then, characterizes providence. But Burke also has more specific ideas: his aesthetic implies a metaphysic. "I know of nothing sublime," he writes, "which is not some modification of power" (64). The sublime "is built on terror, or some passion like it, which has pain for its object" (134); it generates "delight" from the moral exercise it stimulates (135–6). Sublimity is an essentially "masculine" quality, associated with "the authority of a father" (111) and with such virtues as "fortitude, justice, wisdom, and the like." "Never was any man amiable," Burke adds—and he intends the root sense of "lovable"—"by force of these qualities" (110). The sublime stimulates admiration rather than love; "we submit to what we admire, but we love what submits to us" (113).

Hesitantly but distinctly, the writer acknowledges that God provides the ultimate example of sublimity. Contemplation of the Deity necessarily affects the imagination—and, as Burke goes on to specify, the passions.

Now, though in a just idea of the Deity, perhaps none of his attributes are predominant, yet to our imagination, his power is by far the most striking. Some reflection, some comparing is necessary to satisfy us of his wisdom, his justice, and his goodness; to be struck with his power, it is only necessary that we should open our eyes. But whilst we contemplate so vast an object, under the arm, as it were, of almighty power, and invested upon every side with omnipresence, we shrink into the minuteness of our own nature, and are, in a manner, annihilated before him. And though a consideration of his other attributes may relieve in some measure our apprehensions; yet no conviction of the justice with which it is exercised, nor the mercy with which it is tempered, can wholly remove the terror that naturally arises from a force which nothing can withstand. (68)

Providence (or "God," "Godhead," "Deity") exemplifies the ultimate extension of the father's authority, power, and terror for the
son. Both "comprehension" and "management," to return to Trilling's terms, inhere in Deity. This paternal being ordains the laws of
consequence: as a man sows, so shall he reap. God's benignity and
His terror alike belong to His paternal nature. He provides the
ultimate sanction for coherent narrative.

The structures of many early novels—*Robinson Crusoe, Tom
Jones, The Vicar of Wakefield* provide conspicuous examples—insist
on a process of testing through which divine justice manifests itself.
The good man discovers his own moral powers and, after more or
less severe trials, comes into his true inheritance, perhaps supplant-
ing an earthly father but implicitly or explicitly acknowledging the
dominion of that father's divine counterpart. But even fictions less
overtly aware of theological pattern suggest the same point: while
God the Father presides, plot can control the novel. Burke's analogy between the relations of fathers and sons and the link of God
to humanity suggests the moral structure of a God-dominated universe: a structure formed on principles of justice, providing an orderly system of rewards and punishments in this life or the next. A
comparable moral structure long dominated fiction.

The collapse of plot in important novels after the middle of the
eighteenth century calls attention not only to new fictional possibilities but also to changing theological and moral hypotheses. The
philosophical and theological concomitants of literary sentimentalism are by now well established. Late seventeenth-century Latitu-
dinarian divines announced the themes of sentimentalism; a line
of British moral philosophers from Shaftesbury to Hume and
Adam Smith elaborated such themes by insisting on the relation
between moral thought and sensitive feeling.[1] Methodism and
other dissenting religious sects also stressed the importance of the
emotions in establishing and declaring a proper relationship to
God. Simultaneously, sentimental novels (and poetry and drama)
also flourished. *Memoirs of Miss Sidney Bidulph*, written by Frances
Sheridan in intervals between bouts of housework, described by
Ernest Baker as "a banquet of woe deliberately provided for the
epicure of sensibility" (119), was a best-seller—and only one of
many sentimental popular successes.

Providence continues to operate in these novels, but sometimes
in ways that do not in all respects correspond to Burke's elucidation. If God retains the power of the father, He may assume also
attributes of the mother. Plots and characters change; so does the
presiding force of the universe. The "tenderness and affection"

Burke associates with women and with the beautiful come to characterize male protagonists; the "melting" that Burke often links rhetorically with these qualities permeates fictional action, implying weakening or loss of ego boundaries; the straight line of novelistic plot gives way to Tristram Shandy's squiggle. God has not died in order to authorize that squiggle, but He has perhaps become "beautiful" as well as "sublime": feminized.

By way of offering my own elucidation for these assertions, I shall turn to specific novels, beginning with Henry Brooke's *The Fool of Quality* (1765–70). Harry Clinton, its eponymous hero, has few obvious problems of his own. Most of his narrated progress from infancy to adulthood consists in encounters with life's victims. His education derives not from active participation in life—not, like Tom Jones's, from mistakes made in the course of a self-initiated journey—but from passive observation and sympathy. In one typical episode of *The Fool of Quality*, a beautiful, pious, young married woman, Arabella Clermont, raped by wicked Lord Stiver, kills her attacker with a kitchen knife. Subsequently arrested for robbery and murder, she remains serenely convinced that Providence will save her. An unexpected witness testifies to her innocence, but she and her family are left destitute, their children starving and on the verge of death. Arabella educates her husband in Christian submission and tells him of the happiness of Christian death. Just before such death overtakes them all, Harry appears as rescuer; earthly happiness then rewards goodness.

As Janet Todd observes, sentimental works typically depend for their effects on the situation of virtue in distress. "The distressed are natural victims, whose misery is demanded by their predicament as defenceless women, aged men, helpless infants or melancholic youth" (3). Providing reiterated spectacles of desperate people and circumstance, sentimental novels, orthodox definitions of literary sentimentalism claim, demand of their readers response in excess of that merited by their renditions. But surely such events as those in the narrated career of Arabella Clermont fully deserve the intense response that everything in the texture and substance of the novel prepares for and encourages. We find this sort of thing "sentimental," perhaps, because the victims of disaster have not been made richly known to us. Unlike Clarissa (or, for that matter, Lovelace), Arabella appears to have no interior life. She and her husband and children, unrendered as personalities, simply represent suffering and virtue. Their misfortunes therefore seem gratuitous, generated for the harrowing of our sensibilities.

The demand that characters possess "interior life" or rendered

individuality derives from ethical assumptions—assumptions typically unexamined—of a secular age. We may find it hard to take
Arabella's misfortunes seriously because of our highly developed
individualism as well as because we no longer collectively believe in
an attentive, intervening Providence. But the kind of rendition of
character and event exemplified by the Arabella vignette permeates the late eighteenth-century sentimental novel, which depends
on a set of beliefs briefly powerful in Anglo-Saxon literary and
ethical tradition.

Intellectual historians have long distinguished between the kind
of providentialism associated with the Augustinian tradition and its
"optimistic" counterpart. As Jacob Viner points out, both Catholics
and Protestants in the Augustinian line found "the doctrine of the
Fall of Man, the curse of Adam, the second Fall of Man and the
Flood . . . insurmountable barriers to acceptance of optimistic pictures of the destiny of man while on this earth" (25). The sentimental novel, on the other hand, is commonly associated with
the optimistic strain in religion. The story of Arabella suggests,
though, that sentimental "optimism" hardly implies uniformly
pleasant earthly destinies for good people. The optimism of *The
Fool of Quality* and other works of its genre inheres rather in their
implicit faith that moral education can take place by means of the
passions. "If a discourse on the use of the parts of the body may be
considered as an hymn to the Creator; the use of the passions,
which are the organs of the mind, cannot be barren of praise to
him," Burke wrote (52). To consider the passions "organs of the
mind" bridges the abyss between thought and feeling. By the end
of the eighteenth century, novelists, like moralists, preached the
necessity of controlling "sensibility" by "reason." Brooke, Mackenzie, Sterne, and the rest explored a less hierarchical relationship.

The story of rape and murder associated with Arabella does not
constitute Brooke's plot; his novel hardly *has* a plot. Arabella's
story, rapidly presented, functions in the narrative to arouse
the "passions" of the protagonist—and, by extension, those of the
reader. Harry Clinton feels no need to know details about the
characters or personalities of those he helps. On the contrary, their
situation alone defines their right to sympathy, and thus to benevolence. The idea has radical implications, negating the defining
force of social hierarchy. "As our Creator has designed we should
be united by the bond of sympathy, he has strengthened that bond
by a proportionable delight; and there most where our sympathy
is most wanted, in the distresses of others" (Burke 46). Moral spec-

tacles such as Arabella's stimulate the "delight" of sympathy for Harry and presumably for the reader.

The notion of moral spectacle helps to locate the problems that the sentimental novel creates for modern readers by its apparent moral insensitivity. To turn human suffering into a series of exempla for the hero's enlightenment allows Harry to declare his involvement in the universal "bond of sympathy," but, paradoxically, it also dramatizes the separation between victims and agents of providence so forcefully as to make them seem virtually members of different species. Harry, bestowing largesse, serves as God's instrument of justice and mercy. He feels intense emotion and weeps copious tears as he witnesses the varieties of human suffering. But, never suffering deeply himself, he remains an emotional aristocrat: the class system is not after all far away. Misery establishes no democracy.

Many sentimental novels of the late eighteenth century, I propose, struggle to obviate the emotional gap that their reliance on moral spectacle creates. Hence their "plotlessness," hence their protagonists' striking passivity, hence their peculiar treatments of sexuality: all ways to deny separation among people, the power of the self, the existence of the Other—ways, in short, to close the gap.

Contemporary thinkers noted the incongruity between the benevolent human being's utter separation from the object of benevolence, a separation dependent on the dramatic difference in their fates, and the impulse toward merging implicit in the idea of "sympathy." Adam Smith, for instance, in his *Theory of Moral Sentiments*, published two years after Burke's essay on the sublime, reveals the discrepancy although he does not acknowledge it. The idea of "spectacle" dominates his theory. We "see" others as resembling ourselves; we must try to see ourselves as though from another's point of view.

We can never survey our own sentiments and motives, we can never form any judgment concerning them; unless we remove ourselves, as it were, from our own natural station, and endeavour to view them as at a certain distance from us. But we can do this in no other way than by endeavouring to view them with the eyes of other people, or as other people are likely to view them. (110; III:i:2)

To judge ourselves, we in effect divide ourselves into two persons (113; III:i:6). "The man within"—identical with "reason, principle, conscience"—assumes increasing importance as "the great judge and arbiter of our conduct" (137; III:iii:4). *Manhood* provides an important standard, a reiterated term, for Smith, whose stress on the need for judgment implies a stern ethical system. He emphasizes not the softness but the force of "sympathy."

It is not the soft power of humanity, it is not that feeble spark of benevolence which Nature has lighted up in the human heart, that is . . . capable of counteracting the strongest impulses of self-love. It is a stronger power, a more forcible motive, which exerts itself upon such occasions. It is reason, principle, conscience. . . . (137; III:iii:4)

Later he elaborates the distinction here implied, and labels alternative virtues peculiarly male or female:

The propriety of generosity and public spirit is founded upon the same principle with that of justice. Generosity is different from humanity. Those two qualities, which at first sight seem so nearly allied, do not always belong to the same person. Humanity is the virtue of a woman, generosity of a man. The fair-sex, who have commonly much more tenderness than ours, have seldom so much generosity. That women rarely make considerable donations, is an observation of the civil law. Humanity consists *merely* [my italics] in the exquisite fellow-feeling which the spectator entertains with the sentiments of the persons principally concerned, so as to grieve for their sufferings, to resent their injuries, and to rejoice at their good fortune. (190–91; IV:ii:10)

Novels give more importance to "the soft power of humanity" and assign it greater force than Smith allows. The "mere" fellow-feeling characteristic of women also marks such fictional figures as the Fool of Quality. Ernest Baker goes out of his way to observe of Brooke's novel that "in spite of the floods of tears, this is not an effeminate but a manly book" (116). If so, it implies a new concept of the manly. In one of the interpolated dialogues between "Friend" and "Author," the former inquires, "why has the world, through all ages and nations, universally ascribed heroism and glory to conquest?" The answer connects this apparently secular issue to the theological:

Through the respect, as I take it, that they have for power. Man is by nature weak; he is born in and to a state of dependence; he therefore naturally seeks and looks about for help; and, where he observes the greatest power, it is there that he applies and prays for protection [precisely Freud's view]. . . . In the present case, it is with man, as it is with God; he is not so awful and striking, he is not so much attended to, in the sunshine and gentle dews of his providence and benignity, as in his lightnings and thunders, his clouds and his tempests. (Brooke 1: 155–56)

Later, "Friend" complains about the unrealistic fortitude of Arabella, whose story, he fears, will encourage vanity in other women. "Women," he concludes, "unquestionably, have their becoming qualities; in the bed-chamber, kitchen, and nursery, they are useful to man; but beyond these, my friend, they are quite out of the element of nature and common-sense" (2: 83). "Author" responds with several pages citing examples of accomplished women from antiquity. He defines a female mode of heroism strikingly different from that associated with thunder and lightning. "She comes not against you in the hostility of weapons, or fearfulness of power. She comes in the comfort and mild light of beauty; she looks abashed and takes you captive; she trembles and you obey" (2: 89).

Woman, too, then has her disguised form of power, its manifestations corresponding to God's "sunshine and gentle dews" rather than His tempests. Harry Clinton likewise practises forceful gentleness. Occasionally he knocks someone down—in self-defense or in defense of the right: hence, perhaps, Baker's praise for the fiction's manliness. More typically, he weeps for the sorrows of others and donates money. And he tends to make people "melt." In one representative scene, Harry's father and his tutor weep to watch him at work in his benevolence: "their tears were the tears of sympathising humanity; or rather tears of delight on observing the sweet sensibilities of their darling" (5: 7).[2] Harry's "sweet sensibilities" correspond precisely to the "exquisite fellow-feeling" that Smith considers typical of women.

As David Marshall observes in his provocative essay on Adam Smith, the "combination of identification and difference" that I believe constitutes the crux of the sentimental novel "provided the standard eighteenth-century explanation for the pleasure audiences take in watching tragedies" (180). In other words, the period's aestheticians found this paradoxical combination not only viable but fruitful. For later readers, it often seems either superficial or disturbing. When father and tutor enjoy the spectacle of Harry's sensibilities, at once demonstrating their own delicacy of feeling and experiencing the pleasure of their separateness, the reader may think the scene mawkish, but it presents no great moral difficulties. But when the sensibility-arousing spectacle involves real suffering, the combination of identification and difference seems more troublesome. A notorious instance from Sterne illuminates the problem:

—Dear sensibility! source inexhausted of all that's precious in our joys, or costly in our sorrows! thou chainest thy martyr down upon his bed

of straw—and 'tis thou who lifts him up to HEAVEN—eternal fountain of
our feelings!—'tis here I trace thee—and this is thy divinity which stirs
within me—. . . all comes from thee, great, great SENSORIUM of the world!
which vibrates, if a hair of our heads but falls upon the ground, in the
remotest desert of thy creation.—. . . Thou givest a portion of it [i.e., sen-
sibility] sometimes to the roughest peasant who traverses the bleakest
mountains—he finds the lacerated lamb of another's flock—This moment
I behold him leaning with his head against his crook, with piteous inclination looking down upon it!—Oh! had I come one moment sooner!—it
bleeds to death—his gentle heart bleeds with it—(Sterne, *A Sentimental
Journey* 141)

Yorick's rhapsody on sensibility explicitly links the tender feelings of man and of God. Sensibility constitutes a form of divinity.
Despite the moral claims here implied for it, however, in practice
it amounts to emotional luxury at the expense of others. Yorick
imagines the suffering peasant and the dying lamb in order to
indulge his own sensibility. Had the peasant arrived a moment
sooner, thus preventing the bleeding of the lamb and of his own
gentle heart, he would have forestalled Yorick's emotional satisfaction. When Yorick contemplates mad Maria, a wretched young
woman he encounters in his travels, he falls into comparable extravagances of emotional masturbation—extravagances the more
shocking because elicited by human rather than animal misery.
The aspect of "divinity" in such indulgence perhaps consists most
essentially in the utter safety of separation between observer and
observed. Cost-free identification, self-protective difference: a dis-
quieting combination.

Novels like Sterne's and Brooke's attempt to counteract such disturbance by making their protagonists virtually helpless, passive,
"feminine." The innocence and ineffectuality of the child, as G. A.
Starr points out in a provocative essay, constitute the sentimental
hero's ideal. Yorick, bursting "into a flood of tears," comments
"—but I am as weak as a woman; and I beg the world not to smile,
but pity me" (Sterne 45). *The world*, in other words, the reader, is
invited to participate in emotional indulgence comparable to the
protagonist's, with the protagonist himself providing a supernu-
merary object of emotion. No alternative to passivity exists for the
reader, who cannot, of course, actively intervene. Yorick and Harry
(the Fool of Quality) *can*. Sometimes they actually *do*. But even
Harry's consistent benevolence, his endless distribution of money,
hardly counteracts the impression of his passivity. He need never
make hard decisions, since his resources—other people's money
given to enable his charity—appear inexhaustible; he must only

listen and learn. Moreover, what he sees suggests that action has no necessary value, given the mysteries of Providence. In the characteristic pattern, someone moves from ease and comfort to misery and loss, compelled to accept human insignificance and helplessness, states revealed through the victim's experience of harshly reversed worldly fortunes. Then Providence, operating through Harry, manifests itself by providing worldly rewards.

A Sentimental Journey and *The Man of Feeling* likewise suggest the dubious value of action. Yorick, explicitly woman-like, explicitly dedicated to the pleasure of his own sensibility, travels, but he does little more. *A Sentimental Journey* opens with his refusal of alms to a needy monk, followed by several pages of luxurious regret for the refusal. The anecdote exemplifies Yorick's stance: failure of action allows him to enjoy his own mental and emotional operations by contemplating rejected possibilities. The more active protagonist of *The Man of Feeling* helps others and even displays willingness to engage in physical combat, although he in fact never fights. But he too leaves an overwhelming impression of passivity because his main form of action, like Harry's and Yorick's, consists in his responsiveness. The ethic of responsiveness—reaction rather than action—in eighteenth-century terms links itself with femininity: to recur to my earlier terms, with the beautiful as opposed to the sublime. Thus Harley, the Man of Feeling, defines beauty: "A blush, a phrase of affability to an inferior, a tear at a moving tale, were to him, like the Cestus of Cytherea, unequalled in conferring beauty" (Mackenzie 8; ch. 13). He alludes here to Miss Walton, the object of his devotion, but he also describes himself, an inveterate blusher and weeper—as well as many of his male fictional contemporaries.

To define characters by their responsiveness raises potential questions about the status of the ego. *The Fool of Quality* makes such questions almost explicit in a series of meditations on the problem of *self*.

SELF appears to us as the whole of our existence, as the sum total of all in which we are interested or concerned. It is as a NARCISSUS, self-delighted, self-enamoured. It desires, it craves, and claims, as it's right, the loves, attachments, and respect of all mankind. But does it acquire them, my Harry? O never, never. SELF never was beloved, never will be beloved, never was honourable or respectable in the eye of any creature; and the characters of the *Patriot*, the *Hero*, the *Friend*, and the *Lover*, are only so far amiable, so far revereable, as they are supposed to have gone forth from the confines of SELF. (Brooke 5: 230)

As an account of narcissism ("It desires, it craves, and claims, as it's right . . ."), this isn't bad. But the intensity with which it rejects the claims of self reflects a powerful anxiety characterizing many sentimental novels. The speech by Mr. Clinton quoted above begins with reference to "the very horrible and detestable nature of SELF in your soul" (5: 229). Much earlier in the novel, Mr. Meekly offers a longer account of selfhood, extending the issue to the physical universe by suggesting that "every particle of matter . . . has a SELF, or distinct identity," but that "the DIVINE INTELLIGENCE" can draw these particles from selfhood into a state of natural harmony, incorporating them into systems which alone make them "capable and productive of shape, colouring, beauty, flowers, fragrance, and fruits"(1: 124–25). "This operation in matter," Meekly continues,

is no other than a manifestation of the like process in mind: and . . . no soul was ever capable of any degree of virtue or happiness save so far as it is drawn away in its affections from self, save so far as it is engaged in wishing, contriving, endeavouring, promoting, and rejoicing in the welfare and happiness of others. (1: 125)

All virtue and happiness depend on selflessness. Yet we have already seen the self-insistence of the spectator in such novels as *The Fool of Quality*; we have encountered Adam Smith's rejection of "the soft power of humanity" in favor of "stronger" forms of virtue in which ego, mingled with what Freud would call "superego," predominates. Moreover, only the self can experience happiness. But despite Adam Smith, despite the period's glorification of the masculine sublime, sentimental novels flirted, in form and in content, with denial of the self. Their protagonists evade the moral problem of their titillation at the suffering of others by extravagant identification with victims. Faced with the enraged father of the prostitute he has befriended, Harley kneels side by side with the wretched young woman, prepared to suffer paternal wrath as fellow victim. To an old soldier's tale of suffering, Harley responds, "call me also thy son, and let me cherish thee as a father" (Mackenzie 66; ch. 34). Yorick hears a caged starling cry, "I can't get out"; he identifies with the bird, then imagines several other victims of imprisonment with whom to merge in fantasy. He also submerges himself in fictional characters—Dido, for instance: "I lose the feelings for myself in hers" (Sterne 111).

If the boundaries of self appear permeable, so do those of form. One dialogue between "Friend" and "Author" in *The Fool of Quality* concerns the proposed length of the novel itself. "Friend" inquires repeatedly how long "Author" plans to make his tale; after some evasion, the author responds, "My good friend, the reader may make it as short as he pleases" (1: 70). Because it is composed of infinitely duplicable pathetic vignettes, the fiction can plausibly stop at any point. The disjunctive structure of *The Man of Feeling* yet more emphatically denies coherent form. An unnamed narrator begins the story—if story it can be called—by reporting his finding and transcription of a fragmentary manuscript that has been used as gun wadding by his hunting companion, a curate. Given the curate's depredations, one thing rarely leads to another in this narrative. The novel begins at chapter 11; chapter 19 follows chapter 14; and so on. *A Sentimental Journey*, comparably disjunctive in sequence, justifies its ostentatious formlessness as product of the narrator-protagonist's sensibility.

Since Leo Braudy's important 1973 essay, few commentators have attempted to account for the formal anomalies of eighteenth-century sentimental fiction. Braudy connects the disjunctiveness of such fiction with its stress on the value of emotion. "In general, the sentimental novel opposes intuition to rationality; disjuncture, episode, and effusion to continuity and plot; artlessness and sincerity to art and literary calculation; and emotional to verbal communication." He believes that "the self conditions the form of the fiction rather than the other way around" (12). Marilyn Butler elaborates and complicates Braudy's position, considering the meaning of the contrast between early and later forms of eighteenth-century novelistic plot.

> The replacement of the plot based on the protagonist's conscious actions—the plot equally of *Robinson Crusoe*, *Clarissa*, and *Tom Jones*—with an impressionistic sequence of scenes reflects the mid-century flight from rationalistic abstraction, its interest instead in mental activity as it can actually be observed. At its best the old type of plot is both consecutive, and deeply significant for the ethical life of the hero. . . . But this kind of action really belongs to an older universe, sure of its moral absolutes, in which the fallen individual has to make a positive action in order to be saved. Mackenzie's generation sees human activity not in terms of black-and-white ethical choices, but neutrally, naturalistically, as a behavioural fact. The changed attitude to plot is not perverse, but the reflection of a sophisticated new perception of psychological reality. (*Jane Austen and the War of Ideas* 14–15)

Both these accounts call attention to important aspects of the experimental sentimental novel. They leave unexamined, though, the ethical implications of this new form of fiction, and they do not question the nature of the "self" whose mental activity or whose movements of consciousness shape the inconclusive plots of such novels.

The novels by Sterne, Brooke, and Mackenzie deny the effective presence of a separate shaping intelligence sufficiently single and powerful to ordain coherence. Such denial of power amounts to a denial of self understood as unified and unifying consciousness, of self as constituted by what Freud would call *ego*. Yorick asserts himself energetically in the operations of his imagination, manipulating and teasing his reader, implicitly declaring his dominance over those whose lives he imagines. But Yorick's mind, as rendered by Sterne's novel, works by emotional associations. He cannot count on his own stable presence, he hardly knows his own identity. "There is not a more perplexing affair in life to me," he explains, "than to set about telling anyone who I am—for there is scarce anybody I cannot give a better account of than of myself" (109). In *The Man of Feeling*, external circumstances account for documentary incoherence, but that incoherence corresponds to the protagonist's ever-shifting responsiveness. *The Fool of Quality* relies on the trope of repetition, repudiating more complicated formal principles. Harry's consciousness responds in consistent ways, yet his personality seems singularly lacking in force.

   Not only do these fictions reject orderly movement from introduction through climax to conclusion, their protagonists deny climax in their erotic experience. "Sexual consummation," Starr suggests, speaking of Harley, the "man of feeling," "would be a betrayal of his essential childlikeness and an assumption of all the compromises, grossnesses, and responsibilities of adulthood in a fallen world" (516). Again, Starr observes that in sentimental novels,

sexual impotence is a bold but apt emblem of being outside the compromising fray, of ultimate irreproachability. Like the more common sentimental device of swooning, it is a way of absenting oneself from threatening situations, or of admitting at most an altogether passive presence. (521)

That is to say, in the typical sentimental novel the principle of desire, in the form most often apparent in fiction, is deflected.

   Harry Clinton, to be sure, marries at the end of *The Fool of Quality*, by what seems an authorial afterthought. Only in the last few pages does the possibility of romance emerge. Two devoted male attendants successively reveal themselves as female; one conveniently dies; Harry marries the other. Her identity as woman is suppressed by the narrative as well as by her disguise. The marriage carries little erotic suggestion; it transforms and celebrates male friendship rather than confronting any distinctly female principle. Since the important males of these narratives resemble females in the first place, gender differences hardly matter. The principle of sympathy allows movement from spectacle to identification; it apparently subsumes erotic distinctions as well. *A Sentimental Journey* notoriously depends on frustrated erotic expectation. Not only does Yorick never seek sexual satisfaction when he might be expected to, the novel ends in the prolonged anticlimax of his sharing a bedroom with two young women. As Yorick appears about to touch the lady in the next bed, the *fille de chambre* intervenes. The novel's last fragmentary sentence reads, "So that when I stretched out my hand, I caught hold of the fille de chambre's—" (148). The reader may choose to incorporate into that sentence's meaning the word that follows on the page: "END." Yorick, however, taking no responsibility for such a possibility, provides no completion. (Biographical knowledge tells us that Sterne's death prevented the novel's completion, but that fact does not alter the literary argument.) In *The Man of Feeling*, Harley loves Miss Walton from afar. Two pages before the novel's end, he confesses his love; she acknowledges her reciprocal devotion; and he—drops dead: surely the most dramatic example of sexual avoidance in western literature.

At stake in each of these instances is traditional masculine aggression, dominance, power. Like the glorification of responsiveness and the repudiation of climactic form, the refusal to stress usual fictional indices of masculinity emphasizes a new ethos controlling these novels and suggests its metaphysical implications. I use the word *controlling* advisedly: unlike twentieth-century novels of antiplot, these fictions after all assert a principle of order. They imply an order of feeling rather than reason; they show what it really means to understand the passions as organs of the mind. *Robinson Crusoe* provides complicated movements of narration, with its retellings of events, its peculiarities of chronology. Nonetheless, its plot arrangements finally suggest the dominance of God the Father at His work of justice. *The Man of Feeling* allows the possibility of a deity arranging His creation not by the stern logic of justice but by more protean emotional principles. Eighteenth-century philosophers recognized the troubling implications of belief in a God Whose nature seemed the product of humankind's fearful fantasies (Manuel 52–71). Certain novelists, it appears, attempt to evade those implications.

Sentimental novels of the late eighteenth century depend on attitudes and assumptions that thinkers of the period associated with women. The society and the universe they posit modify the moral implications of Burke's dichotomy between the sublime and the beautiful. As Trilling summarizes Burke's argument, the sublime, working through "terror," "stimulates an energy of aggression and dominance"; the beautiful, on the other hand, "seduces men to inglorious indolence and ignoble hedonism" (95). Sterne, Brooke, and Mackenzie demonstrate the inadequacy of an energy of aggression; they construct images of a more loosely focused energy of benevolence.

"It is the nature of narration to explain," Trilling writes; "it cannot help telling how things are and even why they are that way" (135). In telling how things are, sentimental narratives acknowledge the corruption and malignancy alive in society. As R. F. Brissenden points out, "The belief that man was naturally capable of acting benevolently if given the chance was often held [in the eighteenth century] in company with extremely pessimistic ideas about the nature of the world and society" (29). More remarkable than this kind of political awareness is the implicit understanding conveyed by sentimental fiction that narrative form, erotic convention, and heroic individualism all imply a patriarchal ideology of power. Trying to imagine how things *might* be, they dramatize the struggle of narcissism with altruism to insist on altruism's viability. They argue for taking feelings seriously, for valuing the "beautiful" as highly as the "sublime." They imply a deity more feminine—or at least more androgynous—than Burke's God or Smith's, because they take seriously God's sunshine and gentle dews as well as His power.

Sentimentalism implies a set of ethical principles, if not quite those that governed *Clarissa*, and a theological scheme that supports such principles. It is not sufficient, in my view, to note the moral evasiveness of sentimentalism or its tendency to create a black-and-white world that makes moral distinctions unrealistically simple (see, e.g., Brissenden 55). The schematic moral arrangements of the sentimental novel function, as it were, diagrammatically, to call to mind the essential impossibility of resolving life's experiential inequities. In fiction, one can make matters simple, creating remorseless villains to prey on virtuous beauties; and one can create rescuers for the beauties and even, theoretically (surprisingly seldom in practice), punishers for the villains. The insistent multiplication of pathos does not merely solicit multiplied tears. It also suggests the infinite duplication of distress in the world. Fictional plot can alleviate the misery it manufactures, but it may also make its readers uneasily aware of the presence of irremediable wretchedness in the society to which, in stylized fashion, it alludes.

Political implications, in other words, are always latent in senti- ⸀
mentalism. Mackenzie, quite conscious of such implications, conveys a vivid awareness that power inheres in wealth and that the
inequities of existing social arrangements create the miseries that
arouse his protagonist's tears. At one point, Harley, in London on
his vain quest for financial betterment, meets a plausible "gentleman" who introduces him to urban tavern life. The man turns out
to be an erstwhile footman and pimp, at present employed as
gauger. Harley reflects about this gauger's deceit and concludes
that he himself has learned as much from the fraudulent gentleman as he might have learned from the kind of man the former
footman chose to impersonate. The narrator comments,

> And surely the fault may more properly be imputed to that rank where
> the futility is real than where it is feigned: to that rank whose opportunities
> for nobler accomplishments have only served to rear a fabric of folly which
> the untutored hand of affectation, even among the meanest of mankind,
> can imitate with success. (19; ch. 19)

In other words, rank implies power to improve society. Only because representatives of high rank fail to use their power properly
can they be readily imitated by their social inferiors.[3] The narrator's judgment also implies that those without the power of rank
and wealth can hardly hope to accomplish significant good. Harley's increasing melancholy stems partly from contemplating the
relative futility of his own endeavors to help. As Brissenden points
out, "In so far as a vision of society is made manifest in *The Man of
Feeling* it is of a society which is morally dislocated and disintegrat-
ing" (256). Mackenzie knows at least as well as Robert Markley does
that individual acts of benevolence make no substantive difference
in a corrupt society. His protagonist's education in urban life, like
that of Matthew Bramble in *Humphry Clinker*, teaches him of social
disorders fully acknowledged in the text. One fragmentary chapter
(entitled "The Man of Feeling Talks of What He Does Not Understand") begins, "I have a proper regard for the prosperity of my
country: every native of it appropriates to himself some share of
the power, or the fame, which, as a nation, it acquires, but I cannot
throw off the man so much as to rejoice at our conquests in India"
(72; "A Fragment"). The narrator thus launches into a denuncia-
tion of colonialism, predicated, the sentence above hints, on a new
definition of "the man." Neither Harley nor his creator is a twentieth-century Marxist, but both acknowledge political issues that individual benevolence fails to confront.

Harley's inability to make a real difference in the world, and

Yorick's, and even that of the Fool of Quality, despite his vast financial resources, tacitly reiterate the theme of feminization. "The female cause is the cause of virtue," Euphrasia confidently asserts in *The Progress of Romance* (Reeve 1: 136). Inasmuch as men make virtue their cause, they become, like females, unable to affect significantly the public world. Amelia could not by herself energize the plot of Fielding's novel; Yorick and Harley likewise lack the capacity to generate conclusive plot. Plot is nourished by desire. These sentimental protagonists, having refocused their desires toward benevolence, dramatize altruism's futility, its incapacity to produce sustained, complex action, even as they assert its necessity. Sentimental novels declare the inadequacy of plots of power, but they do not appear to develop an adequate alternative.

Yet their fragmentary, inconclusive structures do not only deny the possibilities of Fieldingesque plot or only assert the generalized value of individual feeling. In a brilliant essay on *A Sentimental Journey*, Martin Battestin has demonstrated that Sterne's final novel differs from *Tristram Shandy* in "asserting more confidently than before the possibility of relationship, achieved through the sensuous and imaginative apprehension of what I will call the syntax of things" (Battestin, "*Sentimental*" 223). Battestin argues that form mirrors content in Sterne's eccentric work. The narrator learns to develop harmonious connections with others; he strives also "to achieve a closer, ameliorative relationship with his reader" (224). A grammatical paradigm of syntax models ideal relationship, but "the notorious syntactical eccentricities, ambiguities, and interruptions of *A Sentimental Journey* will remind us that, in art as in life, such relationships are seldom so easily accomplished" (224). Nonetheless, Yorick progresses "from solipsism toward communion, from self-love toward a felt apprehension of the syntax of things" (225). His final incomplete gesture, his grasp of an unspecified portion of the fille de chambre's anatomy, serves "as the dramatic correlative of the human desire for another sort of syntactical completion, the subjective ego set apart, yet reaching out to close the gap that separates us" (237).

Battestin does not attempt to extend his compelling demonstration beyond Sterne's text, but in fact many sentimental novels lend themselves to comparable analysis. The problem of self-love versus social, as I have already demonstrated in the case of *The Fool of Quality*, is thematized in all these fictions. In the kind of sentimental novel I have been calling experimental, truncations, inconsequentialities, inconclusiveness of plot mirror difficulties of relationship partly constituted by the gap between givers and receivers of benevolence, partly implicit in the inadequacy of language to feeling.

On the opening page of *The Man of Feeling*, the first narrator—the man who allegedly publishes the fragmentary manuscript given him by the curate with whom he hunts—tells of his dog's false point. The birds to which the dog directs attention have already flown. Then the speaker constructs an analogy, invoking the idea of friendship. In life too, he says, we hurry on in search of the object of our desire, only to "find of a sudden that all our gay hopes are flown; and the only slender consolation that some friend can give us, is to point where they were once to be found" (Mackenzie xi; Introduction). This rather strained similitude conveys a melancholy sense of human relationships, appropriate in tone to the narrative proper. When Harley sets out on his journey to London, he first encounters a cheerful beggar whose life has abounded in hardship. Explaining why he offers to tell people's fortunes, the beggar says he learned by unsuccess "and, instead of telling my own misfortunes, began to prophesy happiness to others. This I found by much the better way: folks will always listen when the tale is their own" (13; ch. 14). The curate calls attention to the generic instability of the tale told by the manuscript. "'You may call it what you please,' said the curate; 'for indeed it is no more a history than it is a sermon'" (xii; Introduction). Neither history nor sermon, this narrative of misfortune risks alienating readers who would prefer fantasies of happiness they might apply to themselves.

Subsequent direct references to the reader emphasize the need for emotional identification with the characters depicted and the narrator's skepticism about the reader's capacity for such identification. "We would attempt to describe the joy which Harley felt on this occasion, did it not occur to us that one half of the world could not understand it though we did, and the other half will, by this time, have understood it without any description at all" (47; ch. 29). Narration, in other words, is hardly necessary. The mere notation of happenings will suffice to engage the reader attuned to intensities of feeling. "To such as may have expected the intricacies of a novel," the narrator comments toward the end, "a few incidents in a life undistinguished, except by some features of the heart, cannot have afforded much entertainment" (89; "The Pupil, A Fragment"). Implicitly, the ideal relationship of narrator and reader manifests an intimacy that makes plot and even language virtually irrelevant. Yet the entire novel manifests striking lack of confidence over whether such intimacy can ever be obtained.

Not all sentimental novels express their concern with and anxiety over intimacy by strategies of fragmentation and abrupt narrative shifts. Certain works, especially by women, confront directly the problem of power as the originator of event, hence of plot. Focusing on domestic manifestations of force, they express through the development of their plots anger at female subjection to authority. Given their female protagonists, they do not lavishly exploit the emotional possibilities of benevolence: women, as Adam Smith pointed out, lack the resources for generosity. The use of female protagonists also implies different meaning for the denial of self often characteristic of sentimental novels. Such repression of ego, in the case of women, has been institutionalized. It does not depend on individual temperament or decision. These fictions by women deal openly, sometimes innovatively, with the problems of intimacy. They suggest new directions for fiction.

Frances Sheridan's *Memoirs of Miss Sidney Bidulph* has remained largely unread since its eighteenth-century popularity. Even Jane Spencer has almost nothing to say about it. A recent essay by Margaret Anne Doody, however, calls attention to the novel's great potential interest for twentieth-century readers. Sheridan has, Doody suggests, "in what looks like a feminist novel, taken us beyond feminism, opening out the complexities that arise in human life whenever human beings try to do right" ("Frances Sheridan" 345). The novel's central concern, in Doody's view, "is the effect of the past on the present" (345). Sheridan's fiction also "satirizes the crudity of masculine views, and of the world's views of family life, sexuality, and society's claims" (344).

These comments accurately convey the moral and imaginative complexity of Sheridan's enterprise, but not the curious aggressiveness of the novel's sentimentalism. Intent on wringing from the reader as many tears as possible, the novelist imagines a female career of surpassing pathos. Sidney, a paragon of virtue and obedience, consents to the marriage her brother and her widowed mother want for her, with Orlando Faulkland, a young man eligible in all obvious respects, and the object of her growing love. Shortly before the marriage, a letter reveals that Faulkland has seduced and abandoned another young woman, currently pregnant by him. The event reawakens Lady Bidulph's outrage at her own youthful experience. Her lover, too, abandoned her just before their marriage. After confessing his prior obligation to another woman, the man sank into permanent madness. Horrified, Lady Bidulph reads only cursorily the letter of explanation Faulkland has written to Sidney's brother; she ordains that the wedding cannot take place and that Faulkland must marry his mistress.

A meddlesome old woman suggests, as Sidney recuperates from serious illness, that the world will assume Faulkland jilted her unless she promptly marries someone else. A candidate is at hand: Mr. Arnold, who disapproves of Sidney's reading Horace rather than embroidering, and who manifests no attractions other than a talent for musical performance. But Lady Bidulph wants the marriage. Sidney decides that she no longer loves Faulkland and that esteem for Arnold will in due time turn to love. She marries him, over her brother's strenuous objections. That brother, Sir George, continues to plead Faulkland's cause, claiming that he had not seduced the other woman but had in fact been seduced by her.

Lady Bidulph and Sidney become friendly with Miss Burchell, the pregnant young woman Faulkland has left, and they commit themselves to bringing about her marriage. Meanwhile, Mr. Arnold—whom Sidney has indeed come to love—is seduced by Miss Burchell's wicked aunt and tricked by her into believing Sidney emotionally, if not physically, unfaithful to him with Faulkland. He orders Sidney out of his house, keeping their two children. Through Faulkland's agency, husband and wife become reconciled, but they lose virtually all their money as the result of a fraudulent law suit. Arnold dies, leaving Sidney grief-stricken and poor. Her mother dies, leaving her destitute. Her brother, married to a grasping, heartless woman, provides no help. Her children get smallpox. She becomes ill, but survives. Faulkland proposes once more. She tells him she will never marry him and that he must marry Miss Burchell. He does so, in order to win Sidney's esteem. Then Sir George reveals that Miss Burchell is sexually promiscuous. He has slept with her himself. Now Sidney, for the first time, reads the letter in which Faulkland explained his relationship to Miss Burchell. It reveals his innocence and the woman's guilt. Soon Faulkland shows up, in a state of near-madness. He has killed his adulterous wife and her lover; he demands that Sidney marry him. She complies. Before the marriage can be consummated, Faulkland must flee to France. There he gets the news that his first wife still lives. He dies, probably by suicide. Sidney lives on.

This summary, despite its detail, hardly conveys the intricate interconnections of people and events that control the narrative, but it suggests the thematic insistence of misery in Sidney's story. The causes of that misery are more interesting than its manifestations. Sidney herself invokes Providence as explanation. "What a fatal

wretch have I been to Mr Faulkland! my best purposes, by some
unseen power, are perverted from their ends" (362; March 3). Indeed, the "unseen power" appears to operate, in this novel, only
to what human perceptions must find sinister purpose. Earlier,
though, Sidney offers what we may think another explanation for
what has happened.

You know my match was originally the result of duty to the best of mothers; and though, if I ever knew my own heart, it was absolutely freed from
all attachment to any other person, yet was it not so devoted to Mr Arnold,
as to have made him my choice preferably to all other men, if I had not
resolved in *this*, as in every other action of my life, to be determined by
those to whom I owed obedience. (247; Jan. 23)

This complete disclaimer of moral responsibility calls attention to
an important issue persisting throughout the book: the entire subordination of "good" women not only to men but to other forms of
familial authority. The institutionalized self-suppression of the female becomes an article of faith for the virtuous woman. "Fain
would I bring myself chearfully to conform to my mother's will,"
Sidney writes, "for I have no will of my own. I never knew what it
was to have one, and never shall, I believe; for I am sure I will not
contend with a husband." It comes as something of a surprise, after
this, to find her in the next paragraph complaining, "every body is
combined against me; I am treated like a baby, that knows not what
is fit for it to chuse or reject" (78; Sept. 12). Even a woman with no
will of her own cannot enjoy being treated like a baby. But how else
can one treat her?

The novel represents numerous women who act in fashions far
more self-willed than Sidney's, none of them subject to such misfortunes as hers. Lady Grimston, we learn in retrospect, tyrannized
her husband atrociously. Her beloved daughter contends with her
own husband for mastery. The daughter she has rejected, Sidney's
friend Mrs. Vere, repudiated her mother's authority in making her
own marital choice. Wicked Mrs. Gerrarde, the seducer of Sidney's
husband, shows an Amazonian spirit in contesting with Faulkland.
The more violent these women are in claiming authority over their
own lives and those of others, the more likely they seem to get what
they want. Of course the novel, narrated in Sidney's voice, does not
endorse their procedures. Yet the sequences of cause and effect it
depicts in relation to secondary characters raise questions about
Sidney's choice of absolute submission. She has her virtue to keep
her warm. She has little else.

Given a central character who guides herself by the principle of obedience, this novel necessarily forms its plot largely from operations of power that fill in the moral blank Sidney leaves. Of the characters who exercise power, only Faulkland—the man considered too morally flawed for Sidney to marry—exercises it for good. Lady Bidulph, full of self-will and of confidence in her own acumen (she believes, among other things, in her skill in reading physiognomy), possesses only good intentions, but the narcissistic wound she suffered in her youth has distorted her perceptions of men. Lady Grimston cares mainly about having her way, not about her effects on others. Mr. Arnold exercises his power over his wife most forcefully by ordering her departure. He gradually reveals the flaws of a weak man unfortunately granted social power. Sir George Bidulph uses his masculine force largely for the purpose of rejection. Faulkland alone, controlled by his desire to win Sidney's approval, subordinates his own concerns to another's and employs his force to good ends.

Thus far in my account of it, *Memoirs of Miss Sidney Bidulph* may seem to differ from earlier novels more in its recording of unhappy events than in its imagining of how those events come about. Sidney resembles Amelia in her self-subordination to a husband, although Amelia, unlike Sidney, defied her mother to bring about her marriage. The aggressive women and forceful men who populate Sheridan's fiction hardly differ conceptually from their counterparts in Fielding, and, like their predecessors, they make things happen. But I omitted from my summary one crucial happening that suggests another principle of causality. When Sidney reaches the low point of her economic and physical distress, destitute and ill, a savior presents himself in the guise of a long-absent relative who has lost all his money in the West Indies. Sidney shares her last coins with him and invites him to partake of her family's scanty food. He has previously visited her wealthy brother and that brother's proud wife, only to be brutally rejected. Of course it turns out that he has wished to test his family and that he in fact possesses enormous wealth, which he lavishly shares with Sidney, providing her with a splendidly-furnished mansion, a dependable income, and a rich inheritance.

This redaction of the Baucis and Philemon myth emphasizes not only Sidney's generosity and hospitality but the natural warmth of her human responsiveness. The very form of her narrative stresses her hunger for personal connection. She writes in journal-letters to her most intimate friend, from time to time calling attention to the high value she attaches to friendship, the sustaining force she finds in it. Early in the novel, responding to her friend's teasing suggestion that she really loves Faulkland, she explains that she restrains herself from love "till *duty* makes the passion a virtue; and till *that* becomes my case, I am so much a philosopher in love that I am determined not to let it absorbe any of the other cordial affections, which I owe to my relations and my friends" (25; July 4). Sidney follows orthodox conduct-book advice in preventing herself from loving before marriage, but her insistence on the priority of "the other cordial affections" has special personal meaning. Consistently—even after her marriage—she gives her friendships great importance in her life. The relationship she develops with Mr. Arnold, after their reconciliation, itself resembles an intimate friendship. The tie she forms with her wealthy kinsman, Mr. Warner, not only guarantees her prosperity, it satisfies emotional needs. The desire for intimacy too, then, makes things happen in this narrative. Sidney's acts of benevolence differ from those of Harry, in *The Fool of Quality*, or those of the Man of Feeling in that they do not declare inequality. Her devoted servant, Patty Main, functions increasingly as friend rather than domestic. Sidney has no interest in hierarchy. *Memoirs of Miss Sidney Bidulph* makes some attempt to suggest that nonhierarchical intimacy can serve as an agent of plot.

Yet the weight of disaster in the narrative communicates the inefficacy of friendship as a principle for plotting one's life, and raises questions about its usefulness in plotting a novel. Writing to her brother about the impending marriage to Arnold, Sidney observes that her mother "has used the most irresistible argument to obtain my consent, *viz.* that it would make *her* happy" (84; Sept. 23). Motivated by concern for others' happiness, Sidney generates one misfortune after another, for herself and for those she cares about. Others continue to operate by systems of power; she makes herself their victim. The other sentimental novels thus far considered in this chapter convey anger at existing arrangements by repeated vignettes of social injustice. *Memoirs of Miss Sidney Bidulph* establishes outrage at the female situation of helplessness by the entire organization of its plot. Sidney, in her goodness, possesses no power. Because others do, her sensitivity, her high principles, her impulse toward alliance ultimately achieve nothing but harm.

Faulkland, in the exuberance of his own triumphant plot, sees himself as a hero of romance.

Let no hero of romance compare himself to me, for first making difficulties, and then extricating myself out of them; let no giant pretend to equal me in the management of captive beauties in inchanted castles; let no necromancer presume to vie with me in skill for metamorphosing tigresses into doves, and changing imperious princesses into plain country nymphs.

All this I have brought to pass, without the assistance of enchanted sword or dwarf, in the compass of a few days. (199; Dec. 6)

Able, in the freedom of a masculine imagination, to conceive and—more important—to effect desired outcomes, he feels himself master of the power of plot. If in this respect he resembles Lovelace, Sidney, like Clarissa, possesses a story only by virtue of her suffering. In periods of relative contentment, she recognizes the impossibility of meaningful narrative about a woman's ordinary life. Several times she makes the point. "I have read over my journal of the last fortnight, and am startled to think what a poor insignificant being I am! Not a single act worth recording, even to *you*. My whole life perhaps may have passed so" (271; July 7).

Female protagonists of other late-eighteenth-century fictions by women frequently echo this observation about the tedium of women's lives. Cut off from the possibility of performing acts "worth recording," they can only be acted upon. Sidney's life acquires interest when it turns to misery. The insistence with which Sheridan makes this point has a chilling effect. This heroine's career does not end in the prosperity her kinsman has created for her. Here is the novel's final paragraph:

Gracious Heaven! how inscrutable are thy ways! Her affluent fortune, the very circumstance which seemed to promise her, in the eve of life, some compensation for the miseries she had endured in her early days, now proved the source of new and dreadful calamities to her, which, by involving the unhappy daughters of an unhappy mother in scenes of the most exquisite distress, cut off from her even the last resource of hope in this life, and rendered the close of her history still more. . . . (430; "Cecilia's Narrative." Sheridan's ellipsis)

Still more miserable? Noble? Unfathomable? Sheridan too resorts in the end to fragmentation. She cannot generate a happy ending for this particular story; the story, as Sidney herself implies, depends on its calamities. And the reader could hardly endure further multiplication of misfortune. Whatever form of unhappiness you can imagine, the ending suggests, would be appropriate to the endlessly replicating structure of female wretchedness.

The ethical and theological questions that Robert Markley finds hidden in sentimental novels loom large here. "Gracious Heaven" plays a problematic role in Sidney's career. Unlike Clarissa, this heroine never has intimations of bliss hereafter. Such phrases as "in this life" allude to Christian belief in the subsequent life which will bring justice, and Sidney herself never wavers in her piety, but the realm of heavenly reward remains theoretical. The visible function of Providence in the novel is to make good intentions turn to bad ends, to make Sidney—as both she and her brother explicitly recognize—the agent of harm to all she loves. Is the Father-God here once more, to function as divine tyrant? The bitterness implicit in a fictional scheme that makes the perfectly obedient woman an instrument of reiterative disaster lends bite to Sheridan's version of sentimentalism.

Frances Burney, in her first novel, constructs a plot that moves inexorably toward its conventional happy ending. *Evelina* adapts the comic structure of Fielding's fiction; it does not traffic in disaster. Although rage and aggression abound in the text, they are on the whole strictly compartmentalized; the heroine herself does not directly express them. What she *does* express, more intensely than any fictional protagonist before her, is an overwhelming desire for intimate human connection, a desire so profound that it can become an effective agent of plot. Unlike Amelia or Sidney, Evelina appears to make things happen by the sheer force of her will. Other people bring about important events in her life by various kinds of intervention as if they responded to the emotional energy of Evelina's desire.

This seventeen-year-old heroine differs from most of her fictional contemporaries in her apparent lack of any wish to marry, her failure even to manifest awareness of marriage as inevitable female destiny. Although the text deftly documents her increasing preoccupation with Lord Orville, not until her guardian opens her eyes does she realize that her feeling for the nobleman implies the possibility of marital consummation. If her erotic desire appears undeveloped, though, her yearning for non-erotic human connection displays itself vividly. She early develops a close alliance with Miss Mirvan, whom she characterizes as "my second self, [who] neither hopes nor fears but as I do" (110; letter 26). This kind of intimacy, however, will not suffice. She wants another form of closeness that will include help and guidance. "I know not what to *wish*," she writes her guardian, the Reverend Mr. Villars: "think for me, therefore, my dearest Sir, and suffer my doubting mind, that knows not which way to direct its hopes, to be guided by your wisdom and unerring counsel" (111; letter 26). Better than someone to share one's hopes is someone to direct them.

Quite a different model of virtuous young womanhood from Sidney Bidulph, Evelina lacks a sufficient number of benevolent authority figures to meet her emotional needs. Mr. Villars is an ideal mentor, but Mme. Duval, her newly discovered grandmother, proves tyrannical and self-interested.[4] Evelina begs—fatherless child that she is—for men in particular to serve as loving authorities to whom she can devote herself and be happily obedient. Indeed, she becomes increasingly attractive to Lord Orville precisely by virtue of her appeal to him for loving guidance.

> There is no young creature, my Lord, who so greatly wants, or so earnestly wishes for, the advice and assistance of her friends, as I do: I am new to the world, and unused to acting for myself;—my intents are never wilfully blameable, yet I err perpetually!—I have hitherto been blessed with the most affectionate of friends, and, indeed, the ablest of men, to guide and instruct me upon every occasion:—but he is too distant, now, to be applied to at the moment I want his aid:—and *here*,—there is not a human being whose counsel I can ask. (288; letter 66)

Unsurprisingly, Lord Orville responds by volunteering his services as friend. Before long, he has constituted himself Evelina's "brother." By the end, his role as husband appears to have merged, to Evelina's complete satisfaction, with that of father.

The institutional sources of power in the world of *Evelina* include wealth, rank, and, most particularly, *name* (the word echoes insistently through the text), that sign of family and of social position. Evelina at the outset has no name, forced to pseudonymity by the fact that her father refuses to acknowledge her. Without a name, she can hardly hope for a marriage: perhaps her lack of erotic awareness should be understood as a defense. Lady Howard writes to Mr. Villars—as an argument for trying to force Evelina's father to own her—that "she would have had the most splendid offers, had there not seemed to be some mystery in regard to her birth, which . . . was assiduously, though vainly, endeavoured to be discovered" (112; letter 27). Prophetically, Evelina finds herself several times making use of Lord Orville's name to escape from social dilemmas. Under his name she can shelter. Her vulgar relatives in turn use her name—her made-up name of *Anville*—as means for approaching and exploiting Lord Orville. Nonetheless, Evelina needs a *real* name, a name of her own. "Her own," of course, means her father's, which she successfully acquires just in time to give it up for Lord Orville's.

Her search for intimate association produces multiplication rather than substitution. She acquires a new brother in the impecunious Scot, Macartney, whom she befriends after discovering him in a state of dangerous depression. She finds in Mrs. Mirvan, her friend's mother, a mother-substitute who will take loving care of her, and in Mrs. Selwyn a "mother" to express her aggression. She gains in Lord Orville a lover who functions as friend, guide, and protector. And she captivates her true father without having to relinquish her attachment to Mr. Villars, to whose arms— specified as those of "the best of men"—she hastens at the novel's conclusion, after her marriage to one presumably relegated to the category of second-best (388), though likely, as she has pointed out earlier, to resemble Mr. Villars increasingly with age.[5]

In her self-deprecating preface to *Evelina*, Burney summarizes the novel's action:

a young female, educated in the most secluded retirement, makes, at the age of seventeen, her first appearance upon the great and busy stage of life; with a virtuous mind, a cultivated understanding, and a feeling heart, her ignorance of the forms, and inexperience in the manners of the world, occasion all the little incidents which these volumes record.

"Young female" opposed to "world" creates story. From one set of social problems, the restoration of Evelina's "name" rescues her. Given lineage and social position, she has resources for self-defense. Her multiplication of close attachments combats a more serious set of difficulties, the psychic strains inherent for such a young female as Evelina in a world that operates by assertions and perceptions of power and by acts of aggression. Susan Staves long ago called attention to the remarkable series of threats that confront Evelina herself, making her "predominant emotion," according to Staves, "an acute anxiety which is painful, real, and powerful" (368). Staves goes on to comment that "All the resources of Fanny Burney's art are used to exorcise from Evelina and Lord Orville those qualities which give life to the book and to embody them in characters who are then criticized for their boldness" (379).

Agreeing with both these observations, I would argue further that Evelina's anxiety derives not only from the threats she herself faces, abundant though they are, but more fundamentally from the presence all around her of what Staves calls "boldness": willingness to engage directly in power conflicts. If she acquires several new real and substitute family members to answer her need for intimacy, she also gains a number of unwanted relatives: a grandmother of brutal sensibility and a family of cousins, the crude, insensitive Branghtons, with their equally crude father. Her distaste for them derives partly from her snobbery, but also from deeper feelings. Of a trip to Vauxhall with the Branghtons, she remarks, "a hautbois concerto was so charmingly played, that I could have thought myself upon enchanted ground, had I had spirits more gentle to associate with" (178; letter 46). Gentle herself to a degree that incapacitates her for purposeful aggression (she laughs at the fop Lovel, but only because she knows no better), Evelina places high value on gentleness in others. But her social circumstances make her confront the fact that people often achieve what they want by the very antithesis of gentleness. Not only the crudities of the middle class frighten her—there are also those of the aristocracy, predatory toward helpless women, willing to make even aged, poor females instruments of their brutal competitiveness.[6] Mrs. Mirvan's husband, a sea captain, plays sadistic practical jokes on those of whom he disapproves. Mme. Duval spews out verbal violence.

Staves attributes to the aggressive characters all the novel's "life": which brings up once more the problem of where story comes from. Evelina herself makes it increasingly clear that she attaches the idea of compelling narrative to Lord Orville. When he does not inhabit the scene, she finds nothing of interest to write about. "I fear you will be sick of reading about this family," she observes to Mr. Villars; "yet I must write of them, or not of any, since I mix with no other" (164; letter 42). Unlike Susan Staves, Evelina believes the vulgar provide no narrative material of value. On the other hand, she never imagines that Mr. Villars might be sick of hearing about Lord Orville. Later, to Miss Mirvan, she proclaims herself reduced to total inarticulateness. "You complain of my silence, my dear Miss Mirvan;—but what have I to write? Narrative does not offer, nor does a lively imagination supply the deficiency" (247; letter 60). The point is not that nothing has happened, but that Evelina does not know how to make story out of the happenings provided. She is by this time back at Berry Hill, Mr. Villars's establishment, which has provided sufficient interest for seventeen years; now it no longer supplies the stuff of narrative. Neither aggression nor confined domesticity satisfies Evelina's narrative or emotional needs.

From the point of view of the modern reader, the characters directly engaged in power games indeed generate the best stories. But Evelina, and presumably her creator, dimly apprehend another principle of narrative, one related to but extending the mode of the sentimental novel. Like the typical sentimental novel, *Evelina* suppresses the erotic. Its heroine's interest in Lord Orville purports to center on his virtue and his social graces. Presented as a man with more manners than passion, Orville strikes many readers as sexually uninteresting and unthreatening. Although men constantly make passes at Evelina, her accounts of these episodes emphasize her generalized terror rather than her awareness of specifically sexual threat. (Starr, however, calls attention to the presumably inadvertent sexuality of Evelina's language when she describes Willoughby's menace [526].) Like sentimental novels too, the text makes benevolence the sign of virtue. Evelina—in this respect resembling Sidney Bidulph and Harry Clinton—uses someone else's money as her instrument of generosity, but she unambiguously demonstrates her benevolent impulse in relation to Macartney and in her generosity to the young woman who has usurped her place in her father's household. And Burney's novel conforms to sentimental pattern in making its protagonist strikingly passive, responsive rather than initiatory.

More fundamental than these sentimental conventions is the novel's endeavor, more fully realized than in Mackenzie and Sterne, to reject power and elevate affiliation as the central principle of plot. The many characters in *Evelina* who operate on the basis of aggression and competition accomplish rather little. They succeed in punishing one another: Captain Mirvan's contrivances chastise Mme. Duval and the fop Lovel. But the ludicrous, dreadful race in which two women in their eighties compete in order to settle an aristocratic wager provides a type for competitive activity in the novel (much effort, little achievement), and an indication of narrative attitude toward it. Futility characterizes the activities of Lovel and Sir Clement Willoughby, of the Branghtons and Mr. Smith (one of Evelina's would-be suitors). They generate brief embarrassment or anxiety in Evelina, but little more. Blifil, in *Tom Jones*, appears to have matters all his own way through a good deal of the narrative. Sir Clement, who plays the corresponding role in *Evelina*, gets Evelina to himself for a few minutes in his carriage or in the Vauxhall walks and indirectly causes her illness by his forgery of a letter allegedly by Lord Orville. Not even temporarily does he ever appear to come close to achieving his ends.

Evelina's mainly nonerotic desire, on the other hand, makes a great deal happen, directly and indirectly. She attaches not only Lord Orville but also Lady Howard and Mrs. Mirvan to her and her interests mainly by the power of her naively explicit need for human attachment. Becoming ill to dramatize her mourning over her lost "esteem" for Lord Orville, she finds her illness a means for renewed contact with her idealized lover; clarification duly follows. New expressions of her yearning for affection and guidance draw

Lord Orville more closely to her. Others serve as agents of her desire by bringing about an interview with her true father, but she wins him by her expressed wish to "soothe your sorrows" and by such exclamations as this: "Oh, Sir, . . . that you could but read my heart!—that you could but see the filial tenderness and concern with which it overflows!—you would not then talk thus,—you would not then banish me from your presence, and exclude me from your affection!" (366; letter 80). Evelina's "heart" becomes the instrument of her success, which consists in her possession of one literal and two metaphorical fathers.

In comparison with the other sentimental novels I have considered, *Evelina* assigns a great deal of space to representing the speech and action of "bold" characters. If they do not function to make important things happen in the plot, they nonetheless serve significant narrative purposes. As I have already suggested, they supply the ground for Evelina's pervasive anxiety, because they define possibilities she wishes to reject in her own life and indicate the widespread realization of such possibilities in the "world" she has entered for the first time. Moreover (and this relationship may provide further ground for Evelina's anxiety), they project the negative side of the heroine's desire. Love implies hate, attachment implies repudiation. I have argued elsewhere that Evelina manages herself to express a good deal of aggression on paper (Spacks, *Gossip* 156–63). She does not knowingly permit herself such aggression in face-to-face contact. Captain Mirvan and Mrs. Selwyn between them manage to punish most of the persons who seriously interfere with Evelina's peace of mind. In other words, they act out Evelina's unacknowledged and unacknowledgeable wish to get her own back. Most important, from the point of view of plot and of theme, is the fact that the aggressive characters Evelina encounters everywhere have, finally, so little effective force. This is Burney's most essential fantasy, the one at the heart of her fiction. In Mackenzie's novel and Sheridan's, evil people, evil social forces, determine much of human experience. Burney's new form of sentimentalism declares otherwise.

Evelina's most important self-determined action (one of her few such actions) involves her disarming of a man bent on violence. In removing Macartney's pistols, she condenses the novel's plot: the plot that shows how "feminine" desire for relationship can succeed when "masculine" desire for power fails. "The presence of sentimentality," Philip Fisher writes, "is most obvious at precisely those places where an essential extension of the subject matter of the novel itself is taking place" (93). The "essential extension of . . . subject matter" described in this chapter involves giving centrality to "feminine" values: one of the novel's most radical forms of representation. The female Gothic novel, now widely recognized as a variation of or development from the novel of sensibility, would refine and complicate Burney's new narrative direction.

6

FATHERS AND DAUGHTERS: ANN RADCLIFFE

Among its other contributions to the history of the English novel, *Evelina* called attention to the subject of fathers and daughters. Burney dedicated the novel—her first, published anonymously—to her father, invoked as "Author of my being!" The last stanza of the dedication reads,

> Oh! of my life at once the source and joy!
> If e'er thy eyes these feeble lines survey,
> Let not their folly their intent destroy;
> Accept the tribute—but forget the lay.

Thus the poem whose first line attributes authorship to the father ends by denying it for the daughter: her father is to forget the poem that praises him, remembering only the praise.

The pattern of attributing all significant agency to men persists in the novel itself, as Evelina multiplies literal and metaphorical male relatives. For modern readers, a faintly erotic tinge suffuses the young woman's familial relationships. Lord Orville mistakes her new half-brother, Macartney, for her lover. The novel's final words are, "the chaise now waits which is to conduct me to dear Berry Hill, and to the arms of the best of men" (388; letter 84)—i.e., Mr. Villars, who appears to substitute for Evelina's new husband. Indeed, her use of the first-person- singular pronoun rather than the expected plural might suggest that she has forgotten all about her husband. Her longing for her guardian's "arms" recalls the terms of Mr. Villars's repeatedly articulated fantasy of "closing these aged eyes in the arms of one so dear—so deservedly beloved!" (14; letter 9). Conventional though this formulation is, its repetition and its physicality give it slightly disturbing emphasis in Burney's text.

The vestigially erotic father-daughter (surrogate father-daughter) relationship contrasts with the de-eroticized connection of lovers. Lord Orville values Evelina for her "modest worth and fearful excellence" and because she is "informed, sensible, and intelligent"

(329; letter 75); she adores him for his high moral standards, his intelligent conversation, his wisdom and benevolence. Although Lord Orville speaks of Evelina's beauty, his tone suggests that it too possesses moral weight. The aristocrat's sexuality, like Evelina's, obscures itself behind a screen of propriety.

Of course sexual passion has its place in this novel—disguised, or displaced into the background. The stories of Evelina's mother, who dies in childbirth after an indiscreet marriage, and of Macartney's mother, who dies in miserable exile, having indulged an illicit passion, recall the dire consequences for women of expressed sexuality. Evelina frequently encounters male rudeness, physical and verbal: synecdoche for sexual violence. She even suffers a rather halfhearted attempt at seduction. Episodes in which someone seizes her hand or declares his intention of stealing a kiss carry explosive emotional charge. They call to mind the possibilities of direct phallic aggression and suggest female anxiety corresponding to the male anxiety of *Tristram Shandy* and *The Man of Feeling*.

The desire for intimacy, Evelina's strongest desire, and the desire for power which she occludes and fears both contribute to sexual arrangements—in life and in literature. Both also shape plots. Ann Radcliffe's female Gothic, making sexual threat more explicit and more dangerous than it customarily is in Burney, investigates the passion for intimacy and that for power. Radcliffe also asserts the relations of fathers and daughters as the symbolic heart of her narratives. Her novelistic renditions of intimate connections between powerful men and relatively powerless women provide a focus for reflecting more richly on how different structures of thought generate different fictional patterns.

In Radcliffe's novels, I propose, literal or metaphoric tensions between fathers and daughters suggest a way to understand the new kind of plot that *Evelina* introduced. Radcliffe's plots might be called "daughters' plots"—not simply because they originate in a female consciousness, but because they establish internal principles of action by giving due weight to the psychology and morality traditionally associated with daughters as well as to the assumptions of sons.

In an interesting comment on the subversive potential of the Gothic novel, Robert Kiely observes the form's early concentration on domestic disruption.

The Gothic novel did eventually encourage large-scale social subversion, but, in its earlier forms, the 'natural order' which it disturbed was of a simpler and more fundamental type. The confusion existed not between lawmaker and renegade, but between father and son, brother and sister, lover and mistress. Basic human relationships were thrown into an extreme disorder which was symbolized most commonly in sexual terms—adultery, incest, pederasty. (36)

Kiely's failure to mention daughters and fathers in his loci of "confusion" seems surprising, since symbolic father-daughter incest permeates early Gothic fiction. His general point about the impulse toward social criticism implicit in intimate violations of natural order, however, is illuminating. Radcliffe's exploration of father-daughter relationships extends the radical implications of earlier sentimental novels.

Her male precursors and peers also investigated the subject. In Horace Walpole's *The Castle of Otranto*, for instance, a tyrannical father declares his intention of marrying his daughter's best friend after he divorces his current wife, whose passive compliance with this plan he rightly assumes. Manfred's plots fail, and he accidentally stabs his daughter to death, his dagger striking her where paternal weapons in these novels always seem to land, in her "bosom," thus "effecting both absolute mastery and a type of incestuous violation in a single stroke" (Haggerty, "Literature and Homosexuality" 344). He has intended, rather, to kill his daughter's friend Isabella. David Morris comments astutely on the doubling involved in Manfred's relation to the two young women:

When Manfred in jealous rage stabs the figure he believes to be Isabella, it is not coincidence but the Gothic truth of repetition which substitutes his own daughter, Matilda. Matilda and Isabella—despite their opposite temperaments—are doubles or mirror images, and Manfred's pursuit of Isabella is not simply an expression of unrequited desire but the reenactment of an ancient pattern. What terrifies Isabella as she flees from Manfred through dark, subterranean passages is not the prospect of capture or even rape—however terrible—but sexual violation by the man who, in the repetitions of Walpole's narrative, is the double or dark surrogate of her own absent father. (305)

A more brutal version of comparable events occurs in Matthew Lewis's adolescent fantasy, *The Monk*. As the wicked monk's sexual imaginings accumulate around his innocent girlish victim, she addresses him ever more frequently as "Father"; he combines the authority of all males with the patriarchal authority of the Church. She turns out, after Ambrosio has raped and murdered her (with another stab to the bosom), to be his sister, not literally his daughter (he has also, along the way, strangled his mother to death), but the sexually tinged conflict between paternal power and filial innocence remains central to the Gothic effect.

Neither *The Castle of Otranto* (1764) nor *The Monk* (1796) exemplifies the new "daughters' plot" of the late eighteenth century. Instead, such works recapitulate, with fresh trimmings, the structure of novels by Richardson, Fielding, and early Smollett. Their action derives from struggles of power. Walpole opposes to wicked Manfred two heroic and virtuous male figures: young Theodore, a splendid youth of mysterious birth, like Tom Jones; and a fierce knight eventually identified as the father of Manfred's intended sexual victim. Various versions of male conflict, intensified by supernatural interventions, invigorate the plot. The supernatural, often ludicrously phallic in its manifestations (a sword so big that a hundred men can barely carry it, gigantic human limbs appearing in various parts of the castle), embodies power, a fact implicit in the stress on gigantism. As for the women, they possess no resources beyond obedience and flight. "Perhaps the sacrifice of myself may atone for all," observes Manfred's wife Hippolita—" . . . it boots not what becomes of me" (Walpole 91). "I must not hear a word against the pleasure of thy father," she warns her daughter, as Matilda tries to tell her of Manfred's plan to marry her to her friend's father, yet another version of faintly disguised incest (92). The girls from time to time try to run away, and they depend heavily on male help; they serve only as victims, never as embodiments, of power.

The Monk emphasizes its preoccupation with masculine energy even more, playing variations on the Faust legend to give its villain ever greater resources. An apparently enterprising and self-determined woman—another Matilda—seduces the monk at the outset. In the long run, though, she turns out not to be a forceful female at all, but a demon in disguise, doing the bidding of Satan, the novel's ultimate locus of male power. Neither Ambrosio's sister, his principal victim, nor his mother can comprehend or combat evil. They epitomize the helpless.

Ann Radcliffe, shocked by *The Monk*, set out to rewrite it in *The Italian* (1797), which incorporates new versions of many events in Lewis's fiction. It therefore provides a useful test case for my contention that Radcliffe develops a novelistic structure significantly different from that of her important predecessors. Her most obvious modifications of Lewis's model have little apparent bearing on fundamental conceptions of plot. Committed to Burke's conviction that obscurity provides a crucial element in the sublime, she relies heavily on suggestion. Ambrosio (in *The Monk*) rapes and murders his sister; Radcliffe's wicked monk, Schedoni, only *almost* murders the young woman he believes to be his daughter. Lewis dwells on his protagonist's feelings; Radcliffe diffuses emotional interest. And, as literary histories tend to reiterate, she frequently elaborates details of an imagined Italian landscape, her principles of description based on Burke's aesthetic.

What interests me more is how Radcliffe develops covert moral implications of Burke's theory of the sublime into a foundation for fictional structure. Like other late-eighteenth-century aestheticians, Burke interested himself in "our passions in our own breasts" as the basis for understanding sublimity and beauty (1). Terror and pity, classically defined components of tragic response, particularly concern him. Terror associates itself with the sublime, which "is productive of the strongest emotion which the mind is capable of feeling" (39). Pity seems linked with beauty as "a passion accompanied with pleasure, because [like responses to beauty] it arises from love and social affection" (46). Passion's possibilities, in Burke's view, define themselves by simple opposition, belonging to self-preservation and the sublime (38–39) or to society and beauty (40). Mediating between emotions associated with the self and those connected with society is ambition, a "social" passion arising from man's desire to excel his fellows, planted in man by God in order to ensure progress (50).

Kiely comments astutely on the importance and the fictional possibilities of Burke's dualism.

One finds in Walpole, Radcliffe, Reeve, and Lewis not only Burke's ideas but Burke's problems. Whereas the best romantic poetry achieves, indeed embodies, moments of synthesis, the romantic novel, at best and at worst, is an almost continuous display of divisive tension, paradox, and uncertain focus. The dualism of man's nature—of his taste, his impulses, his ambitions—the deep division in his very way of perceiving reality, seemed an inevitable adjunct to the first romantic stirrings in the young genre. (17)

Ambition, in Burke's system, in its mediating force suggests a possible resolution of division. But as a stereotypically male quality, belonging neither in eighteenth-century fiction nor, apparently, in eighteenth-century society to females (except for *bad* females), ambition does not solve the woman's problem. Radcliffe in her novels found a way to suggest another mode of "progress," based on social feelings, which avoids both the self-abnegation of Hippolita's claim that it boots not what becomes of her and the insane self-assertion of a Manfred, an Ambrosio, or a Schedoni. To convey such a possibility, she devises double plots that imply two different principles of action, two kinds of impetus for fiction. She exploits, in other words, Burke's perception of fundamental division.

The two principles work themselves out on many levels. Not only do individual episodes in Radcliffe's novels embody contrasting moral assumptions, the intricate series of events through which the protagonists of *The Italian* or *The Mysteries of Udolpho* achieve marriage dramatizes opposed systems of value. The crucial sequence in *The Italian* during which Schedoni almost murders his presumed daughter exemplifies Radcliffe's method. Abducted to an isolated, half-ruined house on the seashore, Ellena must sleep in a room with a secret passage opening into it. In the middle of the night, Schedoni steals in, his dagger at the ready. He takes a long time deciding to strike; a highly eroticized scene, with emphasis on the need for denuding the girl, details his hesitations. Sexual innuendo accumulates. "He stooped to examine whether he could turn her robe aside, without waking her." (One might wonder why, exactly, he needs to "turn . . . aside" a robe made of lawn, a particularly fine, sheer fabric.) Again, "as often as he prepared to plunge the poniard in her bosom, a shuddering horror restrained him. . . . Vengeance nerved his arm, and drawing aside the lawn from her bosom, he once more raised it to strike. . . . His respiration was short and laborious, chilly drops stood on his forehead, and all his faculties of mind seemed suspended" (234). The lethal assault the monk has in mind appears essentially sexual in nature.

The assault, however, never takes place. Instead, Ellena wakes up. Schedoni drops the dagger, having noted the miniature she wears around her neck, a representation of himself as a young man: he can now understand the young woman as his reflection. Ellena tells him the picture portrays her father. Schedoni then constitutes himself her protector rather than her assassin, but he still proposes to use her in the service of his ambition. If a father exemplifies power, he must concomitantly exemplify danger.

In his person and in his character, Schedoni, a powerful male, represents the human sublime—a concept, in Radcliffe's treatment, permeated with moral ambiguity. The afternoon before the attempted murder, Ellena sees him on the beach, not knowing who he is. "There was something also terrific in the silent stalk of so gigantic a form," the narrator comments; "it announced both power and treachery" (221). Schedoni's physical size, his association with power, and his "terrific" aspect conform to Burkean standards, but the idea of treachery reminds us that human beings, unlike mountains, possess moral natures. Schedoni's actual and potential treachery result from the isolation, the concentration on self, that Burke connects with the sublime and with the masculine. Novelists before Radcliffe had consistently criticized such self-absorption. Radcliffe disapproves too—but she also dramatizes its connection with authentic and inescapable power. From one point of view, Schedoni precipitates all significant events in Radcliffe's novel. He demonstrates the naked operations of power. The novel's title designates him as its center, but he exists partly to raise questions about power as the governing principle of action or of narrative.

Effectively deprived of moral imagination by his concern with what Burke calls "self-preservation," Schedoni can conceive no interests but his own. Yet in discussions with his female co-conspirator, the Marchesa, he repeatedly invokes "justice," which, he argues, requires Ellena's death. Thus he taunts the Marchesa: "though the law of justice demands the death of this girl, yet because the law of the land forbears to enforce it, you, my daughter, even you! though possessed of a man's spirit, and his clear perceptions, would think that virtue bade her live, when it was only fear!" (168). Like Carol Gilligan, he appears to believe women less susceptible than men to justice's claim; in fact *his* perverse version of justice subordinates all to his desires. As he sees it, "Strong minds perceive that justice is the highest of the moral attributes, mercy is only the favourite of weak ones" (111). ("Weak ones" we may take as a periphrasis for women.) Justice is the instrument of power, in the monk's view. Mercy betrays power's absence.

Schedoni employs the phallic dagger in his obsessive efforts to dominate. As plotter, as father, as would-be and as successful murderer (he manages to dispatch a rival monk and has in the past killed his own brother and only accidentally avoided killing his wife), he proves controlled by passion for political, social, psychological, and financial mastery. In moral terms the sublime comes to only this. Ellena, on the other hand, like her lover, Vivaldi, and her mother, Olivia, governs herself by another system of desire, another structure of value.

The thrust of her psychological and moral orientation, the dimensions of the other system of assumptions shaping the plot, reveal themselves in her reactions to the attempted assassination, its preambles and aftermath. Walking on the shore, in imminent danger of being murdered (although she has avoided full acknowledgement of that possibility), she rejoices "that the fishermen, whose boats she had observed, had escaped the threatening tempest, and were safely sheltered in their little homes, where, as they heard the loud waves break along the coast, they could look with keener pleasure upon the social circle, and the warm comforts around them." This apparent sentimentality reveals Ellena's mode of reflecting on her own condition by displacing her feelings. What troubles her most—since she represents *beauty*, not *sublimity*—is not her danger but her isolation: "I have no longer a home, a circle to smile welcome upon me! I have no longer even one friend to support, to rescue me!" (220). For her, the idea of a father merges with that of a protector. When Schedoni demands to know the identity of the face in the miniature, Ellena responds, "Alas! he is dead! or I should not now want a protector" (235). Believing herself, subsequently, to have found a father in Schedoni, she obstinately interprets his responses as forms of caretaking. When she finds the dagger under her bed, she decides, implausibly, that someone else has tried to murder her and Schedoni has rescued her. "O! my father, do not deny me the pleasure of shedding these tears of gratitude, do not refuse the thanks, which are due to you! While I slept upon that couch, while a ruffian stole upon my slumber—it was you, yes! can I ever forget that it was my father, who saved me from his poniard!" (248).

That pleasure involved in "shedding . . . tears of gratitude" suggests the shape of Ellena's desire. More single-mindedly even than Evelina, she yearns for friendship, affiliation, being taken care of, being able to take care. When, in a situation of extreme danger, her lover shows up to rescue her from a nunnery, she repeatedly returns to her friend Olivia (not yet revealed as her mother) for affectionate farewells, apparently valuing friendship more than love or life. At her own wedding, she reflects on a previous aborted attempt at marriage in terms again suggesting that friends and family matter more than erotic love. Vivaldi expresses similar feelings in less extreme terms. In the Inquisition's dungeons, for example, himself in danger, he worries about the situation of other victims, opposing an ethic of compassion to one of justice and denouncing justice's institutional perversions. And he at least momentarily resolves not to claim Ellena for his wife until his family approves—not because of reluctance to defy his parents, but because he wishes not to deprive Ellena of the new family to which she is entitled: he wants his mother and father "willingly [to] admit her in the rank of their child" (180).

In other words, Radcliffe stresses the moral qualities associated with Burke's category of "beauty" through the responses of at least one male character as well as those of the heroine. Yet the notion of sublimity recurs. The sublime of nature, less morally ambiguous than its human equivalent, extends its strength from the physical to the moral realm. Thus Ellena, abducted into the mountains, reflects, "Here, the objects seem to impart somewhat of their own force, their own sublimity, to the soul" (62–63). Similarly, Vivaldi, on his way to the dungeon, finds inspiration in Roman ruins evoking "a melancholy awe, a sacred enthusiasm, that withdrew him from himself" (195). Moreover, Radcliffe's plot suggests that the human sublime, for all its terrifying aspects, can help to strengthen those committed to softer virtues. Schedoni's manipulations provide a principle of energy; much action derives from the protagonists' efforts to escape or overcome his power and his treachery. In the process, they acquire force. Ellena, at the outset a "good girl," devoted to her elderly aunt, industriously producing needlework as a source of income, turns into a woman with powers of resistance and self-determination. Her integrity displays itself in her refusals: reluctance to marry unless Vivaldi's parents accept her, rejection of nunhood. But she also shows courage and endurance in her repeated ordeals and repeated attempts to escape. Vivaldi, too, who shares her "feminine" concern for other people, learns his own strength and independence by the necessities of resistance.

Inasmuch as the plot of *The Italian* can be defined in these terms—as constituted by the protagonists' resistance of Schedoni— it resembles the plots of previous eighteenth-century novels, although the heroine's development of moral stature from a position of initial passivity perhaps represents something new. (Sophia Western and Clarissa Harlowe of course display moral force—but they clearly possess its potential from the outset.) But the degree to which the plot develops also from the imaginative and emotional capacities of its protagonists—what Radcliffe and her predecessors called "sensibility"—suggests the novelist's fresh direction. The narrator repeatedly calls attention to the deficiencies of a "sublime" consciousness and the resources of one more oriented toward human sympathy. Thus, we learn that Schedoni can interpret other people's responses only by analogy with his own; he therefore makes serious mistakes. As the novel approaches its dénouement, the narrator stipulates, in moralistic terms, the double principle of action.

It may be worthy of observation, that the virtues of Olivia, exerted in a general cause, had thus led her unconsciously to the happiness of saving her daughter; while the vices of Schedoni had as unconsciously urged him nearly to destroy his niece, and had always been preventing, by the means they prompted him to employ, the success of his constant aim. (384)

Radcliffe's notion of the unconscious is not ours, yet we too might say that the novel opposes two forms of unconscious orientation in working out its action. The principle of sympathy, the ethic associated with "beauty," conflicts with the passions of self-sufficiency, the ethic of "sublimity." On the other hand, only by opposing itself to or identifying itself with the sublime does the beautiful acquire strength.

The Mysteries of Udolpho (1794), Radcliffe's earlier and better-known Gothic romance, marks even more distinctly the ways that "sensibility," the emotional structure associated with the beautiful, can develop into a mode of effectiveness—as, in earlier novels, it typically had not. Emily St. Aubert, the heroine, suffers pressure from two different father figures. First her literal father, a paternal paragon, concerned about her tendency to imaginative and emotional excess, tries to effect her moral education by a process of deliberate frustration. He wishes to develop in her—he says it repeatedly—"habits of self-command" (e.g. 5); words like *strength* and *fortitude* recur as he ponders how to construct her character. He teaches her "to reject the first impulse of her feelings, and to look, with cool examination, upon the disappointments he sometimes threw in her way"; he finds himself "often obliged to witness, with seeming indifference, the tears and struggles which his caution occasioned her" (5). For the best of reasons, this model father frequently behaves like a tyrant.

If such a "good" father throws disappointments in Emily's way with pedagogical intent and watches with *seeming* indifference her tears and struggles, the male authority figure who succeeds him after Emily is orphaned (the requisite state for Gothic heroines) replaces appearance with substance. A mysterious Italian, Montoni, marries Emily's aunt, her guardian. Dark, powerful, courageous, brooding, informed with unimaginable purpose—in short, *sublime*—Montoni supplies a steady series of real, important disappointments for Emily and cares not at all for her tears. He assumes, among other paternal prerogatives, that of disposing of her in marriage for his own advantage. Emily's imperative need to resist him educates her more successfully than her benign true father could have done.

Although Emily often relies on male help, she defies the terrifying Montoni, resists the sexual advances of Count Morano, steadfastly refuses to yield her paternal estate, and keeps her head in desperate situations. A typical Gothic heroine, she, like characters in *The Italian*, identifies with the power of sublime scenery while opposing herself to the moral corruption involved in human sublimity. I want, though, to dwell not on these obvious facts but on the plot's other side, the way that Emily's "sensibility," her need for human attachment, defines itself as strength rather than weakness. It fuels her resistance, generates action, and finally undermines male power.

Emily's aunt, who marries Montoni, proves stupid, snobbish, superficial, and misguided; she torments the fatherless girl with unkind suspicions of sexual impropriety. Nonetheless, Emily governs her behavior at Udolpho largely by compassion and sympathy for her aunt, a fellow victim. Undeterred by repeated snubs, she tries steadily to alleviate Mme. Montoni's situation, braving unknown dangers and defying Montoni in repeated efforts to help her aunt. After the aunt finally dies, Emily's concern shifts once more to Valancourt, the man she loves. For his sake she refuses to relinquish her own inheritance until pressed beyond endurance. Safely returned to France, driven to give up Valancourt because of false reports about his Parisian vices, she relies for emotional sustenance and spiritual fortitude on her friends, the text repeatedly emphasizing their importance to her.

Emily's true father thought sensibility enervating, but it fortifies Emily: by considering herself obligated to others, she is empowered to act for herself. Much of what happens in *The Mysteries of Udolpho* happens because of Emily's benevolent concern. Even her commitment to Valancourt involves not merely dependence on him but care for him.

Yet sensibility, that vague term suggesting sensitive responsiveness in its possessor, implies desire. In *The Mysteries of Udolpho*, the figure of Laurentini, destroyed by her passions, emphasizes that fact. Emily indulges sensibility but avoids desire by self-government amounting to repression, and by transforming sexual to altruistic feeling, as "good" women have traditionally done. Clarissa's conversion of sexual to religious devotion exemplifies a comparable transformation.

So far, as my allusion to Clarissa emphasizes, my account of attitudes toward female feeling implicit in Radcliffean Gothic hints that these late-century novels echo assumptions of their novelistic predecessors. The reliance on affiliative impulse to energize plot and to strengthen character (one might contrast the striking passivity of the protagonist in *The Man of Feeling*) constitutes, I have argued, something new, but only indirectly do such attributions of force challenge standard doctrine about the relations of the sexes. But I have so far virtually ignored, in my treatment of Radcliffe, a conspicuous aspect of Gothic novels: their reliance on the supernatural.

As everyone knows, Ann Radcliffe introduces horror only to explain it away. *The Mysteries of Udolpho* provides the most notorious instance: early in the novel, Emily observes behind a black veil something so horrifying that she faints, never revealing to anyone what she has seen. Not until toward the end does the narrator explain that Emily saw a decaying corpse, complete with worms. But the corpse is only a wax image; the mysterious appearances and sounds that generate fear in not one but two castles have originated in relatively unsinister activities of living men.

Ardent imaginations typically prove susceptible to supernatural appearances, and sensibility implies imagination as well as sexuality. I have argued before for the covert equivalence between imagination and sexuality in many eighteenth-century treatments of imagination's dangers for women (Spacks, "'Ev'ry Woman"). In Radcliffe's Gothic, imagination generates a dark and relatively unrepressed version of desire: which brings us back, after a long detour, to the matter of fathers, the question of paternal sublimity. What Emily sees and hears at Udolpho connects itself in her imagination with the character of Montoni, the castle's owner. If she glimpses an apparent corpse, she assumes that Montoni has murdered someone; if she hears inexplicable groans and voices, she believes them to comment on Montoni's immediate wickedness; the eerie figure who flits about the battlements must testify to evil from the past. Only the first of these conclusions ever becomes explicit in the text; the reader's constructions supplement Emily's in the other instances.

That is to say, the reader, male or female, is encouraged, like Emily, to dramatize a conviction of Montoni's badness by associating supernatural possibility with human evil. We need not believe in the actuality of the supernatural; as David Morris points out, "Unlike more subtle shades of feeling or perception, fear is an ancient biological endowment, rooted in human physiology and psychology, as responsive to false alarms or to elaborate fictions as to genuine threats of personal injury" (310). Tzvetan Todorov's notion of "hesitation" is directly relevant. "The fantastic is that hesitation experienced by a person who knows only the laws of nature, confronting an apparently supernatural event," Todorov writes (*The Fantastic* 25); he adds that "the fantastic . . . implies an integration of the reader into the world of the characters; that world is defined by the reader's own ambiguous perception of the events narrated. . . . *The reader's hesitation* is therefore the first condition of the fantastic" (31; Todorov's italics).

Radcliffe's version of the fantastic carries insistent moral implication, but morality appears to derive, in the first instance, from feeling. Struggling to interpret ambiguous appearances, the reader may share with Emily a double response to the human sublime connected with such appearances: moral rejection signaled by immediate fear or revulsion, mingled with compelling attraction. The uneasiness linked to supernatural effects helps the reader to identify with the protagonist. "Gothic writers seemed caught between proving the reality of their fantasy and making that fantasy powerful and real," George Haggerty writes. He links the latter endeavor with the novelists' "attempt to find a vocabulary for inexpressible private reality" ("Fact and Fancy" 381). The ostensibly supernatural for Radcliffe supplies an important part of that vocabulary.

The mingled fascination and terror of the supernatural transfer themselves to the male figure who for Emily epitomizes danger. Critics (most cogently, Cynthia Griffin Wolff) have commented on the attraction and repulsion Gothic heroines feel for powerful villains, and on the sexual components of this emotional pattern. Emily's responses to Montoni and his paternal authority, like Ellena's emotions toward Schedoni in *The Italian*, have an ambivalent aspect. When Count Morano penetrates to her room with the intent of carrying her off and marrying her, Emily announces that she prefers to "remain under the protection of Signor Montoni" (263). Morano, as bemused as the reader may be by this phraseology, given Montoni's brutality, concludes, with outrage, that Emily loves her captor. The narrator encourages us to draw the same conclusion.

Whether or not Emily thrills to Montoni despite her revulsion at his tyranny and injustice, the text urges its reader to identify with or admire Montoni's power while also endorsing Emily's compassionate impulses and her rejection of Montoni's values. The narrator, in other words, invokes in readers a complicated response equivalent to that sensibility overtly characteristic of the heroine: specifically, a symbolic response of daughters to fathers. The reader in effect duplicates a daughter's experience of the sublime.

Thomas Weiskel, in his brilliant study of the "romantic sublime," suggests the relevance of a Freudian model for the sublime experience. Oedipal competition, in his view, lurks in the background; he finds in the poetry of Collins, for instance, vestiges of "family romance" (106–35). Radcliffean Gothic embodies a specifically *fe-*

male view of the family romance: not the competition of fathers and sons, but the dangerous, ambivalent love of daughters for fathers. Mutual attraction governs the relations of fathers and daughters. The relationship, however, also emphasizes women's exclusion from male power.

Emily experiences in slightly disguised form the fear inspired by the paternal sublime. By embodying the object of fear in the shape of the unnatural, the gruesome, the supernatural, Radcliffe hints at the anger connected with such fear and the possibility of malignant paternal intention as well as the punishment lying in wait for daughters too profoundly attracted to dangerous, beloved fathers. Yet Emily's sensibility also facilitates expression of the impulse to closer attachment with the father (always potentially sexual, as is the danger fathers embody for daughters) by converting it into the more generalized, less dangerous, social impulses that we often label "sentimental" in their presentation.

Both in their sentimentalism and in their efforts to evoke terror, then, such Gothic novels as Radcliffe's invite from the reader reactions appropriate for persons defined as attractive (that is, secondary) rather than powerful when the aesthetic universe is dichotomized into the sublime and the beautiful. Sentimentalism and terror alike, therefore, have profound effects on the plots as well as the emotional atmosphere of Radcliffean Gothic. Radcliffe's plots can appropriately be described as "daughters' plots" not only because they accord due weight to the daughter's predictable system of values, her stress on attachment, given her exclusion from power. Even more important is the fact that, allowing attachment to triumph, such plots covertly demystify the father's force. The danger of the masculine sublime, embodied in supernatural appearances, is finally illusory, like the imagined danger of the wax corpse. Men's *social* power remains both real and dangerous: Schedoni can have Ellena confined in a convent, Montoni can carry Emily off to his mountain retreat and dictate her marriage. But *phallic* power, the mysterious potency of the dark male figures, derives largely from the imaginations of its potential victims and proves factitious. Although real dangers remain for Gothic heroines, in Radcliffe's plots the most dreaded menaces can be explained away, the ambiguity of what Todorov calls "the fantastic" resolved into the comprehensible and manageable.

So sensibility—that symbolically female value—can win out, obviating separation after abundantly symbolizing the hidden dangers of excessive filial attachment. Sons' plots declare independence: Tom Jones discovers his origins, then, supported by Sophia, in effect succeeds Squire Allworthy as master of Paradise Hall. Ellena, in *The Italian*, on the other hand, attaches herself not only to a husband but to a substitute father (Vivaldi's); Emily and Valancourt replicate the regime of Emily's dead father and in effect apotheosize him, thus insisting on an enduring family bond (672).

Daughters deal with fathers, these fictions suggest, by indirection and disguise. Radcliffe's plots, through their own indirections, affirm not only that everything turns out all right, but that more was all right all along than appeared to be the case, since phallic power is largely bestowed by the imaginations of others. A wicked father proves not in fact to be a father; a father who appears to have erred has only been misinterpreted; and daughters, as these plots are devised, can prove their fortitude and ingenuity by both resisting and incorporating the sublime, hint at their hidden aggression and their yet more hidden fear, and reaffirm their commitment to the life of the family.

Radcliffe discovers how at once to celebrate and to criticize both the force associated with the sublime and the vulnerable sensibility linked with the beautiful. Her plots explore the relationship of sublimity to beauty (in the wide Burkean sense of those terms) from the vulnerable under side. The double principle of action they dramatize, the notion that affiliative as well as aggressive feeling generates force, and the demystification of purely phallic potency provided a foundation for nineteenth-century English novels by men and women alike. Later novelists found other forms of symbolization than the supernatural to express the darker emotions of the vulnerable, and less ostentatious modes of sublimity than the commanding villains of Radcliffe's fictions. But Radcliffe remains their important precursor.

From Pamela to Evelina, female protagonists in fiction, as we have seen, engage crucially in the activity of interpretation by which they may hope to control stories if not plots. I suggested that Lennox's Arabella approaches heroism in her interpretative fervor, although she finally fails to impose the story she desires on her experience. Pamela and Clarissa achieve control of their stories, though only at the cost of marriage or death; one might claim for them a fuller attainme t of Arabella's kind of heroism. Sidney Bidulph and Evelina, on the other hand, heroines of a different sort, appear far from heroic in their attempts to understand their own stories. A depressed sense of possibility governs them. They interpret on the basis of fear rather than desire.

The same could be said, it might seem, about Radcliffe's heroines, who characteristically torment themselves by false "presentiments" of disaster. Yet interpretation as action assumes new importance in Radcliffe's Gothic. Indeed, it becomes in a sense the center of plot—a fact of special interest in relation to the theme of fathers and daughters. "Some deep struggle for control of the springs of being itself seems to be the issue [in Gothic novels]," Judith Wilt writes, "some struggle by the parent to unmake or reabsorb the child and thus to stop time, keep power, take back freedom and life where it has inadvertently been given away" (*Ghosts* 12). One sees such a struggle in the violence by which a father literally murders a daughter, in *The Castle of Otranto*, or in that which makes an apparent father approach such murder, in *The Italian*. The struggle for control of meaning recapitulates the same contest in subtler terms. If fear appears to form the stories Radcliffe's heroines tell themselves, it sometimes only screens and facilitates desire. And sometimes it uncovers the most sinister dynamics of father-daughter relationships. The Gothic fictions that reveal the ultimate failure of power in the phallus have a more somber aspect; they also show the compromises necessary for daughters in a world controlled by fathers.

Clarissa, I earlier suggested, takes advantage of the gap between ideal and actual. *The Italian* works in the space between nightmare and actuality. With much of the same narrative material as her predecessor, M. G. Lewis (*The Monk*), and her successor, Charles Maturin (*Melmoth the Wanderer*), Radcliffe, unlike them, never literalizes the dire possibilities she announces. Such possibilities remain constantly before the reader, however, because they inhabit the characters' imaginations. Ellena's uncertainties about not only what might but what *can* happen generate an atmosphere more disturbing if less horrifying than either Lewis or Maturin can achieve.

Ellena seems remarkably docile for a heroine. Orphaned, as she believes, she has been told of the identity and the deaths of both parents. No mystery about family or life circumstances plagues her; she possesses from the beginning a palpable sense of security.

Yet the narrative immediately announces its concern with questions of interpretation, and such questions will soon become crucial for Ellena. In the frame story, an Englishman shocked to discover that assassins haunt churches is given a manuscript to help him understand what he has seen. The manuscript contains the story of Ellena and Vivaldi; he must figure out its application. The story the Englishman reads (we learn no more about this character or his reactions) opens with the hero's first sight of the heroine:

The sweetness and fine expression of her voice attracted his attention to her figure, which had a distinguished air of delicacy and grace; but her face was concealed in her veil. So much indeed was he fascinated by her voice, that a most painful curiosity was excited as to her countenance, which he fancied must express all the sensibility of character that the modulation of her tones indicated. (5)

Vivaldi, trying to deduce a woman's nature from her voice, finds possibly moral qualities ("delicacy and grace") in the physical but remains curious about the further moral revelations he imagines in her face. The sequence epitomizes the novel's method. In more momentous matters as well, characters must interpret inadequate and ambiguous appearances. Inevitably, they interpret on the basis of their desire. Their fancies often prove less benign than Vivaldi's.

Ellena's security soon vanishes. Her aunt dies, leaving her alone in the world; Vivaldi's parents bitterly oppose the idea of his marrying her. Mysterious kidnappers abduct Ellena, depositing her in a mountaintop convent where she faces an enforced choice between nunhood and arbitrary marriage. Courageously, she rejects both, though warned of possibly horrible fates as a result. Vivaldi rescues her, but another group of kidnappers wrench her from the altar just before the couple can exchange marriage vows, taking her to the lonely spot where Schedoni shows up to murder her. Yet Ellena is miraculously spared; the nun who earlier befriended her turns out to be her mother; she comes from a better family than she thought, has more money, and proves an appropriate match for Vivaldi, whom, in the final pages, she of course marries.

This partial summary suggests the multiplicity and unpredictability of the novel's events. Beyond the fundamental problem of survival, the heroine confronts the central difficulty of making sense of her experience. She constructs a series of mini-narratives as new happenings refute each successive interpretation. Ellena's ways of "making sense" create fear, the counterpart and equivalent of desire. She imagines herself walled up alive in a convent's dungeon, or separated forever from her beloved Vivaldi, or too weak to travel a few yards. "As they crossed the garden towards the gate, Ellena's anxiety lest Vivaldi should have been compelled to leave it, encreased so much, that she had scarcely power to proceed. 'O if my strength should fail before I reach it!' she said softly to Olivia, 'or if I should reach it too late!'" (134). Olivia points out that the gate is very close, but a few minutes later, "breathless and exhausted, she was once more compelled to stop, and once more in the agony of terror exclaimed—'O, if my strength should fail before I reach it!—O, if I should drop even while it is within my view'" (134). Such extreme anxiety repeatedly defines Ellena's condition. Although her imaginings rarely correspond to actuality, they convey the truth of a woman's essential limitation and oppression.

Matters finally work out well for Ellena, but not as a result of her independent action. Her capacity for resistance—negative action—protects her, and she undergoes genuine terror without being overcome. But she has no power to make anything happen: only to keep things from happening, or to endure the pain of her experience. Her intense anxiety calls attention to the desperation of dependency. Feeling nightmare ever imminent, Ellena dramatizes the predicament of the powerless.

Ellena's special modes of interpretation, which focus attention on her desire, emerge with particular clarity in the brilliant sequence detailing her situation at Spalatro's lonely seaside house, to which she is abducted. Here interpretation becomes urgent. Ellena, driven by the fear that constitutes the obverse of her desire, decides that the villainous-looking Spalatro wishes to murder her. After she rejects the poisoned milk he provides (one of her more important refusals), he tells her she can walk on the seashore. Ellena watches an approaching storm and thinks "of her own forlorn and friendless situation," perhaps tracked "by the footsteps of the assassin." Her female fantasy of friendlessness, isolation, and persecution, which I considered earlier from another point of view, hardly exaggerates; she errs only in her understanding of the source of danger. Failing to see Spalatro, she congratulates herself on a possibility of escaping, then notes a monk walking along the shore.

"His, no doubt, are worthy musings!" said Ellena, as she observed him, with mingled hope and surprise. "I may address myself, without fear, to one of his order. It is probably as much his wish, as it is his duty, to succour the unfortunate. Who could have hoped to find on this sequestered shore so sacred a protector!" (220)

This unique instance of Ellena's hoping when she should fear (still telling the wrong story) emphasizes the degree to which Radcliffe's novel, although it explains away supernatural manifestations, yet deals in the seriously disturbing. Although Ellena will not be murdered, her assumptions and her wishes about the sources of security will be utterly violated. A monk, a "father," functions as symbolic parent; like a literal father, he should help the unfortunate. Ellena trusts in the parental role, *desires* to trust it. But this powerful father seeks her destruction, allied with Vivaldi's comparably powerful mother, who wishes at all costs to prevent her son's marriage. Ellena's experience of parental betrayal exceeds even Clarissa's.

The monk—Schedoni, whom the girl does not know—passes and repasses Ellena, then asks her identity. "I am an unhappy orphan," she replies, her formulation reiterating her concern about parents (221). Schedoni becomes sufficiently explicit about his enmity to make Ellena faint, but he then foregoes his opportunity to lay her unconscious in the surf and thus eliminate her. But of course Ellena's confrontation with a dangerous father continues, in a scene also considered earlier. Imprisoned once more, left "again to solitude and terror" (224), she awakens to a loud call from Schedoni, who has just dropped the dagger with which he planned to murder her. "Be merciful, O father! be merciful!" she pleads. Schedoni reiterates, "Father!" He demands the identity of the face depicted in the miniature Ellena wears. "This was my father," she finally responds, "pressing it to her lips" (235). "Unhappy child!" Schedoni says at last, "—behold your more unhappy father!" (236). Immediately Ellena's voice softens "into tenderness." In a ludicrous but significant escape into the most conventional of female roles, she asks "with the most soothing accents of compassion, and looks of anxious gentleness, what made him so unhappy, and tried to assuage his sufferings" (237). The problem of interpretation baffles her. She inquires why Schedoni has entered her room at midnight and supplies her own explanation: "Did you come to warn me of danger?" (238). Hastily accepting this hypothesis, Schedoni departs.

The narrator, attributing Ellena's subsequent narrative interpretations to "the ingenuity of hope," calls attention to an important principle of her story making: "The suspicions, however, which she had formerly admitted, respecting his designs, were now impatiently rejected, for she was less anxious to discover truth, than to release herself from horrible suppositions" (242). Ellena cannot face an actuality worse than her worst imaginings. As Schedoni realizes that he too has made up a self-gratifying story, about Ellena's inadequacy as a mate for Vivaldi and about the need to get her out of the way, and that he has thus defeated his own best interests, Ellena tries desperately to construct a new narrative that will allow her to love her father. She could sustain no sense of cosmic order if the universe contained a parent who wished to kill his child. For Ellena and for the reader, Schedoni's character threatens fundamental assumptions of coherence.

Ellena's devoutness, through which she reiterates faith in order, consists in sentiment, registered often in her response to sublime landscapes. A strange instance occurs during her captivity, when she gazes out the window at the mountains.

> Here, . . . looking, as it were, beyond the awful veil which obscures the features of the Deity, and conceals Him from the eyes of his creatures, dwelling as with a present God in the midst of his sublime works; with a mind thus elevated, how insignificant would appear to her the transactions and the sufferings of this world! How poor the boasted power of man, when the fall of a single cliff from these mountains would with ease destroy thousands of his race assembled on the plains below! How would it avail them, that they were accoutred for battle, armed with all the instruments of destruction that human invention ever fashioned? Thus man, the giant who now held her in captivity, would shrink to the diminutiveness of a fairy; and she would experience, that his utmost force was unable to enchain her soul, or compel her to fear him, while he was destitute of virtue. (90–91)

The worship of God through the mountains somehow leads to the wishful identification of virtue with power. More curious is the location of Ellena's enemy as "man"—at first apparently generic man, but more clearly masculine as the passage continues. The specific location of "man" on the battlefield, armed for destruction, suggests maleness; and the final image of man as a giant, shrinking to a fairy, makes gender more specific. In fact a woman, the abbess, holds Ellena in captivity, and the only clearly identified enemy so far is Vivaldi's mother. Yet the battle of the sexes informs this novel as it does *Clarissa*—and as in *Clarissa*, it is a battle of the opposed values clearly identified by Burke.

Ellena's interpretation of landscape in this instance exemplifies what is at issue in all her interpretations. Her desire to embody "virtue"—meaning especially sympathy, compassion, concern— and to find support for her "feminine" convictions motivates her. I have already argued that such "feminine" ideas of virtue control Radcliffe's plots. Ellena's reaction to what she sees from her window suggests her awareness that these ideas necessarily exist in tension with alternative systems. The sheer energy of her alogical progress from pieties about the Maker and His works to fantasies about virtue's unmanning of power declares hidden anger. It also exemplifies the symbolic as well as literal force of interpretative acts: the force of embodied feeling. Ellena's vision of warrior turning to fairy betrays her awareness that she is engaged in struggle. The plot of Radcliffe's novel turns on the same struggle.

Although *The Mysteries of Udolpho* does not announce interpretation as its subject so conspicuously as *The Italian* does, it works out yet more intricate relations between interpretation and plot. In a thoughtful examination of the interplay between "reason" and "sensibility" in Radcliffe's novels, Gary Kelly has argued that the novelist's fictional structures embody a "typology of emotional states . . . associative in nature," and thus lack "any principle of organization based on moral development or progress."

> All aspects of the novel's formal technique are motivated by the need to create occasions of sensibility or perplexity, but even the description of different kinds of sensibility can be seen as motivated by the need to high-light the perplexities. Here already is the principle of alternation in the overall temporal pattern of the novels, and it is in fact the only strong organizing principle present in any of Radcliffe's fictions. The alternation need not, as in the cruder kinds of Gothic, be between diametrical oppo-sites, but only between differences, and so throughout the novel the hero-ine merely goes through a variety of emotional states in more or less rapid succession. (Kelly, "A Constant Vicissitude" 55)

Although Kelly considers that Radcliffe's plots lack progressive form, he sees them as inculcating consistent doctrine: reason must control sensibility to create happiness.

Such is the conviction of St. Aubert, father of the heroine in *The Mysteries of Udolpho*. Emily repeatedly proclaims his rightness; she believes herself to have learned, by arduous experience, exactly what Kelly believes her to have learned. But *Udolpho* embodies other kinds of meaning as well: specifically *female* meanings that qualify the official doctrine. Emily faces repeated challenges to interpret ambiguous appearances. The sequence of her inter-pretations provides the "organizing principle" Kelly misses in an assembly of happenings that, as Kelly rightly observes, seems hap-hazard and repetitive. But external happenings do not altogether define reality in a novel centered on the interplay between external and internal.

St. Aubert himself early announces the importance of this rela-tionship. "Store [the mind] with ideas," he advises, "teach it the pleasure of thinking; and the temptations of the world without, will be counteracted by the gratifications derived from the world within" (6). Much later in the novel, when Emily is imprisoned at Udolpho, she awakens to thoughts of the various disasters that threaten her, all of which she feels herself helpless to combat. "She rose, and, to relieve her mind from the busy ideas, that tormented it, compelled herself to notice external objects" (241). "Ideas," it seems, may prove tormenting rather than gratifying; "the world without" offers valuable distraction as well as dangerous tempta-tion. Only by paying close attention to actualities of the external world can Emily hope to check her fantasies; conversely, only the interpretative force of imagination enables her to make sense of what she sees.

Formulated in general terms, these notions sound commonplace. But the struggle to find a plausible balance between the claims of inside and outside makes arduous demands on a heroine who, because of her age and her gender, possesses importance in the world only as an object of male love, a pawn for male manipulation. She knows from the beginning the demands of social propriety; she always behaves well. She must learn how properly to interpret her own feelings and how to turn them to her own ends in a social context that declares acceptable only a limited emotional range.

In the course of her career Emily writes a good deal of bad verse. A glance at the developing concerns of this verse may suggest the change in emotional atmosphere that helps to validate the young woman's growth. Indeed, the sequence of verse sketches the structure of the novel's plot, inasmuch as that plot concerns Emily's progress. The girl's earliest poetic effusions, written under the influence of anxiety about her parents' health, display understandable obsession with sickness and grief. Later, she turns to narrative. On her way to Italy with Montoni and her aunt, she composes a sonnet about a young man traveling, like her, in the Alps. Its final couplet reads,

> Desperate, at length the tottering plank he tries,
> His weak steps slide, he shrieks, he sinks—he dies!
>
> (165)

This transparent metaphor for her own psychological inadequacy to face the realities of her current situation economically conveys her depressed interpretation of possibilities. Later, leaving Venice by boat, she composes a more elaborate versified story of attempted murder narrowly averted: objectification of her fears and hopes, hope, by this time, only to avoid disaster. Escorted, at Montoni's behest, from Udolpho by a man whom she discovers to be an assassin, she writes a narrative poem in which a pilgrim, stabbed by a concealed "ruffian," breathes a prayer for his murderer as he dies (415). The poem vividly delineates the temptation to virtuous passivity, the temptation of victimization so prevalent among eighteenth-century fictional females. The goodness of a victim may declare moral superiority to active villains, but it does not rescue him or her from destruction. Emily might languish for years at

Udolpho. Yielding to Montoni does not imply salvation; only by resisting can Emily hope to achieve equanimity.

The last of Emily's narrative poems, allegedly composed on board the ship carrying her back to France and to safety, is her most self-indulgent. Compelled and titillated by images of hopeless, death-implying love, she resembles Sterne's Yorick and Mackenzie's Harley in her insistent pathos. Her highly derivative verses tell of a young sailor parted from his bride, promising her that they will meet again, perishing in a storm as he faintly proclaims, "Farewel, my love!—we ne'er shall meet again!" The bride, predictably, dies too.

> And oft, at midnight, airy strains are heard
> Around the grove, where Ellen's form is laid;
> Nor is the dirge by village-maidens fear'd,
> For lovers' spirits guard the holy shade!
> (464)

The Collins-like excursion into hints of the benign supernatural implies an alternative to the dark supernatural intimations associated with Montoni and with Udolpho, but this poem too suggests that Emily is heading down the path of sensibility, she and the novelist who has created Emily's verse both content to indulge the fine feelings associated with victimization, separating themselves from the machinations of power.

After returning to France, the young woman turns her talents to lyric. Her lyrics evince no more remarkable literary gifts than do her narrative poems, but a new theme at least dimly informs them. If they speak obsessively of melancholy, they also return consistently to the subject of force. The last two in this series of poems—the final one occurring only six pages before the novel's end—epitomize the emotional ambivalence characteristic of the lyrics. Having just heard that mysterious, troubled Sister Agnes lies at death's door, Emily rests on a cliff looking at the water and composes an "address" called "To the Winds." Evoking the power of the tempest, the first sixteen lines stress the sublime and terrifying aspect of the wind. The final nine lines explicitly reject the terrible:

> Oh! then I deprecate your awful reign!
> The loud lament yet bear not on your breath!
> Bear not the crash of bark far on the main,
> Bear not the cry of men, who cry in vain,
> The crew's dread chorus sinking into death!
> Oh! give not these, ye pow'rs! I ask alone,

As rapt I climb these dark romantic steeps,
The elemental war, the billow's moan;
I ask the still, sweet tear, that listening Fancy weeps!
(641)

The "still, sweet tear" relates oddly to the "elemental war" requested in the line immediately preceding. Emily declares herself not to want the winds' destructiveness, to desire only their emotional stimulation. But her sweet tears apparently flow, sympathetically, at the violence of "elemental war." She would preserve the decorum of sensibility, incorporating, somehow, the primitive energies of nature. Similarly, her last lyric addresses itself "To Melancholy," for several stanzas producing Miltonic sentiments in verse again modeled on Collins. In the next to last stanza, she expresses her desire to be guided to banks laved by Neptune "With measur'd surges, loud and deep," and to hear how "wild the winds of autumn sweep." There she would

pause at midnight's spectred hour,
And list the long-resounding gale;
And catch the fleeting moon-light's pow'r,
O'er foaming seas and distant sail.
(666)

Once more, explicit desire for the wild, noisy, and powerful merges with a wish for gentler forms of self-indulgence.

The "plot" sketched by Emily's series of poems, of movement from passive acceptance of victimization to ambivalent identification with images of force, corresponds to the confused plot of the larger narrative, full of odd duplications and redundancies. At the novel's beginning, Emily exists under the control of a benevolent but autocratic father, concerned to shape her character. Orphaned, she moves into Montoni's sphere of influence. In due time, at an apparently arbitrary moment in the plot, she escapes from Udolpho to France, where she accepts the domination of a new father figure, the Count De Villefort, whose daughter Blanche becomes her close friend. Her true father approved her love for Valancourt, which motivates much of her resistance to Montoni, but the Count, misinformed about the young man's Parisian adventures, urges the cause of another suitor and warns Emily against indulging her love. Convinced that virtue demands her resistance to Valancourt, she sends him away. Once she has had time to hear the warnings against passion delivered by dying Sister Agnes, however, the Count learns of his mistake, invites Valancourt's return, and the two young people can marry at last.

An unsympathetic reading of this sequence might observe Emily's extraordinary docility to moral guidance and Radcliffe's apparent concern to multiply suspense for its own sake. In no obvious sense does character control plot. But if one starts with the notion of plot as a dynamic of desire and seeks the sense in which Emily's desire may be said to drive the plot, matters become rather more interesting. The force of the heroine's *negative* desire—her wish to escape, avoid, reject—plays an important part in shaping the plot. Her *positive* desire, both sexual and nonsexual, remains largely obscure to her, and possibly to the reader as well. But it too helps to dictate the direction of plot.

Gary Kelly economically summarizes an interpretation of plot accepted by many commentators.

> The plots . . . are as conventional as the themes and characters, and are all based on the standard romantic plot: cavalier meets damsel, they fall in love, they are separated by circumstances or the machinations of their foes, they overcome or survive separate strings of difficulties, are reunited, and marry. ("A Constant Vicissitude" 53)

At one level, this description applies accurately to *Udolpho* and to Radcliffe's other fictions. Yet the possibility of describing the same plot in different terms calls attention to the profound ambiguity of the very notion of plot. A "damsel" lives happily with parents deeply concerned for her moral education. When her mother dies, she travels with her father for the sake of his health. On their trip, they meet a young man, a "cavalier" whom father and daughter both find attractive. Father dies, daughter returns sadly to her home, where the young man finds her and declares his love, to be rebuked by the aunt who has now taken charge of the girl. And so on: the Radcliffean plot can be summarized as a drama of literal and symbolic parents and children.

"The feeling which the new form, the Gothic romance, deals with constantly," Margaret Anne Doody writes,

> —feelings which sharply set it off from the older sort of romance—are inner rage and unspecified (and unspecifiable) guilt. These passions are essentially related to all sorts of other emotions—fear, anxiety, loneliness—which are unstable, powerful, and unpleasantly associated with helplessness and with some kind of sense of inferiority. . . . Inner rage and overwhelming guilt are, in eighteenth-century circumstances, very feminine emotions—women have to suppress rage because they cannot control

things; women feel guilty because they continually fail to live up to expectations. ("Deserts, Ruins" 553–4)

Guilt and rage contribute to what I have called Emily's negative desire: her intense wish to escape the supervision of fathers—conflicting and often merging with her wish to avoid the burden of independent moral responsibility.

The pattern manifests itself distinctly in the novel's final sequences. Valancourt's misleading guilty hints about his own corruption corroborate the Count's impression of his culpability, so Emily cannot avoid repudiating him. They meet accidentally at the home of an old servant to whom Valancourt has given financial help. The old woman cannot fathom Emily's repudiation of her lover. "Dear! dear!" she says, "to see how gentlefolks can afford to throw away their happiness! Now, if you were poor people, there would be none of this" (626). She reiterates the point several times, calling attention to the moral luxury of Emily's scruples—essentially aristocratic appurtenances, and, as it will turn out, altogether mistaken.

But of course Emily's scruples are not quite her own. The Count has virtually ordered her to reject Valancourt; she behaves as she has been trained to do, submissive to the authority of an older, wiser man. Before accepting his version of reality, she considers the possibility that he may err in his view of Valancourt. Perhaps someone has misrepresented her lover to the Count; perhaps the Count himself is "influenced by some selfish motive, to break her connection with Valancourt" (509). But the hypothesis cannot persuade her; the Count has too good a character to allow such behavior. Nor can Valancourt have been misrepresented, since the Count has "said, that he spoke chiefly from his own observation, and from his son's experience. She must part from Valancourt, therefore, for ever" (509).

Emily allows her belief in the Count's good character to sway her; she does not trust her earlier conviction of Valancourt's rectitude. She accepts the Count's assertion that he possesses trustworthy evidence from his own observation and his son's experience. In both instances, it develops, she is mistaken. Her own feelings would have guided her better than the Count's assertions. Both he and his son have misinterpreted appearances. Until she yields to male authority, Emily herself interprets better than they do.

In her lurid deathbed admonitions, Sister Agnes claims to see in Emily a hidden flaw. "You have passions in your heart,—scorpions; they sleep now—beware how you awaken them!—they will sting you, even unto death!" (574). Employing less decorous terms than his, Agnes here echoes the concerns of Emily's dead father, who never refers to anything so unladylike as passion but who worries a great deal about his daughter's emotional life, imagined as a potential source of disaster. Feeling, he believes, cannot dependably guide a young woman. He urges her to cultivate reason and discipline. Sister Agnes, soon unmasked as Laurentini di Udolpho, embodies the same warning. Her madness and misery result, the text asserts, from passional indulgence. She too should have exercised moral and rational control.

The announced doctrine of *Udolpho* never varies. Yet the plot implies a view rather different from that of the explicit ethical assertions—or, at any rate, it allows dramatically different interpretations. In the story of Laurentini, the possibility of subversive meaning inheres in omissions of commentary. A French aristocrat, Laurentini's "passionate adorer" (656), makes her his mistress instead of his wife because of her sexual looseness. After he marries a compatriot, Laurentini follows him from Italy to France. Thereupon "all the energy, with which he had first loved [her] returned, for his passion had been resisted by prudence, rather than overcome by indifference" (657). Incited by Laurentini, the Marquis murders his wife: "she fell a victim to the jealousy and subtlety of Laurentini and to the guilty weakness of her husband" (658). Both conspirators die remorseful, but only Laurentini's protracted and agonizing years of guilt and intermittent madness are extensively narrated.

Jealousy and subtlety sound worse than guilty weakness. The account of Laurentini, offered in the narrator's voice, emphasizes the culpability of the woman and of the parents who failed to teach her to control her passions; it dwells hardly at all on the man's guilt. Yet the Marquis's passion, not Laurentini's, initiates the connection between them; he administers the poison that kills his wife. A narrative of shared male and female moral failure has been converted into a fable of wicked womanhood.

Similar suppressions mark Emily's story. Her emotions, against which her father warned her from the beginning, in fact provide reliable indices of her actual situation. Like Vivaldi in *The Italian*, she suffers from what Schedoni calls "susceptibility": willingness (although she struggles against it) to accept supernatural explanations and apparent eagerness in ambiguous situations to believe the worst. Her erroneous interpretations cause her suffering. Thus she allows appearances to convince her, mistakenly, of her aunt's death. She believes during most of her stay at Udolpho that a decaying corpse occupies a room down the hall from her. She expects to be murdered by the men Montoni has ordered to escort her from the castle. Consistently wrong about her ways of accounting for facts, she yet penetrates to more profound truths. Her apprehension of Montoni as a destroyer of women, like her perception of something wrong in the history of the Marquis who effectively adopts her, acknowledges emotional actuality. Often she fails to find appropriate correlatives for her anxiety, yet always the anxiety has sufficient cause.

The text treats the female difficulty in discovering emotional correlatives as though it were equivalent to having no adequate cause for feeling—although it also involves the reader in intensities of anxiety comparable to the heroine's. The text warns against emotional self-indulgence and encourages it. And it demonstrates, without ever asserting, the rightness of the emotional "daughter" in opposition to the wrongness of the rational "father." Emily's heart leads her to know Valancourt's integrity, but she yields to the assertedly superior knowledge of an older man. The Marquis's character may, as Emily believes, be too upright to allow him to lie to her, but it does not prevent his being wrong. Despite its elaborate assertions of the need to dominate feeling by reason, *The Mysteries of Udolpho* dramatizes the power of feeling to guide people accurately. It also dramatizes another kind of power: that of authoritative men to enforce their will and their standards on women.

I pointed out earlier that Radcliffe's novels debunk men's phallic but not their social power. These novels in fact insist on the inescapability of social arrangements that grant dominion to men. They do not insist that men prove wrong—make erroneous judgments and interpretations—in exercising that dominion, but they demonstrate precisely this. Not only do Radcliffe's Gothic fantasies assert the "female" values of sensitivity, reconciliation, family; they also show, in contradiction to their announced doctrine, that female assumptions, feminine sensibility, may provide more accurate guidance than does rigorous rationality.

7

ENERGIES OF MIND:
NOVELS OF THE 1790s

'The last decade of the eighteenth century," J. M. S. Tompkins writes,

saw an increase of intellectual energy in the novel. This energy, though pouring itself into literary form, was extra-literary in origin. It did not express itself in depth of characterization or significance of form, but, taking its source from the ethical, social and political views of the authors, streamed through the novel as through a well-worn channel of access to the public. (296)

Tompkins cites Ann Radcliffe as one of the novelists who "felt the attraction of great energy of character" (285) but notes Radcliffe's political conservatism, describing her as "staunchly clinging to old ideals in the turbulent flood of new ones" (250).

The relation between an author's "ethical, social and political views" and his or her literary practice becomes a vexed matter in the 1790s. Marilyn Butler (*Jane Austen . . .*) and Gary Kelly (*English Jacobin Novel*) have brilliantly specified characteristics of "Jacobin" and "anti-Jacobin" novels and have located late-century novelists on a political spectrum. Their work calls attention to historical specificities concealed within fictions making no overt claim to historical relevance. But, as Tompkins's observations hint, even politically conservative writers might embody radical principles in their novels. A recent essay by Kelly ("Jane Austen . . . ") emphasizes links between Jacobin and anti-Jacobin novelists:

It would be wrong to say that the Anti-Jacobin novel was completely at odds, either thematically or compositionally, with the fictional social criticism of the English Jacobins. They both tend to venerate the "domestic affections" and stoic virtues, though for different reasons. They both tend to mount consistent satire on social conventions and social institutions of certain kinds, and on "Society" or fashionable social life in particular. In brief, they both show a tendency to attack aristocratic cultural and social hegemony by attacking the (to them decadent) institutions of aristocratic court culture. (291)

To investigate operations in the late-century English novel of the principle of energy to which Tompkins calls attention reveals important emotional issues implicit in the political attitudes prevailing in fiction. Butler points out the high emphasis on rationality in "progressive" fiction and the problematic value now attached to feeling.

> In general the most marked trend in the English popular novel of the 1790s . . . is its resolute rationality, its suspicion of the uncontrollable workings of the unconscious mind. . . . Conservative critics of the novel, and conservative novelists too, see that the true threat to orthodoxy lies in the moral relativism implicit in the sentimental movement. It is therefore cunning of them, though inaccurate, to ascribe to the "jacobins" of the 1790s subjectivity, emotionalism, indulgence towards human weakness, and belief in sexual freedom, all of which the jacobins explicitly renounce. For the time being the English progressive novelist speaks resolutely to the Reason. (*Jane Austen* 33)

If the Jacobins explicitly renounce subjectivity and emotionalism, they yet imply considerable interest in the operations and the performative force of feelings conscious and unconscious. The recurrent notion of "energy of mind" will help to focus the complex implications of that interest. It will also help me to explore ideas about the kinds of meaning plot embodies—plot considered, as usual, not in its technical sense, but more generally as the large structural principle of narrative that organizes representations of sequence and causality. The novels that interest me often contain *characters* who plot—*bad* characters. Plotting makes things happen within the narrative, but it does not alone determine outcome. More effective, ultimately, is that quality referred to as "energy of mind." Its role in these texts suggests new attitudes toward story and plot, a new view of gender relations, and a new understanding of the human psyche.

Let me start with Thomas Holcroft, in the twentieth century an almost completely neglected author. ("I know of no reader who has admitted enthusiasm over the novels of Thomas Holcroft," Harrison Steeves writes [292].) In 1792 Holcroft—47 years old, previously employed as shoemaker, strolling player, secretary—published a seven-volume novel called *Anna St. Ives*. Its plot at the outset would have sounded familiar to its first readers. Anna, a young woman of aristocratic family, loves, without quite knowing it, Frank Henley, son of her father's steward, who also loves her. Her father, however, wishes her to marry a man of high birth,

Coke Clifton, brother to her best friend, handsome, intelligent, and rich. Believing in her obligations to her family, Anna agrees to this match, although she has become aware by the end of the first volume of Frank's virtues and of her feeling for him.

Appropriate twentieth-century terms for discussing this fictional situation come readily to mind. We might speak of female masochism or of female oppression; or allude to eighteenth-century conventions for novelistic plots; or examine changing familial arrangements of the late century and comment on the persistence of old family patterns in fiction. Holcroft, however, conscious of such issues himself, forestalls us. His plot soon assumes an unexpected shape.

Before Anna agrees to marry Clifton, Frank proposes to her, claiming her on the basis of their shared social commitments and convictions. She refuses him, but acknowledges that she loves him, she kisses him (this in an eighteenth-century novel!), and—demands his help in elevating Clifton's character. Clifton, she explains, has great human potential. Properly educated, he might do immense good. Frank will fulfill a social responsibility by helping to turn his rival's energies toward virtuous ends.

This strange alliance does not end the novel's unexpected twists. Ever more intimate with Frank as they pursue their common purpose, Anna tells her fiancé about the relationship, including the proposal, the confession of love, the kiss, and the shared intent of reforming Clifton himself. Pretending to accept her high-minded plan but actually consumed with rage, Clifton decides to seduce her by invoking her own progressive beliefs and then to abandon her: he has his own eighteenth-century novelistic plot in mind. She indignantly rejects him and turns to his rival. Clifton, sounding more and more like Lovelace, plans to imprison and rape her. He manages to confine her and Frank in separate strongholds, but both, drawing on what Anna calls their "energy of mind" (423), escape. (Anna, in the process, climbs over a high wall, commenting that people who think only men can climb walls are wrong.) Clifton, though seriously wounded during his victims' escape, survives to be absorbed into the common purpose and intimate association of Anna, Frank, and his sister Louisa.

Anna St. Ives, extraordinary in many respects, resembles other novels from the 1790s in establishing well-worn fictional predicaments only to resolve them in unexpected ways. Godwin's *Caleb Williams* (1794), for instance, begins with the poor orphan boy helped by a benevolent rich man and develops into a bizarre saga of guilt and retribution. Wollstonecraft's clumsy, poignant fragment, *The Wrongs of Woman* (1798), tries to imagine from the familiar starting point of victimization fresh possibilities of female character. And there are Radcliffe's Gothic romances, with their heavy reliance on the fantastic; and Frances Burney's *Camilla* (1796), which directs attention to the plight of an ugly woman. Such superficially dissimilar works in their experimentation with plot reveal common late-century concerns. Whether their authors hold "conservative" or "radical" political commitments, whether or not, like Radcliffe and Burney, they concern themselves explicitly with their characters' inner lives, they demonstrate a shared preoccupation with how psychic force shapes happening in the external world. Frank Kermode's observation that fictions, unlike myths, serve as "agents of change" (39) seems apropos here. Certain late-eighteenth-century novels, defining new relations between force and feeling, between psychic reality and worldly effectiveness, thus announce change and embody ways that fiction can become an agent of change in modes of understanding the world. The effort to specify these new relations is my present enterprise.

All plots in their nature raise questions about agency and causality: what, or who, makes things happen? Anna St. Ives and her lover Frank share faith in the powerful agency of "energy of mind." Anna, who identifies this energy explicitly with courage, suggests that her extensive possession of it ("I have infinitely the most") entails her necessary triumph over Clifton's base intentions (423); Frank proclaims it more useful than pugilistic training for winning a fist fight (386). Both defeat fierce antagonists. Yet their mental energy accounts for relatively few of the novel's happenings. In this fiction as in Godwin's, Wollstonecraft's, and Radcliffe's, "bad" characters—those opposed to the interests the text appears to support—generate events and stories by *plotting*.

The function of plotting within these novels parallels the attitudes the novels imply toward their own construction. The most "literary" of the schemers is Godwin's Falkland. In his youth, Falkland has killed a man and allowed two others to be hanged for his crime. Yet he maintains a well-earned reputation for wisdom and benevolence, unable to tolerate others' bad opinion. When he realizes that his secretary Caleb has penetrated his secret, he effectively rewrites the story of the younger man's life, constructing a coherent and plausible narrative of Caleb's treachery and thievery. In the nightmarish course of Godwin's novel, Caleb can never regain control of his own life story. As Jacqueline Miller puts it, "Falkland has been the 'author' of Caleb's life, and Caleb's own efforts to be the author of his own history and identity have been impotent"

(368). Like *Clarissa*, Godwin's fiction develops into a competition of stories, Falkland and Caleb struggling for narrative dominance. Finally Caleb wins assent for his "true" story of Falkland's crime, shedding the "false" narrative of himself as criminal. Falkland observes that "the artless and manly story [Caleb has] told, has carried conviction to every hearer" (324). But Caleb, characterizing himself as an "atrocious, execrable wretch," now begins to "endure the penalty of [his] crime" (325): the crime of exposure. He loses interest in his own story and in his selfhood: "I have now no character that I wish to vindicate" (326). (Jacqueline Miller comments on this point: 379.) "Artless and manly," he has defeated a diabolical plotter, only to experience fully the power of the plot.

The force of Falkland's plot for self-preservation derives from that of the fictional plot he manufactures: the force, it proves, of truth. He declares Caleb a criminal; Caleb finally acknowledges himself exactly that. (The relation between fiction and truth is another matter at issue in these novels. Often, it seems, fiction *creates* truth.) Caleb knows himself finally as thief (of Falkland's reputation) and murderer (Falkland dies three days after his accusation). Defeat of the plotter does not entail defeat of the plot. By *plot*, in this instance, I mean (to draw on the *O.E.D.*), "A plan or project, secretly contrived by one or more persons, to accomplish some wicked, criminal, or illegal purpose." In the case of Falkland, this meaning almost merges with the literary sense: "the plan or scheme of any literary creation." The same linkage recurs insistently in other works.

The principal plotter in *The Wrongs of Woman*, Maria's husband George Venables, also rewrites his victim's life story. In Maria's narrative of her life, she remains at the mercy of men, helped by a good uncle, victimized by a bad husband. Venables invents stories—persuasive interpretations—in which she possesses far more power. The plausible tale he tells her landlady has her escaping from a loving spouse; the plausible tale he constructs for the divorce court reports her plotting to commit adultery; his plausible tale of her madness assigns her the force of the irrational. By proclaiming her dangerous power, he destroys any power she might have. He confines her in a madhouse. Maria, helpless, cannot imagine "that, in all the fermentation of civilized depravity, a similar plot could have entered a human mind" (76); she also calls it an "infernal plot" (182). Her imprisonment, like her later defeat in the law court, is entailed by the rigorous logic of the literary plot that Venables constructs. His plot implies an inescapable narrative.

Radcliffe's fiction evokes an oppressive world that refuses wo-

men in particular the opportunity to construct their own life stories. (Montoni, for instance, in *The Mysteries of Udolpho*, mocks
Emily's pretensions of being a "heroine": that is, imagining herself
at the center of the action.) Female protagonists suffer from the
operations of plotters who tell stories to aggrandize themselves as
well as to control others. Control of story implies control of people
and of events. Holcroft makes the same point negatively through
an ineffective plotter. Plotting from frustration rather than, like
Radcliffe's villains, from ambition, Clifton cannot manage even
briefly to impose on Anna and Frank a fictional model in which he
dominates. Both refuse to play out their opponent's plots.

Will coincides with desire in the psyches of the fictional plotters
I have mentioned, and transparent motives drive them. The question of motive becomes more complicated when asked of the novelistic plots themselves. To what ends do Radcliffe and Holcroft
and the rest tell their stories? What is the purpose, the reason, for
their plots? Why do plotters play sinister roles in their narratives;
what is the relevance of other possible relationships to story—the
kind embodied, for instance, in most of the female characters?

Females, in these fictions, cannot plot. Anna St. Ives, the most
powerful and effective of the fictional women, writes to her confidante,

How happy should I be were your brother and Frank Henley to conceive
an immediate partiality for each other! How much too would it promote
the project I wish to execute! I have been taxing my invention to form
some little plot for this purpose, but I find it barren. (69)

Heroines substitute dreams for plots. If they can define for themselves "something to be carried out or accomplished" (I quote once
more from the *O.E.D.* on *plot*), they appear more or less unable "to
plan, contrive, or devise" the means of achieving their goal. Yet
most of them reach that goal nonetheless.

Instead of plotting—trying to arrange other people's lives as
well as their own to fit into a predetermined story—female characters in these books more passively fantasize. Radcliffe's heroines,
confined in an author's Gothic imaginings, can exercise little control, but this fact only encourages them to construct coherent, usually unhappy, almost always inaccurate, narratives of the future.
Emily, in *Udolpho*, Ellena, in *The Italian*, and Adeline, in *The Romance of the Forest*, all feel frequent false "presentiments." Their
projections into the future, and those of other characters, directly
or indirectly express desire. Emily and Adeline, like Wollstonecraft's Maria, imagine only stories of love, or of love's frustration.

Anna St. Ives, with larger visions, dreams of a society without inequities of rank, wealth, or gender, in which men and women alike would communicate with perfect truth and openness. It will not soon flourish, she knows, on a national scale, but she tells herself (and Frank, Clifton, and Louisa) a story about a microcosmic version of it, composed of three or four persons. The problem of desire, however, is more complicated than these summaries suggest. The protagonists of these novels need to clarify their own desire—to discover and acknowledge it. Given their intricate minglings of wish and fear, young female characters in particular often cannot see the full shape of their desire. Anna, for instance, defines her wishes in terms of social vision; she learns to accept the urgency of her love as well. Radcliffe's heroines, on the other hand, who claim to desire union with their lovers, discover their need for a wider community than that of sexual love.

The presence of numerous belatedly revealed stories in these novels substantiates desire's ambiguities. Holcroft, like his characters vividly committed to the present, does not rely on newly uncovered stories as developed parts of his plot. On the other hand, disclosure of a story from the past—a story defining Falkland's dangerous desire—generates the plot of *Caleb Williams*. In *The Wrongs of Woman*, several women's tales of "the oppressed state of women" (120) reiterate the difficulties of female desire and establish the ground of Wollstonecraft's narrative. Radcliffe's intricate fictions, full of secrets, rely heavily on mini-stories of indulged desire that gradually reveal what a heroine needs to know. Like Wollstonecraft's embedded tales, these little stories have cumulative effect. In *The Romance of the Forest*, Adeline first appears in a metaphorically denuded state, with hardly any story of her own beyond that of confinement in a nunnery, and with no apparent relatives or friends. But she accretes stories and people, finding narrative everywhere, learning narrative's power and learning terrors and dangers of thoughtless self-gratification. Even when the stories seem to have no connection to Adeline, they bear on her complex history and situation. *The Mysteries of Udolpho* makes less ostentatious use of its discovered narratives, but only after its heroine learns the story of the dying nun who has allowed sensibility to become passion, only when she hears a revised story of her lover's behavior in Paris, can she find happiness.

These novelistic plots construct themselves, then, with three components: Plotters within the text whose will straightforwardly serves their desire and brings about many happenings; dependent characters unable to plot—thus fully to acknowledge will and desire—but often possessed of conspicuous mental energy to block plots; and embedded stories, which, by uncovering the past, reveal to the characters the meaning of their desires. The workings of narrative conflicts in these terms help to convey new attitudes toward narrative.

Pondering the motives of plot in these late-century novels calls attention to their difference from their predecessors. *Tom Jones*, for instance, also employs a structure opposing a villainous plotter—Blifil—to a less coherent innocent, Tom himself. Blifil wants to consolidate his own position and weaken Tom's. Tom wants to enjoy himself, to help others, to win Sophia, but with relatively little articulated consciousness of his own purposes. One can hardly doubt *Fielding's* purposes, though. Everything in his "perfect" plot contributes to a demonstration that, under the rule of Providence and of comic novelists, the good man will acquire the social and personal power that validates his character. Tom wants Sophia and gets her. But the offhand manner in which she—Wife, in due time Mother, Mistress of the Household—is bestowed on him suggests that she constitutes an emblem of Tom's achieved position more than an emotional necessity. The novel's plot, in all its complications, enacts movements of power. It concludes when Tom wins and Blifil loses.

Caleb Williams lends itself to no such description: in it, no one wins. In *Anna St. Ives*, no one loses. In Radcliffe's novels, good defeats evil, largely by the revelation of old stories, but the resolutions suggest new terms for understanding all that has gone before. When Tom Jones settles down, we realize that his previous good deeds and wild oats inevitably lead to just this form of "maturity," the assuming of a place in society, the accepting of grown-up power. The final pages of *The Romance of the Forest* include this sentence:

Here, contemning the splendour of false happiness, and possessing the pure and rational delights of a love refined into the most tender friendship, surrounded by the friends so dear to them, and visited by a select and enlightened society—here, in the very bosom of felicity, lived Theodore and Adeline La Luc. (362–63)

No inevitability governs the progression from a half-ruined abbey in the forest to "the very bosom of felicity."

Trying to arrive at the motives of late-century plots through the weight of their resolutions leads back to the motives of the female characters. (Caleb can be assimilated to this category, since he fills the structural role of female: dependent, then victimized.) Except for Anna St. Ives (in many respects anomalous), all respond to rather than create situations. Plotters make things happen; the women, and Caleb, react, sometimes heroically. Yet they must eventually realize purposes beyond resistance. "The real affections of life," comments the narrator of *The Wrongs of Woman*, "when they are allowed to burst forth, are buds pregnant with joy and all the sweet emotions of the soul" (193). Like her fictional sisters, Maria wishes most of all to enjoy those "real affections." As for Caleb—after fleeing and resisting and seeking expedients for viable existence in his state of persecution, he realizes the pain of "Solitude, separation, banishment!" "The pride of philosophy," he continues, "has taught us to treat man as an individual. He is no such thing. He holds, necessarily, indispensibly, to his species" (303). Driven to defiance by his lack of fellowship, Caleb violates fundamental human connections by breaking the tie between him and Falkland that Falkland himself has violated long before; self-defeat must follow.

Anna St. Ives's vision of community controls her. Her opponent, Clifton, the plotter, seeks power. Unlike the other plotters, he does not die in the end but joins the "community." The novel's ending hints uneasiness about this outcome. Clifton's vocabulary remains that of power: "And must I submit?" he inquires of Anna, with considerable feeling. "Are you determined to make a rascal like me admire, and love, and give place to all the fine affections of the heart?" (480). As she affirms just this determination, Clifton's sister Louisa enters. "You are my brother!—My brother!" she proclaims—"I have found the way to your heart! Will make it all my own! Will twine myself round it! Shake me off if you can!" The text continues, in Frank's words, "The energy with which she spoke, and looked, and kissed him, was irresistible! He was overpowered: the tears gushed to his eyes, but he repressed them; he thought them unmanly" (481).

Louisa's rhetoric, as she speaks of making her brother's heart all her own and defies him to shake her off if he can, speaks as eloquently of power as does Clifton's. Frank's summarizing description declares Clifton "overpowered." The sequence hints that the vision of community constitutes an indirect strategy of domination; the same possibility reverberates in Godwin's narrative. Radcliffe and Wollstonecraft, on the other hand, like Burney, attempt to construct the way of power and that of community as genuine alternatives.

The male novelists implicitly express anxiety over the "feminization" implicit in the high value attached to sensibility by hinting that female "affiliativeness" means the same thing as male competitiveness. Clifton's concern about the possibility of being "unmanly" suggests such an interpretation. A character in a novel by Robert Bage significantly titled *Man As He Is* provides a gloss for Clifton's worry: "The manly manners of our more immediate ancestors," he observes, "we have exchanged for the manners of women. We have gained in gentleness and humanity; we have lost in firmness of nerve, and strength of constitution" (1: 272). Worry about the high cost of the exchange often erupts in late-century fiction.

But it is important to stress that male and female novelists in the 1790s engage in a common innovative enterprise; their different ways of working that enterprise out matter less than the fact of the endeavor. Novelistic plots now often develop, as we saw in concentrating on Ann Radcliffe's Gothic, toward resolutions of reconciliation (in the case of *Caleb Williams*, of failed reconciliation) rather than of triumph. A new end point for plots implies new kinds of structure—and new narrative motives. Claude Brémond has pointed out that the basic forms of narrative ("the elementary narrative types") correspond to "the most general forms of human behavior" (406). The form of narrative manifesting itself in the late eighteenth century accommodates itself structurally to imagined patterns of female as well as male behavior.

These novels, whether by male or female authors, do not abandon old assumptions of male power. Rather, they attempt to incorporate those assumptions into plots based on noncompetitive notions as well, to preserve both "gentleness and humanity" and "firmness of nerve." In this way among others, such plots imply a new view of gender relations. "Energy of mind" is at the center of this view.

But I have not yet defined the term. The idea of energy does not always imply activity; the pervasive concern with energy in these novels focuses more on potentiality than on achievement. Energy of mind need not correspond to "strength of mind," lavishly praised by various characters as a principle of control (Emily's father, in *The Mysteries of Udolpho*, recommends it to her as the means of mastering her sensibility). Often, on the contrary, "energy of mind" implies fused thought and feeling. Its possession appears to guarantee a character's success.

A possible clue to the term's implications occurs in *Anna St. Ives*, which formulates its own gender issue. Writing to her friend Louisa, Anna praises male courage, perseverance, and endurance. Then she adds, "shall we wholly renounce the dignity of emulation, and willingly sign the unjust decree of prejudice, that mind likewise has its sex, and that women are destitute of energy and fortitude?" (37). The contorted construction of the sentence, entangled in its negatives, suggests authorial uneasiness, but Anna is saying that *if* minds had sexes, the male rather than the female variety would be marked by energy. Since minds do not have sexes, females too can claim energy of mind—claiming it, Anna implies, in a spirit of competition with men. This energy includes both active courage and passive endurance: another vital fusion.

Clifton loves Anna for her physical beauty; Frank claims "relationship to [her] mind" (133). This declaration provokes Anna to kiss him, explaining her action thus: "I find my affections, my sensibilities, peculiarly liable to these strong sallies. Perhaps all minds of a certain texture are subject to such rapid and almost resistless emotions; and whether they ought to be encouraged or counteracted I have not yet discovered" (135). The force of "rapid and almost resistless emotions," conceived as a mental attribute, constitutes "energy of mind": a sexualized, emotionalized transformation of intellect.

Such a fusion implies a revolutionary conception of human psychology, not yet stated in the late eighteenth century, as far as I have been able to discover, in English philosophic or scientific discourse. An older notion of mind also survives in fiction, manifested in such passages as that in *The Romance of the Forest* where the good pastor La Luc observes, "wisdom is an exertion of mind to subdue folly" (269). Here the concept of mental activity implies the effortful dominance of intellect over impulse: a concept vital to earlier eighteenth-century formulations of possibility for the good life. But the same novel contains accounts of quite a different sort: "Her mind had not lost by long oppression that elastic energy, which resists calamity; else, however susceptible might have been her original taste, the beauties of nature would no longer have charmed her thus easily even to temporary repose" (9). The curious equation by which capacity for repose testifies to energy once more implies united thought and feeling. Because Adeline retains her energy of mind, she can be "charmed" by nature. Emotional responsiveness coincides with mental force.

Caleb Williams and *The Wrongs of Woman* play with equivalent forms of merging. Caleb himself highly values energy of mind. He muses, "Perhaps it will be found that the greatest hero owes the propriety of his conduct to the habit of encountering difficulties and calling out with promptness the energies of his mind" (144). *Propriety* is a curious word here: what Caleb appears to mean—he is wondering why he cannot more successfully defy Falkland—is power of resistance. A little later, Caleb, speechless before Falkland's menaces, decides to "fly." "I seemed to be in a state in which reason had no power. I felt as if I could coolly survey the several arguments of the case, perceive that they had prudence, truth and common sense on their side; and then answer, I am under the guidance of a director more energetic than you" (154). He never specifies the nature of this energetic "director," but since the episode in question exemplifes the beginning of his own habit of "encountering difficulties" as promptly as "the greatest hero," we may conclude that he here starts to develop an energy of mind not altogether definable in terms of reason.

Maria, in *The Wrongs of Woman*, writing an account of her own life for her daughter, describes herself as having strengthened her mind by imbibing her uncle's sentiments. "He drew such animated pictures of his own feelings, rendered permanent by disappointment, as imprinted the sentiments strongly on my heart, and animated my imagination." Maria concludes her extended account of mental strengthening—a process involving the heart and the imagination—thus: "These remarks are necessary to elucidate some peculiarities in my character, which by the world are indefinitely termed romantic" (128). By *romantic*, Maria probably means "associated with romance"; "the world" finds her view of reality, largely controlled by feeling and imagination, unrealistic. But twentieth-century readers may think of *Romantic* with a capital *R*. The notion of energy of mind—Maria later calls it "energy of character"—as a power merging thought and feeling, giving imagination parity with reason, calls to mind the great Romantics. Blake, for instance, wrote in *The Marriage of Heaven and Hell*

2. Energy is the only life and is from the Body and Reason is the bound or outward circumference of Energy.
3. Energy is Eternal Delight.

Energy as delight, reason as the bound of energy: recurrent novelistic allusions to "energy of mind" imply just such ideas.

But my present concern centers specifically on the relation between this quality and plot. The plotters depicted within these novels—comic figures like Sir Hugh in *Camilla*, constantly planning people's lives in ways inevitably frustrated by recalcitrant individual wills; darker personages like Schedoni in *The Italian*—employ their intellectual capacities to manipulate others' experience into sequences of events useful to the contriver. Such manipulations violate truth of character and of feeling. The narrator of *The Italian* sums up Schedoni by observing that "In fact he cared not for truth, nor sought it by bold and broad argument, but loved to exert the wily cunning of his nature in hunting it through artifical perplexities" (34). Artificial perplexities always mark a plotter's operations, but Schedoni's plots, of labyrinthine ingenuity, depend also on making the worse appear the better reason.

The other plotters within novelistic texts, with the exception of Burney's benign Sir Hugh, a parody figure, similarly betray sinister motives, typically disguised by lofty terminology. Ronald Paulson notes as characteristic of Gothic situations "in which no one can understand or fathom anyone else's motives or actions" (*Representations* 224). Such mutual incomprehension extends beyond the Gothic to register the gap between plotters and nonplotters. Anna and Clifton will never understand one another unless, as Anna dreams, Clifton changes his character. His manipulations contrast with her innocent "energy of mind" as a way of making things happen. Similar contrasts mark other works of the 1790s.

As they make plotters within the text objects of disapproval, the novels' narrators suggest that their own work of elaborating fictions on the page does not resemble the plotters' activity of imposing fictions on people's lives. I alluded earlier to the new pattern of fictional plot that became important in the 1790s: the arrangement of novelistic events to produce resolutions as dependent on horizontal as on vertical relationship, insistent on the achievement of intimate forms of communal harmony as well as on new alignments of power. Narratorial attitudes toward fiction making call attention to another difference between late-century and earlier fictions. Fielding's novelistic narrators boast of their "masculine" control over their plots, suggesting the novelist's godlike power of manipulating characters and events. Sterne's Tristram takes ostentatious pleasure in his plot's unconventional shape, which follows no pre-existent pattern but reflects the vagaries of his consciousness; his comment on his plot as squiggle reminds us of the artifice inherent in plot.

Later novelists more often try to obscure their artifice, to align themselves in effect with the characters manifesting "energy of mind" rather than with the plotters in their own texts. Energy of mind thus bears, as I suggested earlier, on changing attitudes toward plot and story. Late-century writers like to say that they write out of concern with character—the "wonders of the Heart of man," as Burney puts it on the first page of *Camilla* (7). Godwin's account of the composition of *Caleb Williams*, that highly plotted novel, holds special interest in this connection. The novelist reports how he worked backward, from the third volume to the first, in order

to create a plot of flawless unity. First he imagined Falkland's relentless pursuit of Caleb; then its motive. As he thought his project
through from end to beginning, however, his attention focused increasingly on questions of character. "The thing in which my
imagination revelled the most freely," he writes,

was the analysis of the private and internal operations of the mind, employing my metaphysical dissecting knife in tracing and laying bare the
involutions of motive, and recording the gradually accumulating impulses,
which led the personages I had to describe primarily to adopt the particular way of proceeding in which they afterwards embarked. (339)

That is to say, Godwin does not believe conformity to possibility the
test of plot. He would scorn to rely on Fielding's ostentatious coin-
cidences. Rather, plot expresses truth of motive and impulse, Richardson more clearly than Fielding its progenitor. But even *Clarissa*
relies far more heavily on coincidence than does *Caleb Williams*.

Martin Price has observed that "What primarily distinguishes
Blake as satirist from the Augustans is the shift from moral judgment to a standard of energy," adding that "In fact, . . . any standard of vitality tends to transform itself into one of morality" (*To
the Palace* 430). Novelists writing at the same historical moment as
Blake have not abandoned professions of morality, although the
principles they recommend differ from those emphasized earlier.
They hold to an implicit standard of mental energy, imagined as a
balance of psychic qualities more forceful than ratiocination, more
controlled than passion. Their fictional characters embody the
same balance ideally exemplified by their plots. Within the structure of novelistic actions in the late eighteenth century, those who
plot by attempting to control the actions of others—their behavior
corresponding to the literary conduct of novelists like Richardson
and Fielding—inevitably fail. Successful characters influence outcomes by force of mind or personality.

Plots enact what authors assert. For almost three-quarters of a
century, eighteenth-century novels conformed mainly to three fundamental arrangements of plot: well-made structures inherited or
modified from romance (e.g., *Tom Jones*); episodic plots evincing
little obvious attention to structure (*Roderick Random*); fictions of
sensibility which actively denied plot coherence by ostentatious
claims to follow the movements of consciousness or by insisting on
their own fragmentary or arbitrary ordering (*A Sentimental Journey,
The Man of Feeling*). The active assertion of plot's control in such
writers as Fielding can be associated with the dominance of reason;
the active denial of plot in such as Mackenzie depends on commit-

ment to feeling. Episodic fictions, subordinating plot's importance, also weigh in on the side of feeling—although the doctrine stated in their prose sometimes contradicts that implied by their plots. The new plots of the 1790s structurally suggest the elevation of "energy of mind" as a principle merging thought and feeling; various versions of the same merging would dominate the fiction of Austen and Scott, of the Brontës and Dickens and Eliot. Such plotters within the text as Coke Clifton in *Anna St. Ives*, or Maria's husband in *The Wrongs of Woman*, or even the mistaken tutor Dr. Marchmont in *Camilla* work like Fielding, trying to control persons and events to produce desired outcomes. The creators of the fictions containing these plotters, on the other hand, appear to proceed more as Anna does, or Maria: by acknowledging desire (to achieve "happy endings") and discovering rather than imposing the patterns of its fulfillment. Such appearance of course is *only* that: a Holcroft exerts as much artifice as a Fielding to achieve plot resolution. But the new narrative stance of late-century novelists dramatizes the developing ideology of harmony—between reason and feeling, between power and reconciliation, between socially-constructed versions of "masculine" and "feminine"—implicit also in the novelistic celebration of "energy of mind."

These novelists thus force their imaginations to the limits of the conceivable, given existing social possibilities, and suggest one sense in which fictions may constitute an agent for change. To claim organic development for plot, conceiving a new kind of plot integrity based on parity between reason and feeling implies changing concepts of experience as well as of fictional organization. The mode of heroism based on "energy of mind" suggests shifting valuations of the conventionally male and conventionally female—not just the elevation of the feminine that Terry Eagleton and Nancy Armstrong and others have noted, but a dualistic, balanced ideal. Even conservative Frances Burney in *Camilla* imagines the possibility of romantic fulfillment for a homely woman and implies that the triumph of prudence over feeling embodies weakness rather than strength. Radcliffe, adhering to romance outcomes for her plots, suggests new meanings for romance. Wollstonecraft conceives of sexual liberation as evidence of high female character; Godwin dramatizes the inadequacy of the will to dominate as he shows how much darker the laws of character are than those of circumstance. All demonstrate how fully novelists' psychological and moral assumptions imbue the very structure of their plots; all reveal how plot contains and conveys meaning. They foretell the future; they also remind us once more that ideas not wholly defined by their immediate political implications emerged from the English ferment attending the French Revolution.

If the idea of energy often embodies a fusion of values comparable to that exemplified in new kinds of plot reconciliation, it sometimes calls attention to the difficulty of achieving such reconciliation. Not everyone in the final years of the eighteenth century shared Holcroft's or Wollstonecraft's capacity to imagine characters who combined energetic thought with energetic sympathy. Two novels in which energy flourishes at the expense of sensibility may illustrate how plot can convey a novelist's anxiety about the relation between force and feeling. Dr. John Moore's *Zeluco* (1789) imagines a male character controlled by the energy of his passions. The monstrous consequences of commitment to this kind of personal force shape the novel's plot, but, as we shall see, only recourse to conventionally feminine principles can resolve it. The "masculine" and the "feminine" remain isolated from one another, incapable of reconciliation. In *A Simple Story* (1791)—which is anything but— Elizabeth Inchbald explores negative consequences of energy in male and female embodiments. Although her plot achieves apparent reconciliation, it does so only at the cost of powerful exclusions.

Sexuality is at issue in both these fictions. Twentieth-century readers sometimes experience difficulty in understanding the codes by which earlier writers conveyed sexual feeling. Abducted, sexually threatened maidens appear with such regularity in eighteenth-century plots that they seem hardly more than a literary convention. Both Moore and Inchbald, like Richardson before them, uncover the meaning of such conventions. Both resort to sentimental resolutions. In the narratives preceding those resolutions, however, men and women engage in ferocious power struggles, sexual domination and withholding their implements. A sometimes breathtaking sense of sexual antagonism permeates these fictions.

The eponymous central character of *Zeluco* (one could hardly call him a protagonist) lives only for his own gratification. As a boy, he squeezes to death a tame sparrow that fails to perform its tricks satisfactorily; as a man, suspicious about the parentage of his infant son, he crushes the baby. Once he acquires the vast wealth for which he wishes, he gratifies himself mainly by sexual conquest. Because a virtuous woman resists him, he feels impelled to marry her, using trickery to gain his ends. She cannot satisfy his appetites. He resorts, predictably, to mistresses and, stabbed in the bowels by a lover of one of them, dies ignominiously.

The narrator invites his reader to consider the elaborate tale an exemplum. The novel's first sentence announces its ostensible moral:

Religion teaches that vice leads to endless misery in a future state; and experience proves that, in spite of the gayest and most prosperous appearances, inward misery accompanies her; for even in this life her ways are ways of wretchedness, and all her paths are woe. (34: 1)

The illustration of such a truth of course can hardly be in the usual sense agreeable to a reader. The narrator characterizes his "tasks" as "unpleasant" and warns readers who "cannot bear to contemplate such a picture" not to read the story he has to relate (34: 1). Mary Wollstonecraft, in her anonymous review of the novel, specifies the inherent problem of such a narrative: "when not warped by some mean motive, we are unwilling to become acquainted with a heart we instinctively despise; besides, in the character of a villain, there is so much deformity and want of order, that the contemplation of it fatigues, while it raises disgust in the mind" (*"Zeluco"* 98). She suggests that the reader receives pleasure from the episodes related rather than from the character.

Zeluco's career, as reported, indeed dramatizes the emotional futility of vice, and its "episodes" hold considerable interest. The wicked man, it seems, can allow himself no lasting pleasure. He suffers repeatedly from ennui, incapable of satisfaction. More compelling than the reiterative demonstration of this point is the insistent revelation of how inevitably a villain formulates every situation as one involving a struggle for control. Finding the concept of mutuality inconceivable, he must dominate every man and every woman he encounters. The brutality of his sexual maneuvers epitomizes the limitation and the energy of his conceptualizations. Like liquid compelled into a narrow aperture, Zeluco's obsessive, confined comprehension of possibility generates terrific force.

A characteristic extended episode involves the wife of a Portuguese merchant in the West Indies who excites Zeluco's lust. He works to seduce her; she agrees to meet him at night. Believing (rightly) that her husband suspects her, however, she confesses to him Zeluco's overtures. The Portuguese dresses in women's clothes, meets Zeluco, and stabs him with a stiletto. The would-be seducer survives, guesses his assailant's identity, and elaborates a diabolical plot to make the Portuguese doubt his own fatherhood and to arouse his suspicions of his wife. Only the intervention of a *deus ex machina* in the form of a wise physician averts tragic bloodshed. The physician suggests that Zeluco will fall "sooner or later within the grasp of the laws of society" (34: 107). In fact, the laws of society never exert significant force in this novel, in which individuals combat as though in a Hobbesian state of nature.

So completely does Zeluco's lust for power subsume his sexual lust that one can hardly separate the two. Although he repeatedly asserts his desire in sexual terms, his need for women as affirmations of his potency (both literal and metaphoric) functions mainly as metaphor for his all-embracing concern with domination. Neither the Portuguese merchant nor his wife has a name in Moore's text. Both merely illustrate Zeluco's overwhelming need and its consequences. The merchant's revenge underlines the point. Female disguise declares his threatened masculinity; the wounding stiletto reaffirms the phallic power which focuses male concerns throughout the novel. Rape and seduction alike dramatize operations of male power. From the conventionally male point of view, of which Zeluco provides an instance so extreme as to seem almost parodic, women, like the slaves quite elaborately discussed in the West Indies section of the novel, exist only as occasionally rebellious objects of power. (The narrator, despite his panegyrics to female virtue, often appears to share his character's contempt for women. E.g., "If I am not mistaken, . . . the sex in general are apt to shrink from present inconveniences, even when sensible that by encountering them they would obviate the risk of future misfortunes" [34: 64].) The plot reiterates this attitude to the point of tedium.

Zeluco's boundless, almost machinelike energy guarantees and preserves his capacity to conceive and to execute complex schemes. Tireless in futile pursuit of the pleasure to which he feels entitled, he cannot be deterred by conscience, by rebuke, or by the occasional stabbing. In Zeluco, energy—of mind and of body—becomes monstrosity.

The single-minded perversity of this villain's character presents a potential narrative problem. J. M. S. Tompkins, one of Moore's few twentieth-century defenders, affirms the character's realism: "he is a thoroughly wicked man who becomes wicked by natural means, by a bad education, a selfish nature and the opportunities of power. He is mean, base and dangerous, and quite untouched by grandeur" (179). Moore's narrator argues for the realism of his tale on other grounds. First he expresses uneasiness about Zeluco's unmixed villainy by denying it in rather vague terms. Men and women, he asserts, are "animals of heterogeneous composition" (34: 139).

In a character, such as that of the person whose story we have the unpleasant task of recording, there are, perhaps, fewer good qualities than in any
other, because cruelty was become the basis of Zeluco's character, at least
a total disregard to the feelings of his fellow-creatures, when any interest
or gratification of his own was in question. (34: 140)

This kind of cruelty differs, the narrator continues, from that of
devils because it does not seek others' suffering for its own sake.

The proofs, however, of this degree of cruelty need not be drawn from
the stories of giants, and records of chivalry; they are frequently found in
more authentic history, and may be adduced from the conduct of too
many of the heroes and great men of antiquity; not to mention the great
men of our own days, whose sentiments and conduct, however different
from those of the former in every other respect, have a wonderful resemblance to their predecessors, in this article of insensibility and disregard of
the misery of others. (34: 140)

   This is an important rhetorical move. The narrator claims realism for his account of a man obsessed with his own gratification by
linking an apparently fantastic fable to current political concerns,
suggesting that "insensibility" comprises a public as well as a private
vice. The energy that seeks only satisfaction of base selfhood corresponds to that controlling the affairs of the nation. Politically
organized benevolence can counter it in the public realm. Within
the individualistically organized world of the novel, resistance will
come from the equal-but-opposite principle of sensibility.
   Zeluco lacks a hero but has a heroine, beautiful and virtuous
Laura, whom Zeluco marries mainly because she resists him so long
and so successfully. Only another of his intricate, sinister plots can
bring about such a marriage, since Laura instinctively senses his
evil nature. Although Zeluco soon tires of her, this fact in no way
moderates his intense jealousy. Yet he himself feels quite free to
turn to mistresses. One in particular manipulates his jealousy,
arouses his suspicions, and leads him to murder his only child.
Driven to temporary insanity as a result of the murder, which she
witnesses, Laura finally decides to part from the husband to whom
she has remained true despite her loathing. Zeluco's death, however, solves her problem. She eventually marries the German soldier whom she has idealized since her girlhood.
   Laura displays no active energy, nothing corresponding to that
"energy of mind" characteristic even of Radcliffe's heroines. Her
way of dealing with the world resembles Amelia's. Her salient
moral characteristic is "sensibility," manifest in her tendency to put

the welfare of those she loves before her own. Like Amelia, she must rely on Providence to extricate her from difficulties beyond the possibility of human solution. She embodies a "feminine" principle highly valued in the narrative, as the formulation of Zeluco's villainy in terms of "insensibility" suggests. But it is almost impossible to imagine a conceivable fusion between Zeluco's energy and Laura's sensibility. The two exist as utterly opposed guiding principles. Once Zeluco dies, Laura can operate successfully on the basis of her feelings. Before his death, the incompatibility of their marriage dramatizes the irreconcilability of their motives.

In both positive and negative ways, *Zeluco* demonstrates the importance of plot. Its narrative interest derives largely from the necessity by which in this story character implies action. Both Zeluco and Laura play out the laws of their natures. Each possesses, in a Popean sense, a ruling passion: self-gratification for Zeluco, sensibility for Laura. Their trajectories intersect but cannot coincide. Those trajectories, and the relationship between them, create the plot. Zeluco's constrictive self-referentiality forces him into repetitive patterns without the possibility of meaningful change. He may marry or he may murder, but no happening, however dramatic, makes a real difference to him. His actions never contain the seed of resolution. Laura, on the other hand, responsive to others' needs, only dimly aware of her own desires, embodies greater potential for change though equally little promise of resolution. Only through the agency of another is she likely to achieve closure.

This description may suggest the unsatisfactory aspects of plot in Moore's novel. The plot of power seems visibly to have worn itself out. As strikingly as Mackenzie's evasive fragmentations in *The Man of Feeling,* the repetitive action and arbitrary conclusion of *Zeluco* call attention to the insufficiency of power as principle of action. Zeluco himself thinks of nothing else. Tom Jones, sometimes competitive, is also sometimes generous, sometimes tender, sometimes anxious. His effort to win in every win-lose situation seems healthy, a product of his creator's recognition that the world goes round by virtue of competition. Zeluco as a character derives from no such straightforward recognition. His "insensibility" could only be imagined by someone vividly conscious of sensibility as a competing principle. Given that consciousness, with its implicit awareness of the moral inadequacy of power-hunger as motive, the single-minded struggle for power becomes both narratologically and morally insufficient. Zeluco's monotonous emotional range— excitement as he grasps for power, exhilaration as he achieves it, ennui when cut off from its exercise, rage and frustration when he fails to attain his goals—cannot long compel the reader, nor can the repetitive patterns of his effort. One neither takes satisfaction in Zeluco's achievements nor believes in the finality of his defeats. The narrator's tone declares the character's efforts meaningless. The reader waits only for his death.

But the narrative does not make Laura either into a compelling figure. Like a Gothic heroine, she faints and weeps. She sacrifices her own interests for the sake of her mother. She enacts the patterns of marital fidelity and compliance, and finally events rescue her. Her apparent contentment with the role of victim and the narrator's indulgent dwelling on the details of her victimization may cause discomfort for twentieth-century readers. In any case, the stress on victimization emphasizes the inadequacy of what Laura represents—inadequacy to generate or to resolve story or to make things happen within her world. The novel's tone, like its explicit moral commentary, endorses Laura's ethical position. It does not make that position persuasive.

"Self-sufficiency was no part of this amiable woman's character, however virtuous her inclinations were," the narrator comments approvingly (35: 163). He means that Laura does not trust her own principles to defend her against her feelings if she finds herself alone with the man she loves while married to another. The observation helps to define the novel's narrative problem. Sensibility, as here imagined, implies selflessness. We have seen the permeable self as fictional character in earlier sentimental novels where the envisioning of character in such terms reinforces the implications of fragmentary plots. But *Zeluco* focuses on a character vividly informed by his insistent sense of self. The conjunction of figures so profoundly opposed produces a narrative stalemate. It thus calls attention to the necessity of reconciliation that other novels of the period exemplify in action and in characterization.

A Simple Story, which also treats energy as a problematic quality, organizes its plot toward reconciliation but demonstrates, as few of the decade's other novels do, the costs of harmonizing rationality and emotion, "masculine" power and "feminine" sympathy. *Zeluco* holds its greatest interest in its insufficiencies. *A Simple Story*, as Terry Castle rightly says, is "a small masterpiece neglected far too long. Without exaggeration the case might be made for *A Simple Story* as the most elegant English fiction of the century" (*Masquerade* 290). From my point of view, the novel's interest inheres not only in its fictional power but in its recognition of precisely the issues that have concerned me in this chapter.

Castle's provocative reading of Inchbald's fiction, the most attentive and penetrating interpretation yet offered, provides a good
starting point for examining the text. The reading argues that
Inchbald provides "an unfamiliar image of female plot." "Here,"
Castle continues,

the heroine's desires repeatedly triumph over masculine prerogative; familial, religious, and psychic patterns of male domination collapse in the
face of her persistent will to liberty. In both a social and a literary
sense, Miss Milner (the first and most potent of *A Simple Story*'s two heroines) could be said to embody an unprecedented feminine destiny. She is
never, to borrow a word from *Clarissa*, successfully "enwomaned." (*Masquerade* 292)

The novel, in a fashion frequently compared to the pattern of
Wuthering Heights, combines stories of two generations. Miss Milner, after her marriage, "loses her virtue" and dies, leaving a
daughter, Matilda, with no means of support other than her alien-
ated father's benevolence. That father allows Matilda to live in his
house but forbids her to enter his sight. When she accidentally encounters him, he banishes her. The subsequent need to rescue her
from a lascivious nobleman, however, restores his affections, and
the story ends in *rapprochement*.

Castle understands this second-generation narrative as recapitulating the novel's first half.

Its underlying narrative structure, or what one might call its symbolic plot,
is almost identical to that of the first half. Matilda's story not only resembles
her mother's, it is a displaced recapitulation. For Matilda too transgresses
against patriarchal dictate, and she too is threatened with emotional banishment. Yet she too forms, at the last gasp, an eminently gratifying
union, and with the same man, no less, who figures so prominently in Miss
Milner's history—Dorriforth/Elmwood, her own father.
    The repetition clarifies Inchbald's emotional idée fixe, the obsessive pat-
tern of proscription/violation/ reward. The second half condenses the wish
fulfillment structures of the first. (*Masquerade* 323)

This account, like the rest of Castle's treatment, calls attention to
important patterns of duplication. It ignores, however, elements of
difference that strike me as yet more important.
    Most readers have found Miss Milner a more compelling figure
than her daughter: in Castle's remarkable locution, "most potent."
Jane Spencer complains that "impulsive Miss Milner, a fine and
subtly drawn example of the thoughtless heroine, is replaced by
her dutiful and colourless daughter" (160). J. M. S. Tompkins, in
her introduction to the Oxford edition of the novel, characterizes

Miss Milner as "vital and substantial" and ignores Matilda (Inchbald xvi). Moreover, the version of "female plot" that contains Matilda holds far less excitement than does the working out of Miss Milner's story.

Miss Milner's problem, like that of the Gothic heroines, concerns fathers and daughters. Her literal father dies early in the novel, leaving her to the guardianship of a thirty-year-old Catholic priest, Dorriforth. Seventeen-year-old Miss Milner (assigned no first name), a Protestant, soon falls in love with him. When the death of an aristocratic relative makes it imperative that Dorriforth produce further heirs to the title and estate, he is released from his vows in order to assume his place as Lord Elmwood. The opposition of his Jesuit mentor, Sandford, to a match with Miss Milner suddenly disappears, despite the young woman's self-will and passion, and the two marry. The daughter thus, unlike her Gothic contemporaries, achieves sexual possession of her symbolic father. But matters do not work out well despite—or because of—this bit of wish fulfillment. In a subsequent series of events summarized rather than narrated, Lady Elmwood, during her husband's prolonged absence, proves unfaithful to him. She lives in banishment with her daughter by Dorriforth/Elmwood and a female friend until her untimely death.

Even such a summary of the Milner-Dorriforth plot suggests how radical is its imagining. I agree with Castle about that, and about its effort to provide images of female freedom. Freedom, in Inchbald's version of things, implies power. The first half of *A Simple Story* narrates a series of power struggles, most of them explicitly conceived as such. Miss Milner knows her own beauty and, more astonishingly, her own sexuality. For the male sexual aggression of *Zeluco*, Inchbald substitutes its veiled female counterpart. It is refreshing, in this period, to encounter a heroine who faints only occasionally, and only from love, and who actively pursues the satisfaction of her own desires. She manipulates her admirers for her own purposes; she opposes Sandford as wholeheartedly as he opposes her. And once Dorriforth has acknowledged his love, she takes that acknowledgement as an opportunity for the exercise of power.

The text insists on this point. The first characterization of Miss Milner begins, "From her infancy she had been indulged in all her wishes to the extreme of folly, and habitually started at the unpleasant voice of control—she . . . thought those moments passed in wasteful idleness during which she was not gaining some new conquest" (15). The same account comments on Miss Milner's "quick sensibility" and on the "energy" with which she characteristically speaks (15). It prepares the reader for the young woman's reaction when Dorriforth/Elmwood proposes to her. Despite her delight and her immediate acceptance, she soon reflects complacently on the "force" of her "invincible" charms and regrets that she failed to keep her lover longer in suspense: "my power over him might have been greater still" (138). When he forbids her to attend a masquerade, her confidante, Miss Woodley, reminds her that she has always obeyed her guardian's demands. "As my guardian, I certainly did obey him," Miss Milner responds; "and I could obey him as a husband; but as a lover, I will not." Miss Woodley warns her that she may thus lose her fiancé's affections. "As he pleases," says Miss Milner—"for if he will not submit to be my lover, I will not submit to be his wife" (158).

Such language calls attention to the real issue in the extended struggle between the lovers—a struggle in which Miss Milner affirms her power by frivolous actions and Dorriforth/Elmwood demonstrates his mainly by watchful silences. Miss Milner's disobedience about the masquerade precipitates her lover's rejection of her. Now she adopts silence as *her* mode of conduct, never openly expressing her desolation but conveying it by eloquent details of behavior. At the very moment when the lovers believe themselves parting forever, Sandford intervenes to ordain their marriage, apparently (and improbably) motivated by his recognition of their intense mutual love. "Now then, Lord Elmwood, this moment give her up for ever," he commands; "or this moment constrain her by such ties from offending you, she shall not *dare* to violate" (191). Marriage, the Jesuit reminds his immediate audience and the reader, implies immense social power for its male participants. It provides the definitive means to quell female insubordination.

When Miss Woodley reveals to Lord Elmwood that Miss Milner loves him, she feels "filled with alarm" by the intense emotion she sees in his face. "She wished him to love Miss Milner but to love her with moderation" (130). As immoderate as he in her passion, his wife expects that love will continue to dominate and to motivate both of them. But Lord Elmwood goes away to care for his estate in the West Indies. He conceals from his wife the illness that delays his return; her love expresses itself in "violent anger" at his apparent neglect. An intolerable state of "indifference" succeeds (196). Lady Elmwood's passion must find an outlet. She succumbs to a seducer, thus ensuring her own lasting misery and early death.

The narrator attributes the lady's fall to "that impatient, irritable disposition she had so seldom governed" (196). Emotion without the control of reason guarantees disaster—at least for women. Lord Elmwood, equally passionate, suffers less immediately disastrous consequences of his emotional indulgence. His "love to his lady had been extravagant—the effect of his hate was extravagant likewise" (197). He isolates himself from his own child, with a determination that endures long after his wife's death. That wife, belatedly, acknowledges his absolute right to govern. "She had no will, she said, but what she would wholly submit to Lord Elmwood's; and, if it were even his will, her child should live in poverty, as well as banishment, it should be so" (203). The child in her turn accepts as absolute her father's every prerogative.

By roughly two-thirds of the way through, in other words, the narrative has reaffirmed in detail a traditional social order. No mediation seems possible. Miss Milner in her active energy has struggled with Dorriforth and his powerful restraint. The struggle is resolved not by the reconciliation of these two forms of personal force or by the triumph of one over the other, but by a resort to social assignment of power. After accepting the subordination of marriage, Lady Elmwood blazes into utter insubordination. Then, will-less, she must die. Her daughter knows better than to make any claim for herself. The female "freedom" Castle celebrates has found little scope.

Lord Elmwood embodies a traditional male constellation of authority and apparent rationality. Unlike his wife, he rigidly subdues passion, both before and after his brief excursion into love. If his rigidity strikes a reader as unattractive, the text yet appears to prefer it to—to find it less dangerous than—the woman's failures of restraint. No harmonizing of natures appears possible between Lord and Lady Elmwood, nor are we invited to conceive at any level of abstraction the possibility of that nonhierarchical merging of thought and feeling implied in the ideal of "energy of mind."

The second-generation story evolves from just this failure of conception. Taking a rather less rosy view than Castle's, I find in Matilda's career not a narrative of female freedom and power but one of necessary acceptance and limited reconciliation. The first-generation narrative concerns erotic desire; its successor deals with the taming of eros. True, Matilda's pining for her father has moments of ambiguity comparable to Ellena's feeling for Schedoni, and Lord Elmwood's moral monstrosity, painful to himself as well as to others, at times achieves almost Gothic sadism. But Matilda in relation to her father resembles Evelina in her compliance to Mr. Villars more nearly than she anticipates Ellena. Villars's fantasies of dying in his foster child's arms hint the erotic. Evelina's assimilation of father, guardian, and lover to a single paternal role speaks of what she cannot face—and what she can. Similarly, Matilda's longing for a father by and large conceals its erotic components. When she faints in her father's arms (with a moan of "Save me"), provoking his comic, pathetic cry, "Miss Milner—Dear Miss Milner" (274), she hints at an emotional identity between filial and romantic relationship. But Lord Elmwood's rescue of his daughter from a would-be ravisher reestablishes the appropriate sublimations. When he hears that Lord Margrave has abducted Matilda, he inquires, "Where are my pistols?" The now aged Jesuit, Sandford, cries, "Will you then prove yourself a father?" "Lord Elmwood only answered, 'Yes,' and left the room" (324).

Like the fainting episode, this exchange teeters on the edge of comedy because of Elmwood's verbal limitations. His confined rhetorical repertoire corresponds to his restricted emotional range. When someone offends him, he banishes the offender. Just so, he banishes feelings he cannot confront. He thinks himself, understandably, greatly injured. He is prone to self-pity: "it has been my fate to be used ill" (290). But his demand for the phallic pistols with which he will prove himself a father declares his willingness to restore the kind of familial order he can comprehend. Sandford, knowing Elmwood's propensity for tyranny, forestalls the arrival of others at Elmwood House, trying to trick his patron into the habit of providing "care and protection" for his daughter (332). Indeed, by the time the others come, Elmwood is treating Matilda with "easy, natural fondness" (333). He assumes and she assumes his authority over her. As for her would-be lover, Rushbrook: "The idea of love never once came to her thoughts; and she would sport with Rushbrook like the most harmless child" (334). Like Evelina (and other eighteenth-century literary forebears: see Spacks, "'Ev'ry Woman'"), she displays "the utmost ignorance" and "the utmost innocence" (336). Unlike her mother, whose passionate nature proves her destruction, Matilda reveals no capacity for passion. She achieves cozy reunion with her father. She marries a man with whom she can sport like a child. After one brief moment of a power she has never sought ("he has yielded to you alone, the power over my happiness or misery" [337]), she subsides into a marriage which the reader is invited to "suppose" happy (337). Unlike her mother, Matilda has had "a proper education" in the "school of prudence—though of adversity" (338). She knows enough not to want too much.

Critics do not say much about this resolution, with its precipitous retreat from the witty, daring assertiveness of Miss Milner and the

plot involving her. Matilda faints and weeps and pines like a sentimental heroine. She offers no threat to the social order or to a
reader's sensibilities. Her mother has suffered conventional punishment for conventional female sin; Matilda wins the conventional
reward for female conformity. The extremity of the contrast may
create moral disturbance in the reader's mind. The novel's dénouement asserts limited reconciliation: Lord Elmwood becomes
humanized, softened, by experiencing his fatherhood; Matilda accepts the presence of a masculine principle in her life. But the two-
part plot has eliminated the presence and the possibility of energetic, passionate, individual femaleness and has tacitly endorsed
the necessity of dominant maleness. In contrast to the male-created
fantasy of *Anna St. Ives*, published only a year later, a woman writer's imagining of possibility in *A Simple Story* implies social despair,
despite its evocation of spirited femininity.

Christine Van Boheemen, writing about what she calls "the rhetoricity of plot" (91), finds in the principle of mediation a crucial
strategy of narrative logic. Fiction, she suggests, uses "characters or
objects as things to think with, working out irreconcilable contradictions by means of rhetorical strategies which can only function
or exist when embedded in a narrative process, in language" (94).
Van Boheemen offers this theory as a way of avoiding mimetic assumptions. Verisimilitude, in her view, "is only the indication of a
more artificial displacement of the rhetoricity of plot; and even the
most moral, the most realistic novels such as *Anna Karenina*, can
present their moral message only through the use of an essentially
fallacious narrative logic" (94).

The notion of "energy of mind," as it has been considered in this
chapter, functions as a mediating principle in plots typically far
removed from verisimilitude—either by virtue of their romance-
fantasies, as in the Gothic novels, or because of their political ide-
alism (*Anna St. Ives, Caleb Williams*). Paradoxically, to think of the
idea's function in rhetorical terms may help to clarify its ideological
implications. "Art, culture, and society are not separate or sepa-
rable," John Bender has observed (1). Formal arrangements reflect
cultural assumptions. Katharine Rogers complains about the Matilda section of *A Simple Story* that "the emphasis has shifted from
character to plot" (71). She finds in the later eighteenth-century
novel a characteristic "dissociation of plot from character which has
been noticed as a critical weakness" (66). I would argue, on the
contrary, that the emphasis on plot in these novels calls attention
to sources of their strength.

Zeluco and *A Simple Story*, so close in time to the novels considered earlier in this chapter, so different in political and psychological weight, help to clarify the meanings carried by plot in these works and to emphasize the importance and the limitation of "energy of mind" as a governing idea. The movement toward mediation, which Van Boheemen sees as central to the formation of fictional plot, expresses itself thematically in that idea. Many plots of the 1790s seek resolution in the reconciliation of rationality and feeling, power and intimacy, masculine and feminine. "Energy of mind" epitomizes the force of such fusions. The plots devised by Moore and Inchbald, on the other hand, expose the irreconcilability of oppositions that others obscure.

To claim parity between the desire for power and the yearning for intimacy implies the possibility of social as well as literary reorganizations. Little in late eighteenth-century social actualities suggested realization of that possibility. Yet something had changed since the 1740s. Richardson, Fielding, and Smollett affirm the primacy of power as principle in domestic as well as public politics. So do Moore and Inchbald. Moore, in fact, returns to a form of plotting not unlike *Amelia*, with a compliant woman embodying virtue in opposition to power-hungry men. But by making the operations of power virtually diabolical and by dwelling at length on those operations, Moore expresses an uneasiness he can neither contain nor explore. Inchbald, on the other hand, in her Matilda plot dramatizes the action of giving up and hints at her own profound rage over the typical female necessity of giving up. Gary Kelly argues (and I agree with him) that "Inchbald is really at her best in depicting the struggle to suppress deep feeling, and such passages are among the best things in the second part of the novel" (*English Jacobin Novel* 76). Her plot itself embodies that struggle, between anger at the necessities of female compliance and awareness that no viable alternative exists.

In other words, plots of the 1790s, whether optimistic or despairing in their social implications, call attention to heightened levels of consciousness about the meanings of polarities more readily assumed earlier in the century. The nineteenth-century novel would continue to explore possibilities for mediation between those polarities.

8

"THE NOVEL'S WISDOM":
AUSTEN AND SCOTT

Our discussion of fictional plot began with the mid-eighteenth-century case of Charlotte Lennox's Arabella, unable to distinguish between history and romance, made socially ridiculous by her appropriation of masculine values, her interpretations shaped by her desire. It ends with a group of novels published more than sixty years after *The Female Quixote* but structured by the same polarities: reason/feeling, masculine/ feminine, history/romance, desire/control. Jane Austen and Sir Walter Scott, like their novelistic predecessors, reveal in their plots if not in their stated doctrine the "wisdom of uncertainty" which, according to Milan Kundera, constitutes "the novel's wisdom" (7). Their investigations through fiction of oppositions that their culture could not resolve dramatize the urgencies, the difficulties, and the inescapable ambiguities of reconciliation.

Like their immediate predecessors, Austen and Scott seek to construct fictions of ideological harmony but suggest harmony's high costs. The resolution achieved in Gothic novels, and in the works of Wollstonecraft, Godwin, and Inchbald, constitutes both reconciliation and masking. The vision of harmony between "masculine" and "feminine," between the drive toward power and toward intimacy, allures these novelists but does not entirely persuade them. Their efforts at reconciliation possess ideological and literary importance, yet one detects some sleight of hand in their assertions of harmony. Both the effort and the awareness of difficulty appear greater in Austen and Scott than in their predecessors.

Despite their differences of tone, subject, and technique, these novelists share with one another and with many of their nineteenth-century successors a continuing tendency to invent plots based on the moral oppositions that had interested Burke—moral oppositions bearing aesthetic and political implications. Those oppositions are apparent in *Waverley* and *Sense and Sensibility*, more complexly so in *The Heart of Midlothian* and *Mansfield Park*.[1] The four novels, considered together, demonstrate that Scott and Austen, who admired one another, also had something in common. If the novels cannot "typify" their authors' work, they yet suggest the dimensions of continuing novelistic concerns.

Twentieth-century criticism of Austen has tended to consider her plots the most "conventional" and least interesting aspect of her novels. As for Scott, Judith Wilt evokes a widely held position when she notes "the apparent critical preference for the periphery over the center of Scott's fictions, for their 'life' over their plots" (*Secret* 19). But plots carry meanings, for these novelists as for their predecessors, and their meanings call attention to preoccupations Austen and Scott shared with their forebears. "Conventions," by definition, reflect cultural assumptions.

Compared to novels of the 1790s, particularly Gothic novels, *Sense and Sensibility* and *Waverley* notably disperse the power of the father. The father of the Dashwood family, goodhearted but improvident despite praiseworthy intentions, dies at the outset, initiating the action of *Sense and Sensibility*. He leaves behind one son, autocratic in impulse and wealthy, but hardly effective as a force in female lives. As the narrator comments, "Had he married a more amiable woman, he might have been made still more respectable than he was:—he might even have been made amiable himself" (5). But the softening power of the feminine does not manifest itself in this instance. The men the Dashwood sisters marry both appear passive and depressed through most of the fiction; Marilyn Butler calls attention to Austen's use of *diffident* to characterize them (*Jane Austen* 190). They display neither phallic nor significant social force in the foreground of the action, although Colonel Brandon fights an offstage duel (in which no one is hurt) and reports himself as having briefly played a patriarchal role in the past. The only man with erotic energy, Willoughby, behaves badly, thus excluding himself from romantic alliance. Marianne marries Brandon. "Her regard and her society restored his mind to animation, and his spirits to cheerfulness; and ... Marianne found her own happiness in forming his" (379). Now female emotional power manifests itself to moral as well as emotional effect. Male power seems minimally efficacious.

But these works disperse the power of the father, they do not deny it. If the characterization of the Dashwood sisters emphasizes their emotional and moral energy—sometimes misguided, in Marianne's case, but always conspicuous—the plot stresses their inability to control, except negatively, the courses of their own lives.[2] Like their eighteenth-century fictional forebears, these young women cannot act to large purpose. They can choose between self-discipline

and self-indulgence. Marianne spends an improper morning tour-
ing the country house Willoughby will inherit: self-indulgence.
Elinor finds a mode of courtesy—self-discipline—to encourage
Lady Middleton to exclude her from a card game. The girls choose
to go to London. In due time, they choose to come home. But such
actions, such choices, comprise their utmost possibility. When a
man proposes, they can accept or reject; until he proposes, they
can do little of importance. The contrast between Marianne and
Elinor in relation to the men they love enforces this point. Marianne, open, confiding, and active, reveals her love and encourages
her lover in speech and in action. Elinor, dedicated to repression,
waits for her lover to declare himself and acts only according to the
dictates of propriety. The plot insists that this large difference between the sisters makes little difference in their fates. Both are
jilted. If Elinor eventually gets what she wants, whereas Marianne
must want what she gets, this contrast depends less on the actions
of the women than on the courses taken by the men.

In this respect as in others, the narrative of the two Elizas has
cautionary force. Colonel Brandon relates it. His formulations assign minimal agency to the young women whose story he tells. Eliza
1 "was married—married against her inclination" (205). Misery
overcomes her resolution to remain faithful to her exiled lover.
Her husband's unkind treatment produces its "natural" outcome in
her "fall" (206). After her divorce, she "sink[s] deeper in a life
of sin" (207). Brandon discovers her on her deathbed, sees her
"placed in comfortable lodgings" (207), and shares her final moments. He then takes charge of her daughter, Eliza 2, whom he
places in and removes from various situations. Finally he rescues
her from the consequences of Willoughby's seduction.

Colonel Brandon is a good man. He stresses his subjects' lack of
responsibility because of his desire to exculpate them. He even
comes close to blaming himself for the first Eliza's "fall": "Had I
remained in England, perhaps—" (206). But his role as benevolent
father figure underlines the social force inherent in maleness.
Brandon and the first Eliza alike experience the thwarting of their
early love, but only one of them enjoys subsequent viable choices
about the course of his life. Brandon possesses the power, financial
and social, to "place" others; Eliza cannot even choose her own
place. The Colonel tells the Eliza story to Elinor as a parable about
her sister, a warning of the vulnerability inherent in the situation
of a woman committed to emotional self-expression. The parable
extends further than he realizes: his story miniaturizes the condition of even the best women in relation to even the best men. Men

can act to constructive purpose; women act trivially or to their own destruction. Men supply the authority and the capacity on which women must finally rely.

So although the women in this novel neither long for nor fear the symbolic father, they exist under his shadow. Whether "sensible" in the rational or the emotional meaning of the word, they live subject to the will or the whim of men. Foolish John Dashwood, half-brother to Marianne and Elinor, and the only surviving adult male Dashwood, controls the financial resources that, shared, could make the women's lives easier. He chooses not to bestow any of his wealth. Even self-doubting Edward Ferrars, coming to propose to Elinor after his fiancée's betrayal frees him to marry the woman he loves, reveals a kind of confidence inconceivable in a woman, the confidence derived from awareness of social actualities that make women wait for men to act. The narrator comments on the point in a tone of disingenuous doubtfulness modulating into sharp irony:

By his rapidity in seeking [his] fate, it is to be supposed . . . he did not, upon the whole, expect a very cruel reception. It was his business, however, to say that he *did*, and he said it very prettily. What he might say on the subject a twelvemonth after, must be referred to the imagination of husbands and wives. (366)

Edward preserves the social forms that allow women to pretend to power in the moment of courtship. Once he experiences the dominion culturally assigned to husbands, the text suggests, he will no longer bother with such forms. Gentle, loving men like the Colonel and Edward differ from more ostentatiously commanding "fathers" not in the authority they possess, only in the ways they choose to use it.

Like Radcliffe's Gothic plots, the plot of *Sense and Sensibility* derives from the viewpoint of daughters. Despite its lack of overtly sinister suggestion, Austen's novel conveys a more pessimistic view than Radcliffe's. Phallic power is hardly at issue here. Radcliffe debunks it, Austen barely acknowledges it. But men's social power, recognized though not dwelt on by Radcliffe, in this Austen novel appears as a central fact in female lives. For women, there is no escaping fathers. Even "feminized" males, unambitious, unaggressive, reveal the fundamental arrogance of the masculine position.

Scott's young male protagonist of *Waverley* also experiences the omnipresence of fathers. Edward Waverley seeks adventure in traditional masculine modes, assumes military service as male occupation, and makes his marital choice in lordly fashion, having rapidly recovered from his rejection by another woman. Despite his notorious passivity,[3] he finds several courses of action available to him. Haphazard though his choices appear, they remind us that he inhabits the atmosphere of male freedom. Yet *Waverley* raises serious questions about the prerogatives and the necessities of the "masculine."

Dispersed is precisely the right word to describe the power of fathers in this novel. Like Evelina, Waverley finds so many fathers that one suspects him of seeking them. His literal male parent, a selfish and self-serving man who chooses the Whig cause solely as a means to personal advancement, functions mainly offstage, although his actions have important bearings on the intricate plot. As a small child, Waverley in effect elects his uncle, Sir Everard, as substitute father. A kindly man of Jacobite sympathies, Sir Everard sends the youth on his way to Baron Bradwardine, destined to become his father-in-law, but playing a paternally protective part in relation to Waverley from the beginning. In his subsequent travels northward, Waverley encounters a plethora of male figures who wish to guide and control him and whose guidance and control he at least for a time eagerly accepts. Fergus, although a young man, claims and exercises authority over his visitor by virtue of his own political sophistication and experience. On the battlefield, Waverley saves and captures an English soldier, Colonel Talbot, who promptly constitutes himself his captor's moral mentor and subsequently behaves more and more like Waverley's father, even entering into property negotiations associated with the young man's marriage.[4] Seeing one of his comrades-at-arms prepare to shoot Colonel Gardiner, his previous English commander, who has figured previously in the narrative only as offstage tyrant, "Edward felt as if he was about to see a parricide committed in his presence" (334; ch. 46). Since the shooter does not know his intended victim, the idea of "parricide" derives entirely from Waverley's overheated and overdetermined imagination. Gardiner, who does not actually die until the day after the "parricide" episode, preserves a postmortem paternal role for the confused protagonist. His dying look takes on monitory force in Edward's memory. Finally, Waverley metaphorically embraces the "Chevalier," Prince Charles, as father-king virtually the first moment he sees him.

Their symbolic and literal paternal force varies greatly, but each of the figures I have specified to some degree embodies for Waverley the mystique of the father. The Dashwood sisters find the symbolic father's presence inescapable, they do not actively seek it as Edward Waverley unconsciously does. He, like Evelina, wants guidance, help, and support. But the father's meaning for a young man differs, even in fiction, from his meaning for a woman. Scott's version does not stress Oedipal competition; it emphasizes the urgency of Waverley's need for a male model. Following a well-established pattern of the realistic novel, *Waverley* depicts the experience of a youth trying to learn how to live in the world: trying to learn how *to be a man*. The multiplication of male authority figures suggests the difficulty of that endeavor in Scott's imagining of it—the difficulty of establishing male identity.

Such identity, the father figures indicate, depends on more than personal identification. Although Waverley's metaphorical fathers differ from one another and from his literal parent in many respects, each has allied himself to a political cause. Their reasons for doing so include desire for financial gain, family tradition, political ambition, and military honor. The degree of their commitment varies: Fergus could never change his political alliance, Waverley's father might easily shift his. But all exemplify the traditional connection between manhood and public responsibility. If Waverley chooses a lasting model from among them, he must also choose a cause.

Although the young man swears allegiance first to one cause, then to its enemy, and finally to the first one again, these political commitments have for him only personal meaning. He goes to fight for the Hanoverians because his father tells him to. He joins the Jacobite rebellion because charmed by the Prince who leads it. He abandons the cause because he thinks he can honorably do so and reverts to the Hanoverians to save his life and his property, to create a space in which he can begin adult existence. As soon as he declares his allegiance to the "Chevalier," he appears to feel entitled to the love of the Jacobite heroine Flora. She comments on the lack of passion and depth in his alliance: "Can such lukewarm adherence be honourable to yourselves [i.e., Waverley and his family], or gratifying to your lawful sovereign?" (215; ch. 27). More tellingly, she defines Waverley as essentially a private man, whose values partake of the traditionally feminine. If he were to marry, she says rather contemptuously, he "would for ever refer to the idea of domestic happiness which [his] imagination is capable of painting" (215; ch. 27). To Rose Bradwardine, whom Waverley eventually marries, Flora comments on Waverley as military man. He fights, to be sure, but so, she believes, do all men, who have "when confronted with each other, a certain instinct for strife, as we see in other male animals, such as dogs, bulls, and so forth"

(370; ch. 52). But Waverley fails in heroic responsiveness. "I will tell you where he will be at home, my dear, and in his place,—in the quiet circle of domestic happiness, lettered indolence, and elegant enjoyments, of Waverley-Honour" (370; ch. 52). Despite all his activity and all his posturing, Waverley belongs to the domestic realm.

Although the novel consistently focuses attention on its eponymous protagonist, Waverley's actions generate little of its plot. Waverley lavishly exercises his male freedom. The liberty that allows him to spend his early youth reading romantic literature belongs more often to girls than to boys, as Lennox's figure of Arabella reminds us. But his journey northward, dictated by desire, in all its divagations declares the openness of masculine possibility. Waverley's ever-shifting choices, however, make almost as little difference as do those of the Dashwood sisters. Back in England, his family suffers for his alleged treachery, but not only because of the young man's behavior. Others have manipulated appearances against him. He functions as an instrument for those with stronger conviction or greater ambition. Things happen to him and around him, not because he wills them. Flora and Rose discuss a comic episode in which Waverley ends a dispute over military precedence when he "lifted his head as if he had just awaked from a dream, and asked, with great composure, what the matter was" (369; ch. 52). "If he were the hero you suppose him," Flora tells Rose, "he would interest himself in these matters" (369; ch. 52). The conflict ends because everyone unites in laughing at the young Englishman's absent-mindedness. This trivial event epitomizes Waverley's role in the plot of the novel named after him. Although his existence and his presence sometimes organize other people's behavior, he organizes his own so little, possesses so little coherent motivation, that he rarely bears responsibility for significant happening.

It goes without saying, then, that Waverley does not plot, although he figures as object of others' plots. Thus a token of his familial identity, the seal he carries on his watch chain, stolen by an inveterate plotter, becomes an instrument with which to manipulate soldiers loyal to Waverley and to control others' impression of his identity. The account of this sequence, reported long after the fact, emphasizes its position in an ongoing fiction, a heroic or historical drama: "Donald Bean, supposing himself left out of a secret where confidence promised to be advantageous, determined to have his share in the drama, whether a regular part were assigned him or not" (364; ch. 51). Waverley does not know what the drama is, much less what part has been assigned him. Again and again, someone abducts him, usually to serve political ends; in the plot, to emphasize his lack of agency. Waverley interprets what happens to him, but typically interprets it incorrectly. He creates fictions; he does not understand history.

As one might expect of an inveterate reader of fiction, Waverley tells himself stories. Colonel Gardiner's letter demanding his immediate return to his regiment causes him to conceive a narrative of the Colonel as tyrant. The young man sees Flora once, hears her sing, and constructs his fiction of her as Highland heroine and himself as her consort. His fantasies about himself multiply as his situation changes, but he possesses no developed fiction of his own identity. Flora sees him more distinctly than he sees himself. The typical eighteenth-century narrative of a young man's coming of age requires that he mature by rejecting his own behavioral weaknesses and accepting his social responsibilities. Waverley, although he follows this pattern, also needs to construct for himself a stable identity. His most important, and most interesting, flaw is his failure to know what consistent story he should tell about himself.

In a famous moment of Scott's narrative, we learn that Waverley now "felt himself entitled to say firmly, though perhaps with a sigh, that the romance of his life was ended, and that its real history had now commenced" (415; ch. 60). Waverley formulates self-awareness in terms of literary genre, echoing the narrator's conspicuous generic anxiety. Even less than the narrator does he understand the implications of the genres he assumes as alternatives. Writing of a novelist ostensibly very different from Scott, Sara Suleri observes that in one of V. S. Naipaul's books, "The frightening category of history confronts the archaic category of romance" (35). Her adjectives call attention to what Waverley ignores. To insert himself in history would have its own terrors; to preserve his commitment to romance declares his life irrelevant. And in fact we do not quite know which he does. The narrator does not comment on Waverley's claim of self-knowledge, but the problem of interpreting it becomes central to the reader's experience of the novel.

Waverley's distinction implies that he lives no longer in terms of unrealistic expectations. He will turn his attentions to Rose rather than Flora; the shift implies new understanding of his own nature and possibilities. He will return to London and do what he must to clear the family name. He will henceforth follow a consistent rather than an erratic course of action. "History," at the level of individual experience, implies comprehended causality. One escapes its fearfulness by avoiding its public aspects. But it is not easy to discern the difference between Waverley's life before and after his revelation. Immediately after we learn that he has accepted his life as real history, he reads a newspaper account of his father's death and concludes himself "a parricide" (417; ch. 61). The newspaper has said that Richard Waverley "died of a lingering disorder, augmented by the unpleasant predicament of suspicion in which he stood" (416; ch. 61); Edward's conclusion has scanty basis—except according to interpretations of personal fantasy or archaic "romance." Similarly, he decides that allowing his uncle to remain in danger of conviction for treason would be "worse than parricide," since that uncle "has ever been more to me than a father" (417; ch. 61). He therefore sets out on another romance quest, with another false identity, and that not the last he will assume.

Waverley's enthusiasm for seeing himself as parricide betrays a troubled relation to paternal authority despite, or because of, his multiplication of father figures. Everywhere he sees figures of masculine self-confidence who emphasize his own inability to attain comparable poise. After a final journey northward, replete in images of romance (the Baron Bradwardine hiding in a cave, Waverley himself assuming yet another identity), he achieves the marriage that will solidify his social role. The narrative of this achievement focuses intensely on property, particularly the reaccumulation of Bradwardine property, which will, it turns out, descend to Waverley's imagined second son.[5] With wife, property, and expectation of property as anchors, Waverley can perhaps settle into history of an unfrightening sort. It will be a history of quiet domesticity rather than adventurous accomplishment. The marriage on which Waverley embarks will presumably allow him to fuse the "masculine" position of representing his lineage with his "feminine" taste for settled, eventless existence.

Yet his earlier assertion that his life has become real history instead of romance remains ambiguous. Perhaps Waverley, thinking himself to understand "reality," has in fact only constructed another fantasy. On the other hand, possibly the statement contains its own truth: war, as Scott characters engage in it, may belong to the realm of romance; its aftermath, the process of male "settling down," perhaps involves history, a mundane sequence of one thing after another. Such an interpretation would imply a certain optimism, about war as offering opportunity for heroism more significantly than episodes of destruction, about "history" as reassuring if possibly tedious. Neither the texture of subsequent happenings nor the systems of causality that govern them, however, differ markedly from what the novel has previously presented. To be sure,

Waverley's life now moves toward a kind of emotional closure—but neat resolutions belong more plausibly to romance than to "real history."

By calling attention to these alternative terms, the narrator raises the possibility that the difference between "romance" and "history" inheres not in the pattern of events but in their interpretation. Neither Waverley nor his life changes conspicuously until the novel comes to an end. Only the attributed meaning of the character and his experience alters. The narrator's ponderous introductory expressions of concern about readers' generic expectations call attention from the outset to the narratorial problem. He tries to construct his title appropriately, since it "may be held as pledging the author to some special mode of laying his scene, drawing his characters, and managing his adventures" (33; ch. 1). He specifies alternate possibilities implicit in alternate titles. And he returns to this matter of alternatives: he will not write in the mode of *Don Quixote*, he will rather depict a "more common aberration from sound judgment" (55; ch. 5); he will not draw from all his Highland sources in describing the hunt but will depend solely on "the ingenious Mr Gunn's Essay"—"without further tyranny" over the reader (187; ch. 24). But readers have space to elude even the most tyrannical narrator. The narrator determines what the reader will read, but the reader determines *how*.

Waverley, in his addiction to romances, has lost "for ever the opportunity of acquiring habits of firm and assiduous application, of gaining the art of controlling, directing, and concentrating the powers of his mind for earnest investigation" (46; ch. 3). The comment, in the narrator's most moralistic tone, perhaps registers anxiety about the imaginative freedom implicit in the writing of as well as the response to romance. Assumptions of romance oppose those of logic. To tell the story of Edward Waverley demands not rigorous and "earnest investigation," but speculative liberty to trace mental and emotional processes of a youth imagined not as governed by principles of control and concentration but as primarily responsive to emotional stimuli. As a fictional character, Waverley, reader of romances, can only figure in some version of romance. The laws of his nature forbid him to understand himself, to be understood, in history: unless history is redefined.

Scott acknowledges in his 1829 preface to the Waverley Novels his lack of control over the plot of what he refers to as his "romance." "The tale of Waverley was put together with so little care," he writes, "that I cannot boast of having sketched any distinct plan of the work" (525). Alexander Welsh quotes a more general statement of Scott's on the subject of plot: "I never could lay down a plan—or, having laid it down, I never could adhere to it. . . . I only tried to make that which I was actually writing diverting and interesting, leaving the rest to fate" (qu. Welsh 150). The metaphor of the runaway stone, articulated in Chapter 70 of the seventy-two chapters of *Waverley*, insists within the novel's text on the narrator's lack of control. Here "the course of the narrative" is likened to that of "a stone rolled down hill by an idle truant boy," which moves slowly at first, but gradually becomes "most furiously rapid in its course" (480), thundering over hedges and ditches according to the laws of gravity rather than the will of its thrower. No more than Waverley's reading does the novel's writing seem the result of "firm and assiduous application." The novelist, although he several times in the prefatory material alludes to himself as his work's "father" or speaks of his "paternal" role in relation to it, abjures traditional authority over his text, granting it a kind of inanimate life of its own. The narrator's addresses to the reader, ostensibly Fielding-esque in tone, declare his uncertainties and anxieties—about title, about genre, about the reader's response—rather than his dominion. The authority of authorship, as well as that of fathers, comes into question.

The novel's wisdom is the wisdom of uncertainty. Romance, in Patricia Parker's useful formulation, "as a form . . . simultaneously quests for and postpones a particular end, objective, or object" (4). Waverley's quest, on the other hand, need only discover its true object in order to attain it. The young man toys with various false objectives—the wrong woman, the wrong cause, the wrong relation to authority—before defining his proper ends; then he promptly achieves them. His achievement seems oddly beside the point. The final narrative chapter, reporting events immediately after Waverley's marriage, begins, "The nuptial party travelled in great style" (482; ch. 71). The bridegroom travels concealed in that party; he hardly appears more conspicuously in the rest of the chapter. He speaks two expository sentences to the Baron; his portrait, with Fergus, hangs on the wall, along with his arms from "the unfortunate civil war" (489; ch. 71). But essentially all action and all speech belong to the Baron and Colonel Talbot, Waverley's symbolic fathers. They discuss the disposition of property and of heraldry; they propose the toasts. The Baron affirms his intention of willing his estate to Edward's second son. Talbot, rather perplexingly, explains that he has procured the Baron's heirloom cup in order "to give you some token of my deep interest in all that concerns my young friend Edward" (490; ch.71). Things happen around Waverley, even because of him, but his will, purpose, desire now seem irrelevant.

So the plot's resolution declares the novel's uncertainty about the relative importance of fathers and sons and about the ways in which a son may acquire strength. Waverley implicitly commits himself to the more "feminine" side of his nature in taking Rose as wife. But we know nothing of how he will develop that side of himself, and nothing of what will become of his impulse to fight for glamorous causes. His tentative explorations of romance and his equally tentative insertion of himself into history have eventuated in his marriage, but the text provides no direct evidence that he has thereby assumed adult responsibility or authority or political commitment. Authority remains in the hands of the elders, who wield it benignly (no Schedonis here). Time will bring Waverley more property and more power, but it will not necessarily show him how to authenticate his desire, how to give himself a history with meaningful relation to public history. *Waverley* as a novel appears to have resolved none of the problems it set for itself. It has only announced those problems ever more loudly, in its narrative method and its narrative substance.

Like all of Austen's novels, *Sense and Sensibility*, with its vivid narrative voice, makes its readers conscious of the obvious but often forgotten fact that causality in fiction is a narrative construction. One can say—as I said earlier in this chapter—that important things happen in *Sense and Sensibility* because of male desire or impulse. Such narrative arrangements, however, also participate in the dialectic pattern through which Austen's narrator enforces distinctions that clarify the novel's moral universe. Important things happen in the novel in order to reveal the difference between false appearance and the reality it parodies.

The minor figure of Mr. Palmer illustrates characteristic complexities of causality. Elinor, possessed of considerable discriminatory power, finds herself initially at a loss to understand why he appears so oddly intent on being disagreeable. "Sir John is as stupid as the weather," he remarks of his father-in-law. "As vile a spot as I ever saw in my life," he observes of the estate at Allenham that Willoughby will inherit (111). When he scolds or abuses his wife, she is "highly diverted." "'Mr. Palmer is so droll!' said she, in a whisper, to Elinor. 'He is always out of humour'" (112).

This marital relationship parodies the novel's typical situation in which women choose and act but men possess determinative power.

Mrs. Palmer interprets her husband with utter disregard for what he says. If he sneers at the idea of inviting the Miss Dashwoods to his home, "'There now'—said his lady, 'you see Mr. Palmer expects you; so you cannot refuse to come'" (113). She proceeds blithely on her foolish and good-humored course, in her comments transforming her husband's bad temper to good. On the other hand, he decides where they will go and when. Her resources, only verbal, make nothing happen.

But what *he* says also proves nugatory. His utterances typically bear only a devious relation to his intent. They may convey accurately his contempt for his wife's verbal folly, but they rarely mean what they say. Elinor quickly figures out Mr. Palmer's operations. "It was the desire of appearing superior to other people," she deduces, that governs his speech. Much later, she finds "him very capable of being a pleasant companion. . . . For the rest of his character and habits, they were marked, as far as Elinor could perceive, with no traits at all unusual in his sex and time of life" (304). This last generalization turns out to mean that the man is lazy, selfish, and conceited.

Mr. Palmer has little function in the novel's plot. His effort to make himself opaque, however, mirrors the conduct of those more fully responsible for the web of feeling and action that structures the narrative. Colonel Brandon conceals his relation to the two Elizas and his consequent duel with Willoughby; Willoughby conceals his financial calculations and, for a time, his engagement to another woman; Edward conceals his alliance with Lucy. Nor do the women— even apparently artless Marianne—prove more transparent to the novel's other characters. Marianne conceals the lack of formal commitment between her and Willoughby; Elinor conceals her putative lover's commitment elsewhere.[6] Moreover, the major characters often remain opaque even to themselves. Marianne of course stays unaware of the selfishness masked by her claims of freedom and expressiveness, but even self-analyzing Elinor has moments of blindness: when, for instance, she explains Edward's ambiguous behavior as the product of his mother's cruelty or understands his ring set with hair as a covert acknowledgement of his love for her. Her judgment of Mr. Palmer as possessing the characteristic traits of his age and gender turns out to derive from her desire to assert Edward's superiority, although Edward, as far as she knows, will soon marry another woman. Desire always deceives, this novel suggests.

Given its pattern of intentional and unintentional deception, the novel's action necessarily concentrates on disentangling. Elinor and Marianne must make urgent discriminations (like Waverley's, in a sense *generic* discriminations): between true and false intimacy, language, love, interpretation. The false intimacy claimed by Lucy and her sister, by Lady Middleton's bland social behavior, by Mrs. John Dashwood's invitation to the Steele sisters, contrasts with the saving closeness between Elinor and Marianne. The inauthentic language of Lady Middleton, of the Misses Steele, of Marianne and Willoughby at their worst throws into sharp relief the genuineness of Willoughby's confession, of Elinor's revelation of suffering, of Colonel Brandon's concern for Marianne. Specious interpretations yield to accurate ones, false love gives place to true.

All of which makes *Sense and Sensibility* sound cheerily conventional. In fact, its cheer does not extend far. Although the firm control of the narrator's tone assures the reader that nothing will go permanently wrong in this fictional universe, the novel makes it apparent that only the freedoms of fictionality ensure happy outcomes. The concealments indulged in by virtually every character come to an end. Truth manifests itself, often through operations of self-interest, but it possesses no salvationary force. To know that Edward is engaged to someone else explains his actions and his psychic state to Elinor without providing any help for her own emotional dilemma. To hear that Colonel Brandon has fought a duel attests to his orthodox manliness ("Elinor sighed over the fancied necessity of this; but to a man and a soldier, she presumed not to censure it" [211]), but the knowledge helps no one. Discriminating betweeen actuality and appearance is a praiseworthy activity. Elinor's capacity for fine discrimination marks her moral and intellectual excellence, but it makes no difference to her fate. More emphatically than any of Austen's other novels, *Sense and Sensibility* suggests life's essential unfairness.

That unfairness manifests itself particularly in the distribution of power. Not only do men, as we have seen, possess a kind of power unavailable to women. Women too, given sufficient unscrupulousness or moral blindness, can make others do their will. Edward Ferrars's mother, a bully by virtue of her money, provides one case in point, Lucy Steele another. Mary Poovey points out that "Willoughby's aunt, who is empowered by money and age, is even more tyrannical; and Sophia Grey, Willoughby's fiancée, enacts her passion and her will when she commands Willoughby to copy her cruel letter for Marianne" (189). By relentless manipulation in the service of her ends, Lucy Steele gets what she wants in life: a wealthy and foolish husband. "The whole of Lucy's behaviour in the affair," the narrator comments,

and the prosperity which crowned it, . . . may be held forth as a most encouraging instance of what an earnest, an unceasing attention to self-interest, however its progress may be apparently obstructed, will do in securing every advantage of fortune, with no other sacrifice than that of time and conscience. (376)

Neither sacrifice matters to Lucy. The narrator's irony at her expense affirms the moral order assumed in the novel's tone, but it does not obviate the probability that dislocations of that order will occur as men and women seek and find power that can make life a misery for others.

Sense and Sensibility resembles *Waverley* in the relative helplessness of its protagonists. Lacking the concerted will to self-aggrandizement that motivates such as Lucy, the Dashwood sisters, like Edward Waverley, must depend on others to give their lives ultimate direction. Benign outcomes will develop, within the world of fiction, but the presence of such characters as Lucy and Donald Bean (in *Waverley*) reminds the reader of other possibilities implicit in the presence of powerful plotters. The plots of these fictions deprive figures enveloped in their own romantic dreams (Marianne and Waverley) of romantic outcomes. Scott grants romantic Fergus romantic fulfillment—but only in death. Scott presents a rather chaotic plot, Austen offers an ostentatiously neat one, in which, as Marilyn Butler points out, "the same things happen to two girls in each of two volumes" ("Disregarded Designs" 58). Scott's novel and Austen's, both written in their authors' youth, conform to long-established convention in resolving their characters' problems through marriage, but both also hint that marriage may not after all settle every difficulty. Neatness may prove illusory. Scott's cavalier plotting and Austen's partly ironic control make the same point.

To recur to familiar terms: marriage in these novels does not altogether reconcile "masculine" and "feminine" principles. Both novels give the "feminine" apparent preeminence. Austen depicts an almost completely feminized world, Scott stresses Waverley's repudiation of conflict and his desire for domesticity. But Scott also reminds us insistently of "history," and he knows, if Waverley does not, its danger: the unpredictable pressure of public facts on private lives. Austen's novel invites the reader to contemplate ominous possibilities of what Edward may say to his wife a twelvemonth af-

ter his marriage, ominous implications of Colonel Brandon's unquestioning assumption of authority over women. It may be true,
as Tony Tanner says, that Marianne "is married off to Brandon to
complete a pattern, to satisfy that instinct for harmonious arranging which is part of the structure both of that society and of the
book itself" (*Jane Austen* 100). But the anomalies of male-female
relations in *Sense and Sensibility* raise questions about the nature
of society's (and books') harmonious arrangements. Although a
wealthy woman like Mrs. Ferrars or Sophia Grey may exercise
power, female hegemony remains essentially impossible. "Feminine" consciousnesses typically find themselves power's victims.
The best that can be hoped for the possessors of such consciousness
is that they may not mind the role.

Mansfield Park and *The Heart of Midlothian* continue to explore issues of intimacy and power, "feminine" and "masculine," in more
explicit and self-conscious ways. *Mansfield Park* differs sharply from
Sense and Sensibility in investigating the possibility that power does
not only inhere in social roles or belong only to the wealthy or the
aggressive. The interpersonal constructions of power here become
a fact of plot as well as a thematic preoccupation.[7]

Perceptions of power shift in *Mansfield Park*. From the point of
view of Fanny Price, everyone always possesses more power than
she. She readily accepts hierarchical arrangements, as eager as her
cousins could be to place herself at the bottom of any conceivable
social ordering of those above the class of servants. Mrs. Norris
announces the situation from Fanny's first arrival as a little girl. Her
female cousins, richer, smarter, more cultivated, more beautiful
than she, deserve the best the world can offer. Her male cousins
will in due course rule the world. Her uncle rules the household,
Mrs. Norris herself runs everything. Fanny gets what others do not
want, does what others prefer not to do. Edmund alone considers
her needs and desires, thus demonstrating his benevolence, not her
entitlement. Fanny's apparent inability to claim the slightest authority, the most minimal rights, becomes the salient aspect of her
personality.

Yet it is Fanny whom Sir Thomas Bertram addresses in these
terms:

I had thought you peculiarly free from wilfulness of temper, self-conceit,
and every tendency to that independence of spirit, which prevails so much
in modern days, even in young women, and which in young women is
offensive and disgusting beyond all common offence. But you have now

shewn me that you can be wilful and perverse, that you can and will decide for yourself, without any consideration or deference for those who have surely some right to guide you—without even asking their advice. (318)

She has offended him by announcing her intention to refuse a highly eligible offer of marriage. He interprets her will to decide for herself as a challenge to his authority: she has failed to defer to the father figure in her life, here disguised as "those with the right to guide" her. Although Sir Thomas can readily reduce Fanny— who retains, after all, her "obliging, yielding temper" (17)—to floods of tears, although her own mental constructions continue to assign him the utmost power, he has in actuality lost his power as soon as it is openly resisted.

Indeed, Sir Thomas's dominance, the most conventional and in some ways the most manifest in the novel, proves repeatedly problematic. Precisely because his daughters experience him as tyrannical, they rush to escape his governance. His eldest son evades his father's standards in order to assert his own force in the face of the experienced oppression of paternal authority. Sir Thomas's plans backfire. He knows himself a failure as head of the family, inadequate as a judge of character. In the dénouement, he finds "comfort" in Fanny (472), perceiving her now as giving to him rather than as recipient of his guidance and benevolence.

Sir Thomas's shifting position epitomizes an important pattern in the novel. To trace the vocabulary of control as it figures in the text calls attention to the evanescence of every form of authority among the residents of Mansfield Park. Language of power characteristically associates itself, for instance, with courtship. Women assume it as goal to "captivate" or make "conquests" of men. Mary Crawford seeks from Fanny "some pleasant assurance of her power" over Edmund (289). Men worry about their "danger" from attractive women. On the other hand, when Henry sets out to make Fanny fall in love with him, he is seen as "attacking" her peace of mind. Subsequently, he announces the impossibility that her power over his heart will ever cease (297). Julia and Maria interpret their contest over Henry as one of power; they need to have the experience of dominating men. Edmund, parting forever from Mary Crawford, reports the smile with which she entices him to return as "seeming to invite, in order to subdue me" (459). Men and women alike (as in *Clarissa*, though less emphatically) understand the game of love as analogous to war. The battle of the sexes involves not open antagonism but constant effort toward domination. Victors and vanquished frequently change roles.

The issues alive in the abortive theatrical endeavors of Mansfield Park include questions of power. Tom, asserting his leadership in his father's absence, resents the possibility of competition from Edmund. Edmund wishes to maintain moral preeminence but can find no effective mode of demonstrating it. He appeals to his sister to exercise her powers of leadership. She finds the suggestion flattering—although less attractive, finally, than the opportunity of flirting with Henry Crawford. Mrs. Norris considers herself in charge of everything, entertaining herself with fantasies of control. Every situation—the choice of plays, of actors, of locations, the assignment of roles—provides opportunity for contests of mastery in which individuals reveal their self-conceptions and the extent of their personal arsenals.

But Fanny—so she believes—has nothing to do with any of this. Accepting her position as lowest and least, proclaiming her inability to act, helping others to learn their lines, even when her helpfulness forces her to endure the intimate anguish of supervising a love scene between Edmund and Mary, Fanny has defined for herself a place that obviates all questions of power. She refuses to participate in the conventional games. Her concerns lie elsewhere.

They lie, specifically, in the sphere of intimacy. A crude reading of *Mansfield Park* might maintain that the action turns on a contest between Mary Crawford, concerned always with questions of power, wealth, prestige, and Fanny Price, interested only in "love"— meaning far more than romantic love. Indeed such a contest takes place, and Fanny wins. But that fact of "winning" in itself must complicate any impulse to accept Fanny's claim of utter separation from the realm of power.

From the beginning, Fanny manifests her preoccupation with "everybody she had been used to," the family she has left behind (14), and her yearning to be loved by her new family. Edmund assures her, "you are with relations and friends, who all love you, and wish to make you happy" (15), but he comforts her more by encouraging her to talk of her brothers and sisters and helping her to write a letter to her favorite brother. He characterizes her as "having an affectionate heart, and a strong desire of doing right" and remarks also her "great sensibility of her situation, and great timidity" (17). This summary characterization locates precisely the traits that the narrative will exemplify and stress. Until Fanny refuses Henry Crawford, the reader has acquired no data from which to draw other conclusions. One may, of course, choose a different vocabulary for describing Fanny, speaking, perhaps, of "masochism" rather than "timidity," or wondering about the standards by which she defines "doing right." But on the whole, the girl Edmund helps corresponds to the girl the text describes.

The combination of "affectionate heart" and "timidity" does not at the outset promise much success. Predictably, Fanny falls in love with Edmund; predictably, she does nothing consciously to make him reciprocate her affections. The drawing-room scene in which she talks about the wonders of nature and Edmund moves toward Mary at the pianoforte appears to suggest how it will all come out. Fanny, unable to act significantly on or off stage,[8] unable to consider herself important to anyone, unable to make claims for herself, relentlessly high-minded, will watch in pain as Edmund attaches himself to a less worthy but more glamorous woman. If this were what we in the late twentieth century might more readily consider a "realistic" novel, she would content herself thereafter with devising new ways to be useful. Given the operative fictional conventions, however, she will presumably find someone to marry.

The obvious problem of plotting in the novel is to make it plausible, rather than only conventional, that Fanny in fact gets the man she wants. The narrator accomplishes this end, not only by revealing unexpected toughness of mind in the protagonist but also by calling attention to how much has happened in the story as a result of internal mutation rather than external happening. Fanny herself comments on the determinative force of the inner life, using a familiar language of power. "The memory," she observes to Mary Crawford, "is sometimes so retentive, so serviceable, so obedient—at others, so bewildered and so weak—and at others again, so tyrannic, so beyond controul!" (209). The anthropomorphic adjectives recall a range of behavior in the novel's persons: one can be serviceable and obedient like Fanny herself, or tyrannic and uncontrollable as Maria will self-defeatingly become. They also designate an internal range applicable to more than memory. The substance as well as the action of memory turns out to be problematic. Memory merges readily with fantasy, as Fanny's "remembrance" demonstrates:

The remembrance of all her earliest pleasures, and of what she had suffered in being torn from them, came over her with renewed strength, and it seemed as if to be at home again, would heal every pain that had since grown out of the separation. To be in the centre of such a circle, loved by so many, and more loved by all than she had ever been before, to feel affection without fear or restraint. . . . (370)

This vision of life in Portsmouth draws on presumably false although insistent (tyrannic?) memories and projects impossible dreams. It speaks of desire more than of recollection—desire, among other things, to "be in the centre." It epitomizes the way that psychic truth dominates actuality.

And not only for Fanny. Both Edmund and Mary refer to the theatrical interlude as a "dream," thus characterizing the psychic space that enabled a considerable cast of characters to act out fantasies of love and power. But the novel makes it difficult to differentiate "dream" from "reality," since apparent balances of force shift rapidly. Maria, for instance, throughout the theatricals appears to live under Henry Crawford's sway, her moods and attitudes determined by his responses. Once he leaves, she decides to rely on other resources: "Henry Crawford had destroyed her happiness, but he should not know that he had done it; he should not destroy her credit, her appearance, her prosperity too" (202). Making use of credit, appearance, and prosperity, she succeeds in consolidating a curious kind of dominion over him. He does not love or want her, yet he finds himself eloping with her. She has acquired effective power, however evanescent.

Power exists where people—its agents or its objects—think it exists. Mrs. Norris, although she plays a more important part in the action of *Mansfield Park* than Mr. Palmer does in *Sense and Sensibility*, like Mr. Palmer supplies a parodic view of the novel's concerns. Self-designated organizer and expediter of Mansfield Park affairs, she tyrannizes the helpless and indulges the privileged. Her fantasies reassure her of her indispensable role. Fanny, her victim, fears and placates her. Although the narrator's dry accounts of Mrs. Norris's accomplishments alert the reader to discrepancies between her sense of her own importance and her actual achievement, the narrative also reports the degree to which she recurrently enforces her view on others. When actual disaster strikes, however, Mrs. Norris proves altogether inadequate to it, unable to imagine new ways of consolidating her power or of using what credit she has. Even before Mrs. Rushworth elopes with Mr. Crawford, Sir Thomas has begun to see that Mrs. Norris has less good will and less meaningful force than he had previously assigned her. His change of perception marks a necessary change in her possibility for effective sway.

Sir Thomas himself, as I have already suggested, suffers from his changing understanding of his own power. His children as well as his niece consider him the dictator of action and the limiter of possibility in the Mansfield Park household. Maria and Julia both marry specifically in order to escape his restrictions on their liberty. Sir Thomas comes to realize his failure. His authority has had no force to restrict his children's folly and vice; self-will proves stronger. At the end, Sir Thomas appears dependent on the affections of others, most especially of Fanny. Julia Prewitt Brown goes so far as to argue that "at the close of *Mansfield Park* Fanny is as much married in mind to her surrogate father Sir Thomas as she is in fact to her substitute brother Edmund. . . . Anticipating Freud, Austen implies that for the woman, the classic sex partners are father and daughter" (99). Her captivation of Sir Thomas perhaps constitutes Fanny's greatest triumph: this too is a daughter's plot.

The action of *Mansfield Park* might be summarized as a drama of shifting perceptions about the meanings people hold for one another. Of course Fanny's meanings, for others and for herself, change most radically. Her Portsmouth fantasy—"in the centre of such a circle, loved by so many, and more loved by all than she had ever been before"—economically defines her desire: not for the love of one man alone, but for the love of "all," a position at the center of a circle of affection. A situation, in short, of power as well as of intimacy.

The circle of which she becomes the center exists at Mansfield Park, not in Portsmouth. Sir Thomas comes to think her "a great acquisition" (472). People change their minds, change their feelings, change their views of what color eyes best become a woman. Given "so much true merit and true love, and no want of fortune or friends" (473), Fanny and Edmund must live happily ever after.

Yet the insistent pattern of changing minds, changing feelings, and changing assignments of power that has created Fanny's happiness establishes a ground of uncertainty for it. Everything "within the view and patronage of Mansfield Park" remains "thoroughly perfect in her eyes" (473). But environmental perfection depends quite explicitly on "her eyes," as her perfection depends on the eyes of others. Readers may enjoy fantasies of "unconquerable passions" and "unchanging attachments" (470), but the narrator reports conquest and change. Stories end (nineteenth-century stories end) when plots resolve the problems they have set. The sense of resolution, like other fictional phenomena, depends on the desire and the belief of readers. Austen's narrative reminds us of this fact.

To think of the "wisdom" of *Mansfield Park* as that of uncertainty calls attention to one of the novel's innovative aspects. *Anna St. Ives* suggested that concern for intimacy only masked desire for power, then the novel retreated from that suggestion. *Mansfield Park* demonstrates not only that morally unsound characters (the Crawford siblings, Maria, Julia) confuse love and power, but that love implies power. Both love and power exist by virtue of perception. Men and women alike assign virtue to those they love (Edmund demonstrates the process in detail) and grant them power accordingly. Fanny, who early declares the impossibility of her ever being important to anyone, finally becomes important to many. She will never possess the socially ordained power of Sir Thomas or even of Edmund, but she embodies what might be called properly feminine force.

Nancy Armstrong, writing about English domestic fiction, affirms its ultimately conservative effect.

these stories of courtship and marriage offered their readers a way of indulging, with a kind of impunity, in fantasies of political power that were the more acceptable because they were played out within a domestic framework where legitimate monogamy—and thus the subordination of female to male—would ultimately be affirmed. In this way, domestic fiction could represent an alternative form of political power without appearing to contest the distribution of power that it represented as historically given. (29)

Jane Austen consistently *describes* the subordination of female to male, but I am not so sure that she *affirms* it. Her novels suggest, at least covertly, the strains and injustices of "necessary" social arrangements. As R. F. Brissenden points out, the plot of *Mansfield Park* appears, at least in outline, "almost glibly sentimental" ("*Mansfield Park*" 156). Yet the necessities of indirection that govern Fanny's acquisition of domestic power raise the possibility that the sentimental plot thinly obscures a biting commentary on the existing social order.

The Heart of Midlothian is perhaps the first English novel to represent a female hero who can be taken seriously as a figure initiating significant action. Jeanie Deans in her quest for her sister's salvation unites traditionally masculine and traditionally feminine virtues. Unlike Lennox's Arabella, she does not become ludicrous as a result of claiming strengths more often assigned to men. (The claim is perhaps less threatening because Jeanie belongs to the lower classes.) Scott's narrative depicts an admirable "feminized" man and at least one woman who becomes terrifying in her "masculine" force. Partly as a result of acknowledging ambiguity in the assignment of gender characteristics, the novel conveys uncertain implications about the relation of power and intimacy.

"You are a singular young woman," the Duke of Argyle observes to Jeanie. "You seem to me to think of every one before yourself"

(350). Along with chastity, thinking of others first virtually defines female virtue. Jeanie's role as domestic paragon precedes her heroic quest, and Scott's novel resolves itself in a return to her domestic excellences. She takes care of the cattle, she makes good cheese, she does what her father tells her to do, she loves and tries to care for her young half-sister. Her love relationship with Reuben Butler reveals her patience as well as her continence. Although from early girlhood she has demonstrated her superiority to Reuben in "firmness of constitution," such superiority depends only, the narrator tells us, "on the conformation of the nerves" (84). Reuben rights the balance of the sexes by excelling in "acuteness of intellect" (84). Jeanie eventually proves a compliant wife as well as a compliant daughter, serving her husband and saving money to fulfill his desires. She brings "into the married state the same firm mind and affectionate disposition,—the same natural and homely good sense, and spirit of useful exertion,—in a word, all the domestic good qualities of which she had given proof during her maiden life" (447–48). To be sure, she does not understand her husband's sermons, "but no minister of the presbytery had his humble dinner so well arranged, his clothes and linen in equal good order, his fireside so neatly swept, his parlour so clean, and his books so well dusted" (448). The narrator goes out of his way to establish the heroine's conformity with orthodox expectations about female uprightness. Although "singular," she is not rebellious.

If the feminine norm in Scott's novel involves sweeping the fireside, the masculine norm, often ironically treated, implies both contentiousness and obtuseness.[9] An early scene between Reuben Butler and Mr. Saddletree shows the two of them walking down the street, "each talking as he could get a word thrust in, the one on the laws of Scotland, the other on those of Syntax, and neither listening to a word which his companion uttered" (48). The same combination of self-assertion and imperviousness to the needs or desires of others manifests itself again a few pages later, when Mrs. Saddletree cogently observes to her husband, "it wad far better become ye, . . . since ye say ye hae skeel o' the law, to try if ye can do ony thing for Effie Deans, puir thing, that's lying up in the tolbooth yonder, cauld, and hungry, and comfortless" (51). Moral blindness and self-display apparently inhere in the male character. Only the idealized Duke of Argyle is exempt.

The Saddletrees, figures of minor importance in the action, demonstrate the disparity between perception and power for women. Mrs. Saddletree, with female penetration and compassionate female priorities, possesses no capacity to do what she considers important. She must go through the motions of deferring to her husband—of whom she remarks, with contempt for masculine ignorance of the essential, "he might be in a lying-in hospital, and ne'er find out what the women cam there for" (52). He prides himself on, boasts of, keeping his wife under control. Mr. Saddletree is a fool, he hardly matters. Yet his chilling unawareness of the Deans family's desperate misery in the courtroom where Effie is condemned speaks of moral dangers implicit in the stereotypical masculine position.

Reuben Butler, Jeanie's lover, a physically weak and morally "feminized" man, with the feminized role of clergyman/schoolteacher, uses metaphoric rifles and bayonets in trying to persuade Jeanie's father of his point of view. Even he, as the earlier episode with Saddletree hinted, operates by principles of male aggression. Effie's lover, George Robertson/Staunton, employs literal weapons (as well as, troublingly, a female disguise). He explains his criminal career as the result of his having been deprived of opportunity for a military profession by his father's situation as clergyman.

I did not so much delight in the wild revel, the low humour, the unconfined liberty of those with whom I associated, as in the spirit of adventure, presence of mind in peril, and sharpness of intellect which they displayed in prosecuting their maraudings upon the revenue, or similar adventures,

he claims, adding,

Had it not been for this cursed rectory, I should have been permitted to follow the bent of my own inclinations and the profession of arms, and half the courage and address that I have displayed among smugglers and deer-stealers would have secured me an honourable rank among my contemporaries. (325)

George feels cheated, in other words, of respectable opportunity to display his manliness and of respectable rewards for it.

But manliness as aggression, with the associated values of courage and adventurousness, solves few problems in Scott's fictional world. George can cut down his friend's body from the gallows, but the friend has already died. He can break into the prison and offer Effie a chance to escape, but Effie refuses the opportunity: he cannot restore her good name. George tries to keep himself at the center of events by telling Jeanie to sacrifice his life for that of her sister; Jeanie does not need him. Finally he suffers the logical consequence of aggression, dying probably at the hand of his only son, who lives by the same values as he. Conversely, the Duke of

Argyle, who sublimates aggression into diplomacy, can accomplish his aims.

Those aims, inasmuch as they are relevant to the plot of *The Heart of Midlothian*, are defined for him by a woman who believes in action but not in aggression. From the beginning to the end of the novel, Jeanie demonstrates the utility of her "active and undaunted habits of virtuous exertion" (501). She rejects the courtship of a lord, yet obtains his financial help. Her lover claims the right to protect her on her perilous trip to London; she points out, accurately, that her capacity to take care of herself far exceeds his to take care of her. Both the help she gets from men (Lord Dumbiedikes's money, Ratcliffe's free passage among criminals, the Duke's intercession) and that she refuses (Reuben's protection, George's self-sacrifice) attest to her moral power. The combination of physical endurance and moral force marks Jeanie's superiority to the novel's other characters, male and female alike.

Her moral force derives partly from her absolute certainty (in marked contrast to Waverley, and to several of the male characters in *The Heart of Midlothian*) about her identity and her purpose. She identifies herself first of all with reference to her femaleness. When Reuben threatens to break their engagement because she refuses to explain why she plans to meet a man at midnight, she expresses regret at the misunderstanding and explains it as resulting from the fact that she is a woman and he a man: they inhabit different cultures. Womanlike (I allude, of course, to traditional notions of womanhood), she accounts for her important actions as results of injunctions from outside herself.[10] Relying always on "faith in Providence, and a resolution to discharge her duty" (200), she finds in prayer the sense of direction she needs. Even the imperative to go to London to save her sister can be interpreted as the suggestion of Heaven. Although she claims no agency for her accomplishments, she acts ingeniously to get the help she needs, beginning with her father's blessing on an endeavor she has not told him about. She speaks to the Duke and to the Queen out of her unquestioning conviction about good and bad, right and wrong; then she relapses happily into conversation about cheesemaking. Others declare her remarkable; she claims no specialness for herself. She needs no such claim.

In all these respects, she contrasts vividly with Madge Wildfire, whose clothes and persona George adopts in leading the Porteous mob. Madge, who has a past history of sexual indulgence, reveals her madness by her radical uncertainty about her own identity. She can play child, highwayman, coquette, virago. Often she presents herself in a muddle of male and female costume, male and female roles. Her purposes fluctuate. Although she has an aspect of pathos, she functions in the narrative as a horrifying image of the "bad"—unmaternal, undutiful, sexual—woman. As Judith Wilt accurately observes, she is a spiritual ancestor of Bertha Mason, Rochester's first wife in *Jane Eyre* (*Secret* 119). But no one confines her to an attic; she roams the landscape of Jeanie's life, appearing when least expected, a dire figure of the woman ungendered because excessively sexual.

And because she is ungendered, she is unstable. Why, then, do the *men* prove so incapable of sustained action—almost as incapable as Waverley? Reuben, unwilling agent of others' male enterprise, gets himself in trouble at the outset partly by taking circuitous routes: a physical representation of his typical inability to get directly to the point of action. When Jeanie needs him, he fails to appear: he is sick, or under legal restraint. Incapable of understanding how others react to him, he inadvertently and repeatedly offends Jeanie's father. The text asserts his virtue and demonstrates his ineffectuality. As for George Robertson/Staunton, he shows an extraordinary propensity to blame his inadequacies on others, the counterpart and opposite of Jeanie's tendency to explain her noble actions by external causes. His criminality is the fault of his wet nurse: he took in evil propensities with her milk. Or it is his father's fault, for forbidding him a military career. Fertile in expedients, he manages, however, to injure himself seriously by a horse's fall just when his energy and courage might have helped Jeanie. Nor can he assist his beloved Effie in her desperate need: when she gives birth, he lies in prison. Aside from his avenging of his friend's death, his exploits, by his own account, seem merely phallic display, with no end in view to engage him. His mature life as "Sir George" simply extends the aimlessness of his misspent youth.

Less important male figures reiterate the sense of masculine limitation. David Deans, Jeanie's father, devotes himself to sectarian doctrine. A successful farmer, he proves far less successful as a father. Effie reacts to his moral severity and lack of demonstrative affection much as Sir Thomas Bertram's daughters respond to him: with a need to get away. Jeanie reveres him, his history, and his principles, but when a problem needs solving she does not turn to him. She recognizes his rigidity as limitation, and she evades it. Lord Dumbiedikes turns the theme of masculine inadequacy into a joke. His pony, which will walk only a single limited circuit, provides an appropriate emblem of its master's character. Only money occurs to him as a means for resolving difficulty, and only his money makes him useful to the heroine.

Even so cursory a summary of male roles in *The Heart of Midlothian* suggests that the narrative attenuates the power of fathers. Two literal fathers, both upright, devout, and well-intentioned, play meaningful parts: David Deans and George Robertson/Staunton's clergyman parent. Like Deans, the senior Staunton discovers that his child has responded to moral restraint by immoral indulgence. He can rebuke and fulminate, but he cannot control George's propensities or his will. Scott uses David Deans at times for comic relief, at times as a sentimental stock figure, but his plot suggests, through Deans and Staunton, that fathers make no difference at all. Madge Wildfire has no father, only a mother of more than masculine terrifying force. Robertson/Staunton, as father of an infant, possesses no effective power whatever. After the birth of Effie's son, he cannot again achieve fatherhood. As father of an adolescent son, he becomes victim to his son's energy.

Tony Tanner comments, in a long footnote of *Adultery in the Novel*, that "the fate of the Father, as depicted in nineteenth- and twentieth-century literature, would make a subject of study in itself. Increasingly the father tends to be either absent, inefficacious, or simply 'asleep'—see Jane Austen's novels, for example" (322). *The Heart of Midlothian* abounds in literal fathers wide awake but inefficacious, yet it also contains a symbolic father figure who, serving as *deus ex machina*, resolves virtually all the narrative's problems, gathering together the threads of the plot. The narrator introduces the Duke of Argyle in terms suggesting that he has assumed a paternal position for the entire kingdom of Scotland. (Claire Lamont suggests that Scott wished to celebrate the Duke's "patriarchal generosity" [Scott, *Heart* xviii].) Argyle feels no interest in achieving personal power "at the risk of throwing a kingdom into confusion" (344). Supporting the "just and lenient" (344), he is "rewarded by the esteem and affection of his country in an uncommon degree" (345). His people respond to him with gratitude and with love. They turn to him in all distress. Jeanie, with her faith in his power and his rectitude, exemplifies her compatriots in her attitude toward the Duke. He responds by engineering not only her sister's salvation but her own translation to prosperity and comfortable domesticity. He provides gainful employment for Reuben Butler and for David Deans and a plausible place of refuge for Effie. He even supplies Jeanie's wedding dress.

I have not yet answered the question I raised earlier: why, in the narrative economy, do the male characters prove incapable of sus-

tained fruitful action? The plot of *The Heart of Midlothian* implies
the answer that male characteristics are inherently self-cancelling.
The Duke of Argyle, exception to the rule, by his effectiveness
helps to elucidate the point. He is, the narrator explains, "not without ambition, but 'without the illness that attends it'"; he displays
the talents of soldier and statesman without the vices associated
with stereotyped notions of masculinity (344). In other words, his
character separates male moral strength—the virtues of the human
sublime—from its corresponding weakness. That a man who rejects personal power as an end in itself should be made the agent
of plot resolution corroborates the implications of other works we
have considered from the late eighteenth and early nineteenth century. Like the authors of those other novels, Scott in *The Heart of
Midlothian* develops a plot based not only on power relations but on
the energies of intimacy as well. Jeanie and the Duke, the idealized,
at times almost allegorical, female and male personages of the
novel, both exemplify the capacity to operate within the existing
social systems of power and the willingness to govern their actions
by principles of interhuman obligation. Both make power instru-
mental to moral purpose. Jeanie functions naively, unconscious of
any need to flatter or to appease. It is Reuben who tells her that
access to the great is difficult and that powerful men and women
may prove hard to persuade, the Duke who devises a system to
warn her of offenses she may unwittingly commit. The Duke himself acts with full knowledge of what he does, hence with far more
verbal deviousness than Jeanie. Together, he and Jeanie can bring
peace and comfort to at least a few who deserve it. (The large social
questions in the background remain unresolved and only vaguely
acknowledged.)

Yet in this novel as in the more tentative *Waverley*, Scott, like
Austen, not only questions the power of fathers, he questions the
possibility of full plot resolution. The attitudes toward "story" (and
toward "romance" and "history") in *The Heart of Midlothian* underline this point. Like its predecessor, this novel conveys uneasiness
about the proper place of fiction and of fact, even about the status
of narrative.

The prefatory section, in which Jedediah Cleishbotham reports
his encounters with two young advocates accidentally stranded in
his village by a coach accident, includes a discussion of the novel as
genre. As one of the young men explains,

the inventor of fictitious narratives has to rack his brains for means to
diversify his tale, and after all can hardly hit upon characters or incidents

which have not been used again and again, until they are familiar to the eye of the reader. . . . The end of uncertainty . . . is the death of interest [i.e., the wisdom of the novel is the wisdom of uncertainty]; and hence it happens that no one now reads novels. (21)

He offers this argument in support of the proposition that "the real records of human vagaries" (21) hold far greater interest.

Scott in effect makes the same claim. His prefatory material to the novel emphasizes its basis in historical fact. Narratorial interventions throughout the text claim historicity not only for public events and characters—the Porteous riots, the Duke of Argyle— but for Jeanie's nature and action. "The tale is well known" (28): thus the narrator introduces his account of Porteous, his fate, and the events preceding it. At once history and "fantasy," the narrative of hangings and riots, like that of Helen Walker/Jeanie Deans, allows the writer to draw on "real records of human vagaries" and to avoid the predictability of romance.

Yet the matter of romance keeps coming up. "She was no heroine of romance," we are told of Jeanie Deans, as she visits Lord Dumbiedikes (251). On the other hand, a few pages later, "There was something of romance in Jeanie's venturous resolution" (268): it is foolhardy and unrealistic. Mr. Staunton accuses her of telling a "romantic story" of herself (333); he means that she has lied. "A romantic heroine might have suspected and dreaded the power of her own charms," the narrator comments, when Jeanie finds herself alone with the Duke of Argyle; "but Jeanie was too wise to let such a silly thought intrude on her mind" (359). Not only mendacious, romances, it seems, are silly as well. But the recurrent allusions to romance suggest a tension in Scott's mind about what kind of fiction (or "history") he has chosen to write.

Notoriously, he diverges from history in the last, eminently forgettable, section of the novel. Effie's prototype, Isabella Walker, according to John McDiarmid, whom Scott quotes in a prefatory section, "saved from the fate which impended over her, was married by the person who had wronged her, (named Waugh,) and lived happily for great part of a century" (7). The historical Isabella worked as a servant. Effie, on the other hand, lives in misery in high society, as does her husband, for most of her mature life and suffers the loss of her husband at the hands of her son: a melodramatic dénouement, a *romance* dénouement.

The difference between actual and fictional outcomes depends on the novelist's plotting. Plots do not present much of a problem for characters within the text of Scott's novel. Meg Murdockson,

Madge Wildfire's mother, plots and has plotted for her daughter's welfare, but her plots never fulfill their intents. Other wills thwart hers; plotting proves only temporarily effective. But the novel itself, unlike *Waverley*, is highly (if sometimes rather randomly) plotted. George Levine observes that "History in Scott is the great plot maker and yet also the redeeming province of fact rather than of his own creative imagination. Yet it manifests itself often in the conventions of romance" (93). The story of Effie's condemnation and Jeanie's rescue of her sister follows the plot of history, adding to it a structure of imagined personal motives. The narrative of the sisters' after-life turns to the conventions of romance, seeking historical fact to justify them. Thus Scott draws on traditional rivalries between Lowland and Highland Scots and on the historical actuality of outlawry to rationalize a narrative sequence that declares the inevitability of harsh punishment for sin.

My earlier description of Scott's effort to find plot structures not based on principles of power alone hardly describes his fictional arrangements for the narrative of Effie's marriage and her husband's death. Now ideas about hierarchy, rivalry, and social antagonism govern the course of events. Effie's loving concern for others may enable her husband to buy land he wants, but it cannot help her sister, her nephew, her sister's husband. The final words of the narrative proper allude to the familial order Effie has established ("Meanwhile, happy in each other, in the prosperity of their family, and the love and honour of all who knew them, this simple pair lived beloved, and died lamented."). But the narrator immediately appends a "moral": "READER—This tale will not be told in vain, if it shall be found to illustrate the great truth, that guilt, though it may attain temporal splendour, can never confer real happiness . . . " (507). The manifest inadequacy of these sentiments to the moral and emotional weight of the story they follow emphasizes Scott's apparent confusion about the implications of his own plot: he does not understand its "tendency."

The dichotomy between plot and story that proved illuminating in relation to *Clarissa* has some bearing here as well. Considerable talk about "story" takes place in the course of the action. Jeanie sets out on her mission with every expectation of accomplishing her end by telling her sister's story. "Their hearts maun be made o' flesh and blood like other folk's," she says of the king and queen, "and Effie's story wad melt them were they stane" (266). The Duke of Argyle, once he hears Jeanie's version of that story, agrees about its power to "melt." He advises Jeanie to tell her story once more, to the unknown "lady," just as she has told it to him. And of course the story—of Jeanie as well as of Effie, the story that Mr. Staunton has rightly called "an extraordinary, and not a very probable tale" (318)—has precisely the desired effect.

Jeanie has no doubt about the shape of Effie's story and no concern about the shape of her own. Effie herself, in prison and before, sees the narrative of her life much less clearly, her ignorance of futurity making it difficult for her to interpret past events. Is hers a story of seduction and betrayal or of disastrous accident? Of true love or of frivolous deviation from rectitude? A tragedy ending in death at eighteen or a narrative of miraculous salvation? The indeterminacies of Effie's situation forbid narrative certitude. But her lover, George, in less desperate circumstances, also has difficulty telling his own story. "Story did I call it?—it is a tissue of folly, guilt, and misery" (324)—and therefore, by implication, not really a story at all: because it doesn't make sense. Partly for similar reasons, Madge Wildfire, whose story Jeanie intensely wishes to hear, cannot tell a coherent tale of herself.

Jeanie understands the almost magical power of stories. She refuses to allow George to tell his father anything about Effie. "My family and friends have nae right to hae ony stories told anent them without their express desire," she insists (334), and the two Staunton men yield to her conviction. Story, which defines identity, here as in *Waverley*, appears to Jeanie identity's essential sign, not to be lightly transmitted. For her as for Clarissa, stories are interpretative narratives of past happenings which help to shape the possibilities of future happenings. Her ability to tell the right story at the right time determines her success.

The split in Scott's narrative between the account of Jeanie and her quest and the record of that quest's aftermath confirms the value of story—as opposed, in this case, to plot. Story as interpretation corresponds to the representation of Jeanie's heroic journey, a re-imagining of history which, as Levine suggests, frees the novelist, paradoxically, by making him accountable to fact. The story ends with Effie's redemption. Afterwards, in the last section of the novel, Scott relies on plot, a structure of willed happenings designed to make (rather than to discover) a point.

The line between "making" and "discovering," like that between desire for intimacy and for power, often dissolves on close examination. The discovery of meanings in life which makes story possible may suspiciously resemble the imposition of meaning on event. But a difference of emphasis remains. Those concerned with story interest themselves in acts of reconciliation with the existent; those focused on plot impose themselves on futurity. *The Heart of*

Midlothian divides between a narrative primarily concerned with and issuing from Jeanie's involvement with her own and her sister's story and a narrative formed from the novelist's obsession with plot and with respectable meaning. That formal split duplicates the ambiguity of value that the fiction promulgates: the power of the father versus the daughter's insistence on the primary importance of attachment. Like other novelists of the period—and with increasing sophistication as he matured—Scott reveals the wisdom of uncertainty about how to value opposed patterns of action and feeling, patterns corresponding to the formal arrangements of fiction.

AFTERWORD

The difference between the truths fiction proclaims and those it tells roughly corresponds to Godwin's distinction between "moral" and "tendency." Carol Kay provides an illuminating instance of the possible contrast between novelists' claims and readers' perceptions when she notes the gap between Richardson's achievement in *Pamela* and his summary of that achievement.

> The convincing account of learning morality—the mixture of the desire for moral approval with other kinds of desire, the odd ways people affect one another, the uncertain birth of a new form of social life—is a more moving, more interesting account than Richardson was ever able to summarize. The list of lessons at the end of *Pamela*, like so many of Richardson's efforts to define his achievement, wretchedly betrays it. (160)

The truth *Pamela* tells us, complicated and compelling, differs from the truth its author saw in it. Of course, the truth fiction tells must depend partly on who is listening and on what equipment the listener brings to the task of comprehension and interpretation. My account of eighteenth-century fiction has emphasized the kind of truth I located first in *The Female Quixote*, a kind steadily recurring in other fiction: the truth of desire, appearing under many aspects.

Immersion in eighteenth-century discourse must tempt the reader to think in polarities. Self-love and social, reason and feeling, sublime and beautiful, art and nature: over and over the period's writers divide the moral, psychological, intellectual, or aesthetic universe in half. Many of the divisions subsume themselves readily under the fundamental separations of socially contrived gender. To the "masculine" realm belong self-love, reason, sublimity, art. Social sentiment, emotion of all kinds, beauty, and nature associate themselves with the "feminine." The patterns of desire rendered by fiction fall readily into comparable classifications. In a crude sense, self-love, reason, and sublimity can be understood as categories of domination, their "feminine" counterparts as emblems of community. The large development traced in this study depends on the diverse possibilities of representation implicit in the relation between these large categories.

If desire deceives, as *Sense and Sensibility* and many works before and after suggest, it also enables. Desire drives plot, impelling writers, readers, and characters within a fiction. And desire, too, frequently expresses itself in terms either of "masculine" or "feminine" categories. (To describe them thus corresponds precisely to eighteenth-century practice, although of course it was by no means ever true that commentators assigned, for instance, all reason to men, all feeling to women.) The large structural patterns organizing eighteenth-century fiction, I have argued, follow a general historical sequence in depending centrally on desire for dominance, desire for relationship, or a vision of unified possibility in which both desires might not only peacefully coexist but cooperate. Inasmuch as these shifting patterns imply changing concepts of conceivable social organization, they speak of ideological possibility if not of historical actuality or necessity.

To structure fiction on the basis of competitive strivings seems the most obvious and easy arrangement of plot. Such a structure corresponds in straightforward fashion to what I remember being told in my first creative-writing course: plot always depends on conflict, between "man" and nature, "man" and "man," or "man" and himself. The structure corresponds also, as Marxist critics have pointed out, to the arrangements of capitalist society. As Lovelace and Clarissa compete for power, as Tom Jones seeks his economic and social destiny, as Fanny Hill makes her fortune, all reinforce an ethical and economic system that assumes the necessity and the value of competition as an end in itself and as an incentive to achievement.

Novels organized by the struggle for power loom large in literary history. With the exception of *Tristram Shandy*, no eighteenth-century fiction after Richardson's and Fielding's enjoys quite the same canonical status as *Tom Jones* and *Clarissa*. *Tristram Shandy* in its aggressive experimentalism, its preoccupation with questions of identity, its sophisticated narrative awareness, seems "modern" to us—even, perhaps, "postmodern" (and concerned with questions of power, although the key of their asking differs from that of Richardson and Fielding). None of these descriptions applies to *The Man of Feeling*.

But this book's argument has been that Mackenzie must be taken as seriously as Fielding for an adequate history of the novel's development. The third quarter of the eighteenth century generated many works now grouped—and often dismissed—as "novels of sensibility." Experimental after their own fashion, such books as *The Fool of Quality* and *Memoirs of Miss Sidney Bidulph* do not

deny the omnipresence of power relations, but they reject the necessity of organizing narratives or governing lives by them. Men
and women need not seek dominance, such characters as Harley
and Sidney imply, and novelists need not rely on hierarchical
structures. Given the realities of competitive society, tragic fates
may overwhelm individuals refusing to participate in the struggle:
neither Harley nor Sidney can finally "succeed"—and the "success" of the novels themselves remains problematic. Only by oc-
cluding the connection between money and power can novelists
resolve plots of sensibility happily. Evelina and the Fool of Quality
achieve or possess the wealth that allows social security. They
inhabit imagined worlds controlled by power struggles, but as characters they embody authorial fantasies of other possibilities. Sentimental novels do not resolve the social problems they at least dimly
acknowledge. They do, however, reflect consciousness not only of
irresolvable difficulties implicit in capitalism but of the close relation between social and fictional arrangements. Rejections of organized plot and efforts to use the yearning for intimacy as a
structural principle both constitute important developments in the
novel's history.

More important still is the late-century movement toward a reconciliation of principles that might allow coherent, even "realistic,"
narrative structure without yielding to the assumption that striving
for power provides the only principle for orderly fiction. The com-
partmentalizing by which Ann Radcliffe receives assessment only
as "Gothic" innovator, Thomas Holcroft as radical political thinker,
Wollstonecraft as protofeminist, has obscured what these novelists
have in common: their effort to reconcile "masculine" and "feminine" principles of organization and of action. Such efforts do not
always produce persuasive plots. At the end of *Anna St. Ives*, the
reader may feel that revolutionary rhetoric obscures but does not
obviate the fact of power as central motive for human action; at the
end of *The Italian*, one may reflect that massive difficulties brought
about by social and individual insistence on dominance have dis-
solved with implausible alacrity; at the end of *Zeluco* or even *A
Simple Story*, one realizes that desire for power and for closeness
inhabit disparate moral universes. Yet Austen and Scott would soon
demonstrate rich fictional possibilities, both structural and substantive, in double awareness of power and community as simultaneous
if conflicting human impulses.

Among the most potent human desires, one must number the
desire for teleology, afflicting readers and writers alike. Fictional
plots appear to move toward appointed ends, and so do the nar-

ratives of literary history. If Fielding and Richardson provide, in my account, the thesis against which Mackenzie and Sheridan attempt an antithesis, Austen and Scott must seem to offer the grand synthesis. And implicit value judgments lurk in such an ordering of the facts.

But I do not mean to suggest that the nineteenth century resolved the problems of fictional structure with which the eighteenth century struggled. I have only attained the end of my story, not its goal. All locations of desire contain the potential for instability. The balance of conflicting desires that I have posited as structural principle for Austen and Scott in due time gave way to new formulations. If the Brontës, like their immediate predecessors, investigated and relied upon reconciliations of the drive for control and for intimacy, George Eliot would explore new aspects of desire—for significance rather than dominance, among other things—and transform them too into structural systems. The point is not to celebrate any particular version of how plot supplements substance in telling the truths of desire, but to recognize the shifting necessities by which novelists incorporate in the deep structure of their plots motives like those that impel their characters.

The specific shapes of plotting in the eighteenth century, however, hold particular interest because the assumptions that order plots appear to coincide with sets of values that the period's thinkers had declared "masculine" and "feminine." Others have commented on a literary process of "feminization" in the late century, as sensibility assumed an important place in imaginative literature, exploiting implications of doctrine expounded earlier by Shaftesbury. The superseding of sensibility strikes me as a more interesting phenomenon than its efflorescence. By the last decade of the century, even those who celebrated the force of sensibility (Radcliffe, for instance) also criticized it. Wollstonecraft's denunciations of sensibility as female pose make explicit the association of fine feeling with weakness, "femininity" in its most trivial sense, and the moral and social dangers of that association for women. The novelistic effort to combine what had been declared polar opposites, under some such rubric as "energy of mind," and to find bases for plot in the combination, has revolutionary implications. It tacitly asserts an end to polarities. Women can climb walls too, as Anna St. Ives pointed out! The universe need not be conceived as a series of binary oppositions. The very structures of novelistic plot, at the end of the eighteenth and beginning of the nineteenth century, speak of reconciliation: not of the elevation of "feminine" over "masculine" principles briefly attempted in sentimental fiction (and drama and poetry) but of the obviation of difference.

A utopian moment, to be sure. And in fact Austen and Scott, for all their deft manipulation of double principles of plot, openly express their skepticism about the possibility of social arrangements based on attempts to ignore culturally created and defined difference. If Fanny Price triumphs in the moral sphere, her triumph effects no fundamental change in the hierarchy of Mansfield Park. Waverley will have to cultivate his "masculine" side in order to achieve public status. But the structure of the novels' plots conveys a potential for change never openly acknowledged, never socially fulfilled.

Plotting, in other words, creates not only stories but meanings. Inasmuch as acts and purposes of plotting supply both the means of telling and the partial substance of what is told in the novels here considered, those represented acts and purposes reiterate a complicated double truth. Lovelace stands as the paradigmatic figure of the plotter, laboring to impose his will on the future, to shape events into meanings that will declare his power. Plotters abound in other eighteenth-century novels as well: Pamela and Mr. B, Blifil, Arabella in *The Female Quixote*, the wicked peer and Colonel James in *Amelia*—indeed, the wicked in many a fictional context: *The Castle of Otranto, Sidney Bidulph, The Italian, Anna St. Ives*, all the way to Henry Crawford in *Mansfield Park*. The efforts of "bad" plotters typically meet defeat. The "good" succeed by other means than plotting. The pattern intricately developed in *Clarissa*, by which concern with story (meaning the interpretation and ordering of past events) proves more effectual than obsession with plot, duplicates itself in less highly elaborated fictions.

One may feel tempted to conclude that the imposition of will and desire involved in fictional as well as political, amorous, or economic plotting arouses anxiety in novelists themselves professionally committed to a socially acceptable version of the activity they deplore in its non-literary manifestations. In the mid-eighteenth century, when plots of power flourished in fiction, many novels contained intrusive narrators whose intrusions often spoke their awareness of the absolute power exercised by the novelist-as-plotter. Readers may choose not to read, or may choose to dislike what they encounter on the page, but their choices do not modify the plot-maker's total control of what happens to the characters he or she has imagined. Explicit self-consciousness about this control largely disappears by the century's end (although Austen, particularly at

the conclusion of *Northanger Abbey*, and Scott recapitulate it), but
the criticism plots convey of plotters within them reiterate concern
about the claim—Lovelace's claim, but also Fielding's—of power to
control future happening.

The anxiety about plotting touches on the relation between fiction and actuality, desire and truth. When Arabella, in *The Female
Quixote*, attempts to translate the power of plot from romance on
the page to romance in her direct experience, she potentially creates a terrifying elision. Her desire to close the gap between fiction
and life perhaps speaks of a wish latent in all acts of narrative plotting. For seventeenth- and eighteenth-century moralists, history
and life supplied to the individual different forms of experience; a
person could enlarge knowledge and increase capacity by relying
on either. *Feigned* history, another mode of vicarious experience,
thus presented obvious dangers (as the clergyman explained to
Arabella). Plots manifestly shaped by human desire might, even for
readers more sophisticated than the young female Quixote, encourage confusion of fantasy with actuality. The power of plotting,
by extension, becomes imaginably the power to change the dimensions of the real.

Even Lord Kames appeared to think that fiction *might* alter the
course of events in the world, as he discusses the effect of fiction
on "man, so remarkably addicted to truth and reality," who nonetheless can be so completely possessed by the reading of a "fable"
as to find "no leisure for reflection" in his response (53–4). If fiction can sway individuals in this way, it can change a great deal. To
take the plots of eighteenth-century novels with full seriousness,
allowing room for "tendencies" as well as for "morals," understanding the ways in which desire creates and records its own truths, can
disclose ideological ferment and ideological possibility, the imaginative and moral vitality of the novel's early development.

NOTES

1. Volume and page citations for the Yale Edition will be supplied for all citations of *The Rambler*, in addition to the number and date of the original publication.

CHAPTER ONE

1. Langbauer and Ross have both discussed the degree to which Arabella's position implies social criticism.

2. Michael McKeon has lucidly set forth the complexities of the debate over romance and history, with its constantly shifting terms.

3. As McKeon perceptively writes, "From Dante on, the fear that women's morals will be corrupted by reading romances is quite conventional, and its articulation [in the early eighteenth century] may provide evidence less of the rise of the reading public than of the persistence of anxiety about women" (52). Johnson's anxiety about women is manifest and massive.

4. Barbara Herrnstein Smith notes that people's summaries of a given plot "will be different if the motives and purposes of their summarizing are different" (217), and she brilliantly discusses the theoretical implications of such differences (217–22).

CHAPTER THREE

1. All citations of *Clarissa* are from the text of the Shakespeare Head Edition. Page references are given first to this edition, then to the more readily available Dent (Everyman) version.

2. For a provocative discussion of Clarissa's relation to "law," see Kay, especially 163–68.

3. Margaret Anne Doody observes that Lovelace "is incessantly eager for power, which is both his object and his function" (*A Natural Passion* 100). Elizabeth R. Napier has examined Lovelace's pervasive language of power. She shares my view that Clarissa "wins" in the novel's struggle for control.

4. Sheldon Sacks writes brilliantly about the kinds of "marker" Fielding provides to reveal to the reader his comic intent.

5. Like other sequences intended to stress Lovelace's despicable nature, this narrative does not occur in the first edition. And, like other such sequences, it turns out to generate more ambiguous effects than Richardson presumably intended.

6. For a provocatively different view of the Harlowes, see John Allen Stevenson, "The Courtship of the Family: Clarissa and the Harlowes Once More," *ELH* 48(1981), 757–77.

7. Sacks offers the fullest discussion of Fielding's use of digressions. See especially 193–229.

8. Rader argues for the metaphysical importance of this desire. "[Tom's] quest for Sophia functions as the motor of the subsequent action, for the force which moves him moves the novel also; so that the meaning of that force becomes bound up with the larger issues of the book" (260). These issues involve man's passionate longing "to be like God" (263).

9. Charles A. Knight provides an interesting discussion of the way Fielding relates problems of individual politics to those of the nation. He sees the central issue of politics not, as I do, as one of power, but as one of service. But he makes the important point that "Once politics is established as a topic, it becomes the subject of a number of predications that also have a status independent of politics, statements concerning epistemology, or etiology, or independent moral behaviour" ("'Main Design'" 393).

CHAPTER FIVE

1. R. S. Crane's 1934 essay on a proposed genealogy for the "man of feeling" remains a particularly useful historical account of sentimentalism's foundations. With a different vocabulary and different purposes from mine, Crane anticipates some of my general conclusions.

2. Crane documents "anti-stoical" praise by mid-century thinkers of the pleasures of sensibility. See especially 205–6.

3. See Markley for an extended treatment of the aristocratic bias of Shaftesbury's altruistic ethics.

4. Margaret Anne Doody writes emphatically about Mme. Duval as "the focus for everything that makes female life seem hopeless or depressing" and as the terrifying image of "the Mother, the buried author of one's being" (*Frances* 51).

5. Kristina Straub suggests that the desire of an eighteenth-century young woman to remain with her father "seems as much an intelligent choice as Freudian regression," given the social realities of marriage (66).

6. Straub writes particularly well about the meaning in Burney's fictional pattern of the horrifying race between two old women (43–46).

CHAPTER EIGHT

1. *Waverley*, published in 1814, was partly written as early as 1805. Austen began work on what was to become *Sense and Sensibility* in late 1797; the novel appeared in 1811. Both fictions, therefore, were partly composed during the era of Radcliffe and Godwin.

2. Claudia Johnson makes the same point, in a splendid essay on *Sense and Sensibility* that emphasizes the novel's criticism both of the conventional ideology of family and of conventional fictional patterns (49–72).

3. Alexander Welsh, interestingly, describes the passivity of Scott's heroes as "a function of [their] morality—the public and accepted morality

of rational self-restraint" (36). This view does not altogether account for Waverley's position, but it suggests at least a partial justification.

4. Robert Gordon argues that Talbot "is not another father-substitute like Sir Everard, or, later, the Baron of Bradwardine," since "Edward and Talbot often speak as equals, . . . and their relationship is founded upon a balance of indebtedness, for each has saved the other's life" (21). Clearly, I do not agree.

5. Alexander Welsh emphasizes the importance of property in the imaginative structures of Scott's fiction.

6. Tony Tanner (*Jane Austen* 80) and Susan Morgan (116) emphasize the importance of secrecy and deception in *Sense and Sensibility.*

7. With different emphasis from mine, Claudia Johnson explores operations of power in *Mansfield Park* (94–120). Among her astute observations is the comment that here neither the beautiful nor the sublime works "the way it is supposed to" (99)—i.e., the way Burke claimed it did.

8. In a paper given at the English Institute, David Marshall demonstrates how inevitably Fanny, despite her protestations, participates in theatrical performance.

9. Judith Wilt has discussed the problem of male and female identity in *The Heart of Midlothian*, linking it to Scott's concerns in the other Waverley novels. She also calls attention to a remarkable statement by Andrew Hook, praising Scott for giving to the novel as genre "a new masculinity" (Wilt, *Secret* 116–42, 218).

10. I do not mean to suggest that only women, in fiction or in actuality, refer their decisions to Providence. Jeanie's disclaimers of responsibility for her own heroism, however, have a very "feminine" ring.

WORKS CITED

Aikin, John and Anna Laetitia. *Miscellaneous Pieces, in Prose*. London, 1773.
Alter, Robert. *Fielding and the Nature of the Novel*. Cambridge: Harvard Univ. Press, 1968.
———. *Partial Magic: The Novel as a Self-Conscious Genre*. Berkeley: Univ. of California Press, 1975.
Armstrong, Nancy. *Desire and Domestic Fiction: A Political History of the Novel*. New York: Oxford Univ. Press, 1987.
Austen, Jane. *Mansfield Park*. 1814. Vol. 3 of *The Novels of Jane Austen*. 3d ed., ed. R. W. Chapman. Oxford: Oxford Univ. Press, 1934.
———. *Northanger Abbey*. 1818. Vol. 5 of *The Novels of Jane Austen*. 3d ed., ed. R. W. Chapman. Oxford: Oxford Univ. Press, 1933.
———. *Sense and Sensibility*. 1811. Vol. 1 of *The Novels of Jane Austen*. 3d ed., ed. R. W. Chapman. Oxford: Oxford Univ. Press, 1933.
Bage, Robert. *Man As He Is*. 1792. New York: Garland, 1979.
Baker, Ernest A. *The History of the English Novel*. Vol. 5, *The Novel of Sentiment and the Gothic Romance*. London: Witherby, 1934.
Bate, W. Jackson. *Samuel Johnson*. New York: Harcourt, 1977.
Battestin, Martin C. *The Providence of Wit: Aspects of Form in Augustan Literature and the Arts*. Oxford: Clarendon, 1974.
———. "The Problem of *Amelia*: Hume, Barrow, and the Conversion of Captain Booth." *ELH* 41(1974): 613–48.
———. "*A Sentimental Journey* and the Syntax of Things." In *Augustan Worlds: New Essays in Eighteenth-Century Literature*, ed. J. C. Hilson, M. M. B. Jones, and J. R. Watson, 223–39. New York: Barnes and Noble, 1978.
Beattie, James. *Dissertations Moral and Critical*. 1783. New York: Garland, 1971.
Bender, John. *Imagining the Penitentiary: Fiction and the Architecture of Mind in Eighteenth-Century England*. Chicago: Univ. of Chicago Press, 1987.
Blake, William. *The Poetry and Prose of William Blake*. Ed. David V. Erdman, commentary by Harold Bloom. Garden City: Doubleday, 1970.
Boone, Joseph Allen. *Tradition Counter Tradition: Love and the Form of Fiction*. Chicago: Univ. of Chicago Press, 1987.
Boswell, James. *Boswell's Life of Johnson*. 1791. Ed. G. B. Hill, rev. and enl. by L. F. Powell. 6 vols. Oxford: Clarendon, 1934.
Boucé, Paul-Gabriel. "Some Sexual Beliefs and Myths in Eighteenth-Century Britain." In *Sexuality in Eighteenth-Century Britain*, ed. Paul-Gabriel Boucé. Towota, NJ: Barnes and Noble, 1982.

Braudy, Leo. "The Form of the Sentimental Novel." *Novel* 7 (1973): 5–13.

Brémond, Claude. "The Logic of Narrative Possibilities." *New Literary History* 11(1980): 387–412.

Brissenden, R. F. "*Mansfield Park*: Freedom and the Family." In *Jane Austen: Bicentenary Essays*, ed. John Halperin, 156–71. Cambridge: Cambridge Univ. Press, 1975.

———. *Virtue in Distress: Studies in the Novel of Sentiment from Richardson to Sade*. London: Macmillan, 1974.

Brooke, Henry. *The Fool of Quality; or, The History of Henry Earl of Moreland.* 1766. 5 vols. New York: Garland, 1979.

Brooks, Peter. *Reading for the Plot: Design and Intention in Narrative*. New York: Knopf, 1984.

Brown, Homer Obed. "*Tom Jones*: The 'Bastard' of History." *Boundary 2* 7(1979): 201–34.

Brown, Julia Prewitt. *Jane Austen's Novels: Social Change and Literary Form*. Cambridge: Harvard Univ. Press, 1979.

Burke, Edmund. *A Philosophical Enquiry into the Origin of our Ideas of the Sublime and Beautiful.* 1757. Ed. J. T. Boulton. London: Routledge, 1958.

Burney, Frances. *Camilla, or A Picture of Youth.* 1796. Ed. Edward A. and Lillian D. Bloom. Oxford: Oxford Univ. Press, 1983.

———. *Evelina, or The History of a Young Lady's Entrance into the World.* 1778. New York: Norton, 1965.

Butler, Marilyn. "Disregarded Designs: Jane Austen's Sense of the Volume." In *Jane Austen in a Social Context*, ed. David Monaghan, 49–65. Towota, NJ: Barnes and Noble, 1981.

———. *Jane Austen and the War of Ideas*. Oxford: Clarendon, 1975.

Carter, Angela. *The Sadeian Woman and the Ideology of Pornography*. New York: Pantheon, 1978.

Caserio, Robert L. *Plot, Story, and the Novel: From Dickens and Poe to the Modern Period*. Princeton: Princeton Univ. Press, 1979.

Castle, Terry. *Clarissa's Ciphers: Meaning and Disrupion in Richardson's "Clarissa."* Ithaca: Cornell Univ. Press, 1982.

———. *Masquerade and Civilization: The Carnivalesque in Eighteenth-Century English Culture and Fiction*. Stanford: Stanford Univ. Press, 1986.

Chambers, Ross. *Story and Situation: Narrative Seduction and the Power of Fiction*. Theory and History of Literature, 12. Minneapolis: Univ. of Minnesota Press, 1984.

Cleland, John. *Memoirs of Fanny Hill.* 1749. Introduction by J. H. Plumb. New York: New American Library, 1965.

Cohan, Steven. *Violation and Repair in the English Novel: The Paradigm of Experience from Richardson to Woolf*. Detroit: Wayne State Univ. Press, 1986.

Copeland, Edward W. "*Clarissa* and *Fanny Hill*: Sisters in Distress." *Studies in the Novel* 4(1972): 343–52.

Crane, R. S. "The Plot of *Tom Jones*." 1950. In Henry Fielding. *Tom Jones*, ed. Sheridan Baker, 844–68. New York: Norton, 1973.

―――. "Suggestions toward a Genealogy of the 'Man of Feeling.'" *ELH* 1(1934): 205–30.

Damrosch, Leopold, Jr. *God's Plot and Man's Stories: Studies in the Fictional Imagination from Milton to Fielding*. Chicago: Univ. of Chicago Press, 1985.

Davis, Lennard J. *Resisting Novels: Ideology and Fiction*. New York: Methuen, 1987.

Dennis, John. "An Essay on the Genius and Writings of Shakespear." 1712. In *The Critical Works of John Dennis*, ed. Edward Niles Hooker, 2:1–17. Baltimore: Johns Hopkins Univ. Press, 1943.

Doody, Margaret Anne. "Deserts, Ruins and Troubled Waters: Female Dreams in Fiction and the Development of the Gothic Novel." *Genre* 10(1977): 529–72.

―――. *Frances Burney: The Life in the Works*. New Brunswick: Rutgers Univ. Press, 1988.

―――. "Frances Sheridan: Morality and Annihilated Time." In *Fetter'd or Free? British Women Novelists, 1670–1815*, ed. Mary Anne Schofield and Cecilia Macheski, 324–58. Athens: Ohio Univ. Press, 1986.

―――. *A Natural Passion: A Study of the Novels of Samuel Richardson*. Oxford: Oxford Univ. Press, 1974.

Eagleton, Terry. *The Rape of Clarissa: Writing, Sexuality and Class Struggle in Samuel Richardson*. Minneapolis: Univ. of Minnesota Press, 1982.

Fielding, Henry. *Amelia*. 1751. Ed. Martin C. Battestin. Middletown: Wesleyan Univ. Press, 1983.

―――. *The History of Tom Jones, A Foundling*. 1749. Ed. Fredson Bowers, introduction and commentary by Martin C. Battestin. 2 vols. Middletown: Wesleyan Univ. Press, 1975.

―――. *Joseph Andrews*. 1742. Ed. Martin C. Battestin. Middletown: Wesleyan Univ. Press, 1967.

―――. *Miscellanies by Henry Fielding, Esq.; Volume I*. Ed. Henry Knight Miller. Oxford: Clarendon, 1972.

Fisher, Philip. *Hard Facts: Setting and Form in the American Novel*. New York: Oxford Univ. Press, 1985.

Flynn, Carol Houlihan. "Defoe's Idea of Conduct: Ideological Fictions and Fictional Reality." In *The Ideology of Conduct: Essays on Literature and the History of Sexuality*, ed. Nancy Armstrong and Leonard Tennenhouse, 73–95. New York: Methuen, 1987.

Fraser, Donald. "Lying and Concealment in *Amelia*." In *Henry Fielding: Justice Observed*, ed. K. G. Simpson, 174–98. London: Vision, 1985.

Furbank, P. N. "The Novel and Its 'Resemblance to Life.'" In *The Uses of Fiction: Essays on the Modern Novel in Honour of Arnold Kettle*, ed. Douglas Jefferson and Graham Martin, 31–40. Milton Keynes, England: The Open Univ. Press, 1982.

Garrett, Peter K. *The Victorian Multiplot Novel: Studies in Dialogical Form*. New Haven: Yale Univ. Press, 1980.

Genette, Gerard. "Frontiers of Narrative." In *Figures of Literary Discourse*, tr. Alan Sheridan, 127–44. New York: Columbia Univ. Press, 1982.

Gilligan, Carol. *In A Different Voice: Psychological Theory and Women's Development*. Cambridge: Harvard Univ. Press, 1982.

Girard, René. *Deceit, Desire, and the Novel: Self and Other in Literary Structure*. Tr. Yvonne Freccero. Baltimore: Johns Hopkins Univ. Press, 1976.

Godwin, William. *Caleb Williams*. 1794. Ed. David McCracken. London: Oxford Univ. Press, 1970.

———. "Of Choice in Reading." In *The Enquirer: Reflections on Education, Manners and Literature*, 129–46. 1797. New York: Kelley, 1965.

Goldknopf, David. "The Failure of Plot in *Tom Jones*." 1969. In Henry Fielding. *Tom Jones*, ed. Sheridan Baker, 792–803. New York: Norton, 1973.

Gordon, Robert C. *Under Which King? A Study of the Scottish Waverley Novels*. London: Oliver and Boyd, 1968.

Haggerty, George E. "Fact and Fancy in the Gothic Novel." *Nineteenth-Century Fiction* 39(1985): 379–91.

———. "Literature and Homosexuality in the Late Eighteenth Century: Walpole, Beckford, and Lewis." *Studies in the Novel* 18(1986): 341–52.

Holcroft, Thomas. *Anna St. Ives*. 1792. Ed. Peter Faulkner. London: Oxford Univ. Press, 1970.

Hunter, J. Paul. *Occasional Form: Henry Fielding and the Chains of Circumstance*. Baltimore: Johns Hopkins Univ. Press, 1975.

Inchbald, Elizabeth. *A Simple Story*. 1791. Ed. J. M. S. Tompkins. London: Oxford Univ. Press, 1967.

Johnson, Claudia. *Jane Austen: Women, Politics, and the Novel*. Chicago: Univ. of Chicago Press, 1988.

Johnson, Maurice. *Fielding's Art of Fiction*. Philadelphia: Univ. of Pennsylvania Press, 1961.

Johnson, Samuel. *A Dictionary of the English Language*. 1755. 3d ed. 2 vols. London, 1766.

———. *The Rambler*. Ed. W. J. Bate and Albrecht B. Strauss. Vols. 3–5 of *The Yale Edition of the Works of Samuel Johnson*. New Haven: Yale Univ. Press, 1969.

Josipovici, Gabriel. *Writing and the Body*. Brighton: Harvester, 1982.

Kames, Henry Home, Lord. *Elements of Criticism*. 1762. Ed. Abraham Mills. New York, 1857.

Karl, Frederick R. *The Adversary Literature: The English Novel in the Eighteenth Century. A Study in Genre*. New York: Farrar, 1974.

Kay, Carol. *Political Constructions: Defoe, Richardson, and Sterne in Relation to Hobbes, Hume, and Burke*. Ithaca: Cornell Univ. Press, 1988.

Kelly, Gary. "A Constant Vicissitude of Interesting Passions: Ann Radcliffe's Perplexed Narratives." *Ariel* 10, no. 2 (April 1979): 45–64.

———. *The English Jacobin Novel*. Oxford: Clarendon, 1976.

———. "Jane Austen and the English Novel of the 1790s." In *Fetter'd or Free? British Women Novelists, 1670–1815*, ed. Mary Ann Schofield and Cecilia Macheski, 285–306. Athens: Ohio Univ. Press, 1986.

Kermode, Frank. *The Sense of an Ending: Studies in the Theory of Fiction*. New York: Oxford Univ. Press, 1967.

Kiely, Robert. *The Romantic Novel in England*. Cambridge: Harvard Univ. Press, 1972.

Knight, Charles A. "The Narrative Structure of Fielding's *Amelia*." *Ariel* 11(1980): 31–46.

———. "*Tom Jones*: The Meaning of the 'Main Design.'" *Genre* 12 (1979): 379–400.

Knox, Vicesimus. "On Novel Reading." *Essays Moral and Literary*. 1778. In *Novel and Romance, 1700–1800: A Documentary Record*, ed. Ioan Williams, 304–70. New York: Barnes and Noble, 1970.

Konigsberg, Ira. *Narrative Technique in the English Novel: Defoe to Austen*. Hamden, CT: Archon, 1985.

Kraft, Quentin G. "Narrative Transformation in *Tom Jones*: An Episode in the Emergence of the English Novel." *The Eighteenth Century: Theory and Interpretation* 26(1985): 23–46.

Kundera, Milan. *The Art of the Novel*. Tr. Linda Asher. New York: Grove, 1988.

Langbauer, Laurie. "Romance Revised: Charlotte Lennox's *The Female Quixote*." *Novel* 18(1984): 29–49.

LeGates, Marlene. "The Cult of Womanhood in Eighteenth-Century Thought." *Eighteenth-Century Studies* 10(1976): 21–39.

Lennox, Charlotte. *The Female Quixote or The Adventures of Arabella*. 1752. Ed. Margaret Dalziel, chronology and appendix by Duncan Isles. London: Oxford Univ. Press, 1970.

Levine, George. *The Realistic Imagination: English Fiction from Frankenstein to Lady Chatterley*. Chicago: Univ. of Chicago Press, 1981.

Lewis, Matthew. *The Monk*. 1796. Ed. James Kinsley and Howard Anderson. Oxford: Oxford Univ. Press, 1980.

Loesberg, Jonathan. "Allegory and Narrative in *Clarissa*." *Novel* 15(1981): 39–59.

London, April. "Controlling the Text: Women in *Tom Jones*." *Studies in the Novel* 19(1987): 323–33.

McCrea, Brian. "Politics and Narrative Technique in Fielding's *Amelia*." *The Journal of Narrative Technique* 13(1983): 131–40.

Mackenzie, Henry. *The Lounger*. 20 (18 June 1785). In *Novel and Romance, 1700–1800: A Documentary Record*, ed. Ioan Williams, 328–31. New York: Barnes and Noble, 1970.

———. *The Man of Feeling*. 1771. New York: Norton, 1958.

McIntosh, Carey. *The Choice of Life: Samuel Johnson and the World of Fiction*. New Haven: Yale Univ. Press, 1973.

McKeon, Michael. *The Origins of the English Novel, 1600–1740*. Baltimore: Johns Hopkins Univ. Press, 1987.

McNamara, Susan P. "Mirrors of Fiction Within *Tom Jones*: The Paradox of Self-Reference." *Eighteenth-Century Studies* 12 (1979): 372–90.

Manley, Mary de la Rivière. Preface to *The Secret History of Queen Zarah*. 1705. In *Novel and Romance, 1700–1800: A Documentary Record*, ed. Ioan Williams, 33–39. New York: Barnes and Noble, 1970.

Manuel, Frank E. *The Changing of the Gods*. Hanover: Univ. Press of New England, 1983.

Markley, Robert. "Language, Power, and Sexuality in Cleland's *Fanny Hill*." *Philological Quarterly* 63(1984): 343–56.

————. "Sentimentality As Performance: Shaftesbury, Sterne, and the Theatrics of Virtue." In *The New Eighteenth Century: Theory, Politics, English Literature*, ed. Felicity Nussbaum and Laura Brown, 210–30. New York: Methuen, 1987.

Marshall, David. *The Figure of Theater: Shaftesbury, Defoe, Adam Smith, and George Eliot*. New York: Columbia Univ. Press, 1986.

————. "True Acting and the Language of Real Feeling." English Institute, 26 August 1988.

Miller, Jacqueline T. "The Imperfect Tale: Articulation, Rhetoric, and Self in *Caleb Williams*." *Criticism* 20(1978): 366–82.

Miller, Nancy K. *The Heroine's Text: Readings in the French and English Novel, 1722–1782*. New York: Columbia Univ. Press, 1980.

————. "'I's' in Drag: The Sex of Recollection." *The Eighteenth Century: Theory and Interpretation* 22(1981): 47–57.

Moore, John. *A View of the Commencement and Progress of Romance*. 1790. In *The Works of John Moore, M.D.*, 5: 1–64. Edinburgh, 1820.

————. *Zeluco: Various Views of Human Nature, Taken from Life and Manners, Foreign and Domestic*. 1789. In *The British Novelists*, ed. Anna Laetitia Barbauld, vols. 34–35. London, 1810. 34–35.

Morgan, Susan. *In the Meantime: Character and Perception in Jane Austen's Fiction*. Chicago: Univ. of Chicago Press, 1980.

Morris, David B. "Gothic Sublimity." *New Literary History* 16 (1985): 299–320.

Mulford, Carla. "Booth's Progress and the Resolution of *Amelia*." *Studies in the Novel* 16(1984): 20–31.

Murry, John Middleton. "Fielding's 'Sexual Ethic' in *Tom Jones*." In *Fielding: A Collection of Critical Essays*, ed. Ronald Paulson, 89–97. Englewood Cliffs: Prentice-Hall, 1962.

Napier, Elizabeth R. "'Tremble and Reform': The Inversion of Power in Richardson's *Clarissa*." *ELH* 42(1975): 214–23.

Parker, Patricia A. *Inescapable Romance: Studies in the Poetics of a Mode*. Princeton: Princeton Univ. Press, 1979.

Paulson, Ronald. "Fielding in *Tom Jones*: the Historian, the Poet, and the Mythologist." In *Augustan Worlds: New Essays in Eighteenth-Century Literature*, ed. J. C. Hilson, M. M. B. Jones, and J.R. Watson. New York: Barnes and Noble, 1978.

————. *Representations of Revolution (1789–1820)*. New Haven: Yale Univ. Press, 1983.

————. *Satire and the Novel in Eighteenth-Century England*. New Haven: Yale Univ. Press, 1967.

Poovey, Mary. *The Proper Lady and the Woman Writer: Ideology as Style in the*

Works of Mary Wollstonecraft, Mary Shelley, and Jane Austen. Chicago: Univ. of Chicago Press, 1984.

Pope, Alexander. *The Iliad of Homer*, Books X–XXIV. Ed. Maynard Mack. Associate Editors Norman Callan, Robert Fagles, William Frost, Douglas M. Knight. Vol. 8 of *The Twickenham Edition of the Poems of Alexander Pope*. London: Methuen, 1967.

Price, Martin. *Forms of Life: Character and Moral Imagination in the Novel.* New Haven: Yale Univ. Press, 1983.

———. *To the Palace of Wisdom: Studies in Order and Energy from Dryden to Blake.* Garden City: Doubleday, 1964.

Pye, Henry James. *A Commentary Illustrating the Poetic of Aristotle.* London, 1792.

Rabb, Melinda Alliker. "Underplotting, Overplotting, and Correspondence in *Clarissa.*" *Modern Language Studies* 11 (1981): 61–71.

Radcliffe, Ann. *The Italian: Or, The Confessional of the Black Penitents.* 1797. Ed. Frederick Garber. Oxford: Oxford Univ. Press, 1981.

———. *The Mysteries of Udolpho.* 1794. Ed. Bonamy Dobrée. New York: Oxford Univ. Press, 1966.

———. *The Romance of the Forest.* 1791. Ed. Chloe Chard. Oxford: Oxford Univ. Press, 1986.

Rader, Ralph. *Idea and Structure in Fielding's Novels.* 1958. Ann Arbor: University Microfilms, 1970.

Ragussis, Michael. *Acts of Naming: The Family Plot in Fiction.* New York: Oxford Univ. Press, 1986.

Rawson, C. J. *Henry Fielding and the Augustan Ideal Under Stress: 'Nature's Dance of Death' and Other Studies.* London: Routledge, 1972.

Reeve, Clara. *The Progress of Romance through Times, Countries, and Manners.* 1785. 2 vols. in 1. New York: Garland, 1970.

Richardson, Samuel. *Clarissa; or, The History of a Young Lady.* 1747–48. The Shakespeare Head Edition. 8 vols. Oxford: Basil Blackwell, 1930.

———. *Clarissa; or, The History of a Young Lady.* 1747–48. 4 vols. London: Dutton, 1932.

———. *The Correspondence of Samuel Richardson.* Ed. Anna Laetitia Barbauld. 6 vols. London, 1804.

———. *Pamela, or Virtue Rewarded.* 1740. Ed. William M. Sale, Jr. New York: Norton, 1958.

Ricoeur, Paul. *Time and Narrative.* Vol. 2. Tr. Kathleen McLaughlin and David Pellauer. Chicago: Univ. of Chicago Press, 1985.

Rogers, Katharine M. "Inhibitions on Eighteenth-Century Women Novelists: Elizabeth Inchbald and Charlotte Smith." *Eighteenth-Century Studies* 11(1977): 63–78.

Ross, Deborah. "Mirror, Mirror: The Didactic Dilemma of *The Female Quixote.*" *SEL* 27(1987): 455–74.

Rothstein, Eric. "'Ideal Presence' and the 'Non Finito' in Eighteenth-Century Aesthetics." *Eighteenth-Century Studies* 9 (1976): 307–32.

—————. *Systems of Order and Inquiry in Later Eighteenth-Century Fiction.* Berkeley: Univ. of California Press, 1975.

Roussel, Roy. *The Conversation of the Sexes: Seduction and Equality in Selected Seventeenth- and Eighteenth-Century Texts.* New York: Oxford Univ. Press, 1986.

Sacks, Sheldon. *Fiction and the Shape of Belief: A Study of Henry Fielding With Glances at Swift, Johnson and Richardson.* Berkeley: Univ. of California Press, 1964.

Scott, Sir Walter. *The Heart of Midlothian.* 1818. Ed. Claire Lamont. Oxford: Oxford Univ. Press, 1982.

—————. *Waverley.* 1814. Ed. Andrew Hook. Harmondsworth: Penguin, 1985.

Sell, Roger D. *The Reluctant Naturalism of "Amelia": An Essay on the Modern Reading of Fielding.* In *Acta Academiae Aboensis, Ser. A,* 62:3. Abo: Abo Akademi, 1983.

"Sentiments of eminent writers in Honour of the Female Sex." *Gentleman's Magazine* 58 (November 1788). In *Novel and Romance, 1700–1800: A Documentary Record,* ed. Ioan Williams. New York: Barnes and Noble, 1970.

Shaftesbury, Anthony, Earl of. *Characteristics of Men, Manners, Opinions, Times.* 1711. Ed. John M. Robertson. Indianapolis: Bobbs-Merrill, 1964.

Sheridan, Frances. *Memoirs of Miss Sidney Bidulph.* 1761. London: Pandora, 1987.

Sherlock, Martin. *Letters on Several Subjects.* 1781. 2 vols. New York: Garland, 1970.

Shklovsky, Victor. "Sterne's *Tristram Shandy*: Stylistic Commentary." In *Russian Formalist Criticism: Four Essays,* tr. Lee T. Lemon and Marion J. Reis, 22–57. Lincoln: Univ. of Nebraska Press, 1965.

Skelton, Philip. Letter to Samuel Richardson. 10 May 1751. In *Novel and Romance, 1700–1800: A Documentary Record,* ed. Ioan Williams, 169–70. New York: Barnes and Noble, 1970.

Small, Miriam Rossiter. *Charlotte Ramsay Lennox: An Eighteenth Century Lady of Letters.* New Haven: Yale Univ. Press, 1935.

Smith, Adam. *The Theory of Moral Sentiments.* 1759. Ed. D. D. Raphael and A. L. Macfie. Oxford: Clarendon, 1976.

Smith, Barbara Herrnstein. "Narrative Versions, Narrative Theories." *Critical Inquiry* 7(1980): 213–36.

Spacks, Patricia Meyer. *The Adolescent Idea: Myths of Youth and the Adult Imagination.* New York: Basic, 1981.

—————. "'Ev'ry Woman is at Heart a Rake.'" *Eighteenth-Century Studies* 8(1974): 27–46.

—————. *Gossip.* 1985. Chicago: Univ. of Chicago Press, 1986.

Spencer, Jane. *The Rise of the Woman Novelist: From Aphra Behn to Jane Austen.* Oxford: Basil Blackwell, 1986.

Starr, G. A. "'Only a Boy': Notes on Sentimental Novels." *Genre* 10(1977): 501–28.

Staves, Susan. "*Evelina*; or, Female Difficulties." *Modern Philology* 73(1976): 368–81.

Steeves, Harrison. *Before Jane Austen: The Shaping of the English Novel in the Eighteenth Century.* New York: Holt, 1965.

Sterne, Laurence. *The Life and Opinions of Tristram Shandy, Gentleman.* 1759–67. *The Florida Edition of the Works of Laurence Sterne.* 3 vols. Ed. Melvyn New and Joan New. Gainesville: University Presses of Florida, 1978.

———. *A Sentimental Journey Through France and Italy.* 1768. Ed. Graham Petrie. Harmondsworth: Penguin, 1967.

Stevenson, John Allen. "The Courtship of the Family: Clarissa and the Harlowes Once More." *ELH* 48(1981): 757–77.

Straub, Kristina. *Divided Fictions: Fanny Burney and Feminine Strategy.* Lexington: Univ. Press of Kentucky, 1987.

Suleri, Sara. "Naipaul's Arrival." *The Yale Journal of Criticism* 2(1988): 25–50.

Tanner, Tony. *Adultery in the Novel: Contract and Transgression.* Baltimore: Johns Hopkins Univ. Press, 1979.

———. *Jane Austen.* Cambridge: Harvard Univ. Press, 1986.

Todd, Janet. *Sensibility: An Introduction.* London: Methuen, 1986.

Todorov, Tzvetan. *The Fantastic: A Structural Approach to a Literary Genre.* Tr. Richard Howard. Cleveland: Case Western Reserve, 1973.

———. *The Poetics of Prose.* Tr. Richard Howard. Ithaca: Cornell Univ. Press, 1977.

Tompkins, J. M. S. *The Popular Novel in England, 1770–1800.* Lincoln: Univ. of Nebraska Press, 1961.

Trilling, Lionel. *Sincerity and Authenticity.* Cambridge: Harvard Univ. Press, 1972.

Uphaus, Robert W. *The Impossible Observer: Reason and the Reader in 18th-Century Prose.* Lexington: Univ. Press of Kentucky, 1979.

Van Boheemen, Christine. "The Semiotics of Plot: Toward a Typology of Fictions." *Poetics Today* 3, no. 4 (1982): 89–96.

Viner, Jacob. *The Role of Providence in the Social Order: An Essay in Intellectual History.* Philadelphia: American Philosophical Society, 1972.

Wain, John. *Samuel Johnson.* New York: McGraw-Hill, 1976.

Walpole, Horace. *The Castle of Otranto.* 1764. Ed. W.S. Lewis. London: Oxford Univ. Press, 1969.

Warner, William Beatty. *Reading Clarissa: The Struggles of Interpretation.* New Haven: Yale Univ. Press, 1979.

Warren, Leland E. "Of the Conversation of Women: *The Female Quixote* and the Dream of Perfection." In *Studies in Eighteenth-Century Culture* 12, ed. Harry C. Payne, 367–80. Madison: Univ. of Wisconsin Press, 1982.

Watt, Ian. *The Rise of the Novel.* Berkeley: Univ. of California Press, 1957.

Weiskel, Thomas. *The Romantic Sublime: Studies in the Structure and Psychology of Transcendence.* Baltimore: Johns Hopkins Univ. Press, 1976.

Wellek, René. *A History of Modern Criticism: 1750–1950. The Later Eighteenth Century.* New Haven: Yale Univ. Press, 1965.

Welsh, Alexander. *The Hero of the Waverley Novels*. New Haven: Yale Univ. Press, 1963.

Williams, Aubrey. "Interpositions of Providence and the Design of Fielding's Novels." *SAQ* 70(1971): 265–86.

Wilt, Judith. *Ghosts of the Gothic: Austen, Eliot, and Lawrence*. Princeton: Princeton Univ. Press, 1980.

———. *Secret Leaves: The Novels of Walter Scott*. Chicago: Univ. of Chicago Press, 1985.

Wolff, Cynthia Griffin. "The Radcliffean Gothic Model: A Form for Feminine Sexuality." In *The Female Gothic*, ed. Juliann E. Fleenor, 207–23. Montreal: Eden, 1983.

Wollheim, Richard. "On Persons and their Lives." In *Explaining Emotions*, ed. Amelie Oksenberg Rorty, 299–321. Berkeley: Univ. of California Press, 1980.

Wollstonecraft, Mary. *Mary and The Wrongs of Woman*. 1788, 1798. Ed. Gary Kelly. Oxford: Oxford Univ. Press, 1976.

[———]. "*Zeluco. Various Views of Human Nature . . . .*" *The Analytical Review* 5(1789): 98–103.

INDEX

Providence (*continued*)
  thority of father, 118; and Burke's
  aesthetics, 117–19; in *Clarissa* (Richardson), 67, 68; and comic novelists,
  182; and cosmic order, 68; and plot,
  9, 194; and sentimental novel, 116–
  17, 119, 125, 135. *See also* Supernatural
Public sphere: as domain of men, 30;
  and domain of novel, 7; female fantasies of, 18; and heroism, 28
Pye, Henry James, 45, 46, 51, 52

Rabb, Melinda Alliker, 65, 75
Radcliffe, Anne, 6, 147–74 *passim*, 175,
  178, 179–81, 183, 184, 193, 227,
  237; on fathers and daughters, 147–
  74; *The Italian*, 150–51, 152–56,
  159, 160, 161, 162–67, 180, 186,
  237, 239; *The Mysteries of Udolpho*,
  152, 156–60, 166–74, 180, 181, 184;
  The Romance of the Forest, 180–81,
  182
Rader, Ralph, 53, 116, 242n
Rape, 58, 60–61
Rape of the Lock, The (Pope), 28
Reader: and acceptance of novel's
  truth, 38, 47–48; and causality, 109–
  10; desire of, 30, 32, 36, 41, 47–48,
  50–51, 237; effects of plot on, 3,
  36–37, 38, 40, 51; and the fantastic,
  158–59; and the Gothic, 160; heroine's role as, 23–24, 25, 26; identification with characters, 30–31, 133,
  150; male, 26; relationship to narrator, 36–37, 40–41, 42, 84, 135, 159;
  seduction by narrator, 42; and sensibility, 124; and the supernatural, 36
Realism, 2, 3, 34
Reason: clash with feeling, 3, 16–17,
  32, 174; clash with imagination, 7;
  and control of sexual passion, 63;
  and plot's control, 188
Reconciliation, as type of plot, 184,
  189, 190, 195, 201–2, 203, 237, 238
Reeve, Clara, 2, 26, 32, 44, 47, 132; *The
  Progress of Romance*, 26, 132
Relationships: affiliation vs. power, 6,
  161, 235, 237; discourse of, 7; of
  domination, 58, 59, 191, 219; and in-

adequacy of plot, 132–33. *See also*
  Sexual relations
Responsiveness, ethic of, 125
Restraint. *See* Self-regulation
Richardson, Samuel, 50, 55–84 *passim*,
  150, 190, 202, 238; *Clarissa*, 9, 31,
  57–79, 81, 85, 87, 92, 95, 107, 114,
  116, 130, 157, 161, 162–79, 188,
  219, 232, 236, 239; *Pamela* 46, 87–
  89, 90–95, 106, 111, 161, 235, 239
Ricoeur, Paul, 2, 12, 30, 52, 75
Roderick Random (Smollett), 113, 188
Rogers, Katharine M., 201
Romance: as criticism of society, 13–
  14; defined, 213; as enabling fiction,
  31; and falsehood, 21; and female
  desire, 14; heroes of, 13, 15, 138–39,
  231; and history, 21, 23, 25, 26, 32,
  35–36, 211, 212, 230; mockery of,
  14, 29; and moral development, 21;
  rules of, 13–14; Samuel Johnson's attitude toward, 21
Romance of the Forest, The (Radcliffe),
  180–81, 182
Romantic, as concept, 186
Ross, Deborah, 24, 241n
Rothstein, Eric, 47, 100
Rousseau, Jean Jacques, 10
Roussel, Roy, 93–94, 96

Sacks, Sheldon, 241n, 242n
Sade, Marquis de, 102
Scott, Sir Walter, 203–34, 238, 239,
  240; *The Heart of Midlothian*, 203,
  218, 224–31, 233–34; *Waverley*, 203,
  206–13
Self: Christian interpretation of, 70,
  71–73; claims of, 125–26; denial of,
  6, 69, 95, 126, 128, 136
Self-definition, 70
Self-development, 96
Self-love, and social, 45, 132, 235
Self-regulation, by men, 19–20
Self-submission, and familial authority,
  136
Self-sufficiency, as ethic of sublimity,
  156
Sensibility, 127: and desire, 157; as
  feminine value, 160, 174; as form of
  divinity, 124; as morality, 46; as op-